AWAKEN, CHILDREN!

Dialogues With
Sri Sri Mata Amritanandamayi

VOLUME I

Adaptation & Translation

SWAMI AMRITASVARUPANANDA

MATA AMRITANANDAMAYI CENTER
San Ramon, California

AWAKEN, CHILDREN!
Volume I

PUBLISHED BY:
Mata Amritanandamayi Center
P.O. Box 613
San Ramon, CA 94583-0613
Tel: (415) 537-9417

THIRD PRINTING

ALSO AVAILABLE FROM:
Mata Amritanandamayi Mission Trust
Amritapuri, (Via) Athinad North, Quilon Dt., Kerala
INDIA 690542

ISBN 1-879410-52-4
LIBRARY OF CONGRESS CATALOG CARD NUMBER: 91-118937

This Book Is Humbly Offered At The

LOTUS FEET OF HER HOLINESS
SRI SRI MATA AMRITANANDAMAYI

The Resplendent Luminary Immanent
In the Hearts Of All Beings

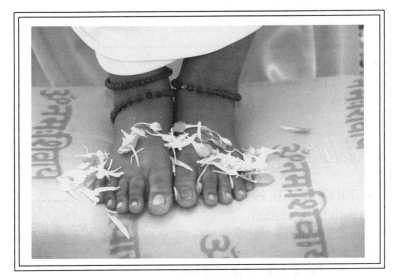

Shôshanam pâpapankasya dîpanam jñânatejasâm
Guru pâdôdakam samyak, samsârârnava târakam

The holy water that has washed the Guru's Feet, dries the mine of
sins, lights the Lamp of Knowledge and helps one cross the Ocean
of Transmigration.

Ajñâna mûlaharanam janmakarma nivâranam
Jñâna vairâgya siddhyartham gurupâdôdakam pibet

It uproots ignorance of the Self, puts an end to rebirth and its
cause, actions. One should sip the holy water of the Guru's Feet
for Enlightenment and Dispassion.

TABLE OF CONTENTS

PREFACE xiv
INTRODUCTION xvi

1 AUGUST 1976 1
God
God is Compassionate
Temples
Mantra
Rituals
Rishis (Sages)

18 SEPTEMBER 1976 18
The Path to Liberation
Elimination of the Mind
The Law of Karma
Sarira Tyaga - Committing Suicide
How to Know the Truth
Do Not Become a Slave to the Circumstances
The Glory of the Guru

19 SEPTEMBER 1976 27
True Knowledge
Monks and Renunciation
Brahman and Jagat
Jivatma and Paramatma
Evolution of the Individual Self
The Signs of Self-Realization
The Way a Satguru Disciplines
Merits and Demerits, Prarabdham

Time Needed for God-Realization
That Which is Needed First

1 SEPTEMBER 1977 45
Prapancha and Vedanta
Vedanta and Image Worship
Pranayama
What is Bondage?

13 SEPTEMBER 1977 49
What is Freedom?
The Grace of Love
Mother's Knowledge and the Purpose of Her Birth

14 SEPTEMBER 1977 53
Mantra Diksha - The Necessity of Initiation
Bhava Darshan - The Divine Mood
The Importance of Acharas - Traditional Customs

15 SEPTEMBER 1977 58
26 SEPTEMBER 1977 59
Tyaga and Bhoga - Renunciation and Enjoyment
Duality and Non-duality

21 SEPTEMBER 1977 65
To Householders
Life After Death
Jnana and Vijnana - The Plane of Pure Consciousness
Name and Liberation
Endless Beginning
Movement - Stillness

14 JANUARY 1978 75
Prabhakara Siddha Yogi

15 JANUARY 1978 77
Taking Disease

1 JANUARY 1980 79
Meditation

5 DECEMBER 1981 88
Easy Path
Purpose of Birth
Kundalini
Satguru - Self-Realized Master

6 DECEMBER 1981 98
10 DECEMBER 1981 99
19 DECEMBER 1981 102
Sahaja Samadhi

22 DECEMBER 1981 103
To the Householders

23 DECEMBER 1981 113
The Mother Hen and Her Chicks

24 DECEMBER 1981 115
Difficult is the Path of Knowledge

27 DECEMBER 1981 124
Subtle Beings
A Real Guru and Disciple

1 JANUARY 1982 131
Disease & Medicine
Intense Dispassion - The Attitude of a Servant

3 JANUARY 1982 133
4 JANUARY 1982 136
12 MAY 1982 138
4 JULY 1982 139
8 AUGUST 1982 141
Vasanas - Tendencies

10 AUGUST 1982 144
Sadhana & Scriptural Study

16 AUGUST 1982 147
18 AUGUST 1982 150
19 AUGUST 1982 152
20 AUGUST 1982 154
Avatar & Jiva - Incarnation & Individual Soul

21 AUGUST 1982 163
Kirtan in the Kali Yuga - Devotional Singing in the
Dark Age of Materialism

22 AUGUST 1982 165
23 AUGUST 1982 166
Control of Food
Ekagrata - One-pointedness

28 AUGUST 1982 168
Dhyana & Brahmanubhuti - Meditation & The
Experience of the Absolute

1 SEPTEMBER 1982 172
Sarvatra Samadarshinaha - Seeing All as One

5 SEPTEMBER 1982 175
Guru Mahima - Glory of the Guru

8 SEPTEMBER 1982 178
10 SEPTEMBER 181
One-Pointedness
Gudakesa - Conqueror of Sleep

18 SEPTEMBER 186
Mother of the House

22 SEPTEMBER 190
13 SEPTEMBER 193
The Guru and Discipline

30 SEPTEMBER 195
1 OCTOBER 1982 196
Complete Faith and Liberation

4 OCTOBER 198
5 OCTOBER 200
6 OCTOBER 201
What is There After Death?

7 OCTOBER 204
8 OCTOBER 208
Control of Food

9 OCTOBER 210
Make Me Intoxicated With Your Love

11 OCTOBER 212
Sadhana & Vasana

13 OCTOBER 1982 215
The Mother Within

14 OCTOBER 1982 217
Taking on Disease

15 OCTOBER 1982 219
Faith in the Guru

20 OCTOBER 1982 219
The Cause of the Mango Tree and the Seed

25 OCTOBER 1982 222
Inaction in Action
Mahabali

28 OCTOBER 1982 225
Unsteadiness
Sraddha - Alertness

7 NOVEMBER 1982 228
The Meditation of a Jnani

12 NOVEMBER 1982 231
The Taste of Work

18 NOVEMBER 1982 232
9 SEPTEMBER 1983 234
Bhava Darshan

7 OCTOBER 1983 243
8 OCTOBER 1983 245
God's Grace
Oblations to the Departed

9 OCTOBER 1983 248
Sraddha & Nishta - Alertness & Discipline
Guru
Customs & Discipline
Discrimination

11 OCTOBER 1983 262
Name and Love
There is No Matter, Everything is Consciousness

12 OCTOBER 1983 266
Story of Sandeepaka

13 OCTOBER 1983 271
Mithya Means Changing
Determination to Reach the Goal

15 OCTOBER 1983 275
17 OCTOBER 1983 277
Scriptures are Billboards
Guru Bhakti

22 OCTOBER 1983 283
23 OCTOBER 1983 288
24 OCTOBER 1983 299
The Hindu Faith and 'I', the Supreme Principle
The Society Which Destroys Itself
Satya Nasti paro Dharma - There is No Dharma
Superior to Truth
Nirvikalpa Samadhi and an Avatar

28 OCTOBER 1983 311

29 OCTOBER 1983 312
Yogaschitta Vritti Nirodah - Yoga is Control of the
Modifications of the Mind
Samatvam Yoga Uchyate - Yoga is Equanimity
The Expansive 'I'

31 OCTOBER 1983 320
To the Sadhaks
Beyond Discipline
Nityanityam - The Eternal and Non-eternal
Worldly Love
Don't Give Up the Intent to Reach the Goal
Manifestation of Siddhis
Avatar
Incarnation and an Ordinary Soul

15 DECEMBER 1988 358
Mother's Talks to Western Devotees

PREFACE

Dear brothers and sisters, herein is contained a direct translation of Holy Mother's *divya upadesha* (Divine advice) into the English language. The tremendous blessing that is bestowed by presenting the Mother's teaching to the English speaking world is not yet fully realized. Now it is left to the reader to sanctify his or her life by a careful reading of the material and a whole-hearted practice of it in daily life.

Several points should be remembered in order that this translation is approached with right understanding. First of all, these conversations have occurred between the Mother and Indian householders and renunciates in the cultural context of India. Also the Mother's advice is given according to the level of understanding of each person to whom she is speaking. Often a word-for-word English translation falls short of conveying the totality of what the Mother has expressed through her mother tongue, Malayalam. One must consider these factors when contemplating her words to achieve deeper insight.

Secondly, the Mother's use of language is direct and earthy. Her words convey an immediacy and intensity of purpose to transmit the Essential, particularly when speaking to *sadhaks* (spiritual aspirants). For instance, when it comes time to bring a point across to a renunciate, the Mother does not mince words. Thus we can understand her expression, "Worldly pleasure is equal to dog excreta," to be sound advice to one whose sole aim is God-Realization.

In a separate conversation with a householder, the Mother's advice takes on an entirely different tone. "Mother does not say that you must give up all desires. You can enjoy them, but do not think that this life is for that only." Keep in mind that in the Mother's language, the word 'world' lit-

erally means 'That which is seen' as opposed to the invisible
Reality or God. Knowing this will be of great help in interpreting her use of the word 'worldly.' When the Mother
contrasts that which is spiritual to that which is worldly, she
refers to the attitude with which actions are done. Spiritual
actions are those actions which lead one to God through
selflessness and purity. Worldly actions are those actions
which lead one away from God, performed as they are in a
spirit of selfishness.

Finally, the Mother speaks to us from the exalted state of
sahaja samadhi, the natural state of abidance of a Self-
Realised Master in the Absolute Reality. The challenge in
translating is to render the Mother's transcendental vision
into English for the layman. The vital ingredient in this process is the contemplative mind of the reader. Abandoning all
superficiality, may our mind and intellect become subtle and
assimilate the eternal Wisdom of the Mother's words.
Firmly established in their practice, may we all revel in the
direct experience of the Supreme Absolute without delay.

My heartfelt gratitude is due to Professor M. Ramakrishnan
Nair, the compiler of *Mata Amritanandamayi Sambhashanangal*,
the Holy Mother's conversations in Malayalam. The present
book, *Awaken, Children! I*, is a faithful translation of the
same, interspersed with some additional materials which
were recorded by me. I would like to thank all of the Holy
Mother's children who took part in producing the book.

Swami Amritasvarupananda

INTRODUCTION

Only in a Great Master who is established in the Supreme Reality can one see the perfect balance of Divine Fatherhood and Divine Motherhood, the beautiful blending of masculine and feminine qualities. Only such a person can transform another and mould the character of others. Integration of one's own inner personality, being higher than anything else, is possible only through discipline motivated by selflessness and unconditional love.

The Holy Mother Amritanandamayi's teachings, sayings and conversations are equally inspiring and throw light on the mystical expressions expounded in the scriptural texts. The Mother's teachings are surcharged with spiritual power and are a tremendous source of inspiration for people from all walks of life, especially for spiritual seekers. The Holy Mother has her own simple and lucid way of expressing spiritual truths with examples which make the points clear and intellectually satisfying.

From a worldly standpoint, she has not attended school beyond the fourth grade, yet her knowledge, wisdom and philosophical insight is immeasurable. In the early days, due to the visitors' lack of spiritual interest, only a few paid attention to the Mother's words. At that time, most peoples' interest was to fulfill their material desires. Thus, they gave less importance to the Mother's precious gospel regarding the Supreme Goal of human birth. Needless to say, her parents, relatives and villagers who were deadly against her 'strange' behaviour considered her as one gone mad and took these words of the Mother to be crazy utterances.

However, at the age of twenty-one, the Holy Mother began initiating some educated young men who had renounced their hearth and home to dedicate their lives to

God-Realisation, and they noticed the depth and simplicity of her explanations and began writing down her teachings. By the end of 1983, Prof. M. Ramakrishnan Nair, an ardent devotee of the Mother, started tape recording the Mother's talks whenever he stayed in the Ashram. Later, he compiled the "Conversations with Mata Amritanandamayi." in Malayalam from the said materials. This English translation of that book is interspersed with other interesting incidents which took place over the course of the last ten or twelve years in the presence of the Holy Mother. From 1979 onwards, at which time I came and settled near the Holy Mother, I recorded many of her conversations and it is from that material that the additional incidents have been woven into the narrative.

1 August 1976

The sun's golden rays blessed the earth on this beautiful day soon after the rainy season. Though sunny, it was not very hot. The trees and plants with their green leaves danced in the gentle breeze which blew from the sea. The melodious sound of the sacred *chakora* bird (Greek partridge) gladdened the ears. The blue waves of the Arabian Sea to the west reverberated with the sound 'AUM' which served as the drone (*sruti*) underlying the song chanted by the fishermen as they pulled in their nets. The large canoes made of wooden planks stitched together with coconut fibers glided slowly up and down the backwaters to the east presenting a charming sight.

At ten o'clock in the morning the Ashram atmosphere was extraordinarily calm and quiet. Peace permeated everywhere. The Holy Mother dressed in pure white was sitting on the verandah of the old temple. A group of college students interested in spiritual life came to see the Mother. They prostrated before the Holy Mother and sat near her. Mother smilingly asked them, "Children, have you eaten anything?" One student replied, "We had breakfast." After a few moments the conversation turned to spiritual topics.

GOD

Student: It is said that there is a God but I am unable to believe it.

Mother: Children, to say that there is no God is like saying "I have no tongue" with your own tongue. Is it possible for a person who has no tongue to say "I have no tongue?" Like-wise, when we say, "There is no God," at that moment itself we agree that there is God. In order to say that a particular object is 'not,' we must have previously had a general knowl-edge of that object. How can we prove the non-existence of something which is not known to us? Truth is only one. That is God. God-Realization is our life's aim.

Student: What is meant by God?

Mother: Son, if you can answer the questions which Mother is going to ask, Mother will tell you what God is.

Student: All right, I will answer.

Mother: Son, what did you eat this morning?

Student: I ate *dosa* (pancakes).

Mother: What other dish was there with it?

Student: Chutney.

Mother: What was it made of?

Student: Coconut.

Mother: Where did you get the coconut from?

Student: From a coconut tree.

Mother: Where did the coconut tree come from?

Student: From a coconut.

Mother: Which came first, the coconut or the coconut tree? That is what Mother wants to know.

The student sat tongue-tied.

Mother: Son, why are you sitting silent? (Pause) Therefore, you should agree that beyond the coconut and the coconut tree there is a power which is the substratum of everything. That is God, a Unique Power which is inexpressible and be-yond words, the First Cause for everything. That is what is known as God.

Student: One can believe if it is said that this building and that coconut tree exist, but how does one believe in something which is not seen?

Mother: Son, would you feel angry if Mother asked you one thing?

Student: No.

Mother: Is your father still alive?

Student: Yes.

Mother: What about your father's father?

Student: He died long before my birth.

Mother: Do any children call their father a bastard because they have not seen their grandfather? Son, do you remember who gave birth to you? When you grew a little older everyone told you, "This is your mother." You believed it, not that you remembered having seen the person when she gave birth to you. Do you believe if it is said that there is cooking gas in cow dung? Cooking gas is not visible but gas is extracted when it is used in the proper manner. Often it is blind faith that leads us to the goal. Son, you left your house to come here and got into the bus. Is it not because of your faith that you will reach the destination? You got into the bus even though there are many vehicle accidents. Was your expectation that you would reach here itself not blind faith? Children, is it not your blind faith that Mother will talk to you that makes you talk to her? Children, all beliefs or faiths are blind.

Student: It is said that God is everywhere. If so, what is the necessity of going to particular places of worship?

Mother: There is wind everywhere, but the person who comes to rest under a tree out of the scorching heat gets a special kind of rejuvenating coolness which filters through the leaves of the tree. Likewise, we can experience a unique peace when we go to *Mahatmas* (Great Souls). The significance of going to other places of worship is the same. The atmospheres in a temple and in a liquor shop are different, are they not?

Student: Mother, how can we see God?

Mother: Children, when there is sunlight we can see numerous dust particles in the ray of sunlight which enters the room through a small hole in the roof of the house. Due to the lack of concentrated light, this is not seen in other places. Our mind is very dim; it has no subtlety. Just like charging a battery, through subtlety we illuminate our mind; we can then see God. Having searched with our external eyes, do not say, "I am not seeing God, therefore, I don't believe in God." We should not make a big fuss saying, "I will only believe in the things that I see." Search, certainly you can see.

Without God's Grace, we cannot see Him. If we want to get His Grace, the ego in us should go. The well would say, "Everyone is drinking water from me. If I am not here, how will they cook food?" But the well does not know that it was dug by someone and that the bricks which make it beautiful were made by somebody else. Our situation is also the same. We become egotistical thinking "I am greater than everything else." But even to move a finger we need God's power. (Pointing her finger at a distance) However powerful a cyclone is, it cannot do anything to a blade of grass; whereas, the huge trees standing with their heads high will be uprooted. All grace will flow to us if a servant-like attitude (*dasa bhavana* or attitude of humility) comes to us. After that, nothing can disturb us. But God will not abide where there is ego. We will be uprooted by the cyclone of ego.

Another student: Mother, what about people who do not have time to go to ashrams?

Mother: Do not say that there is no time. Children, for many years we will sit at the courthouse to litigate for a foot of land. We won't care about rain, heat, or any other impediments. Because of our desire to acquire some land, we find time to try the case and toil for it. Nobody would say that there is no time for that. Similarly, we will wait any number of hours to see a doctor. Children, when you go to the theatre you will buy a ticket, not caring how large the crowd may be or even how many kicks and shoves you may get. That much desire you have to see the movie. These are not difficulties at all if one is intent on the goal (has *lakshya bodha*). Those who sincerely desire to see God will not feel that there is a lack of time.

By this time, a householder devotee and his family had come from Quilon, a town thirty-five kilometers south of the Mother's Ashram. They prostrated before the Holy Mother and took a seat near her. After some light conversation with them, the Mother again turned to the students.

GOD IS COMPASSIONATE

Student: Mother, there are many people who are suffering in this world. Some are rich and enjoy life, but others die from starvation. What is the meaning in saying that God is compassionate? Is God not cruel?

Mother: Children, God is certainly compassionate but we must be deserving of His Grace which is constantly being showered upon us. The river is always flowing, but having constructed a dam, we complain that we do not get water. It is we who make the dam. We will get the constantly flowing Grace of God if the dam of ignorance and ego which we have built is removed. Our mother gave birth to us and taught us the ways to progress. No progress will be made if we do not obey her. Accusing God of being cruel is like blaming our mother for our disobedience. Our case also is similar. God the Creator has given human beings the power to discriminate between the eternal and non-eternal. Yet we commit errors indiscriminately and as a result we suffer. Seeing her son going to the forest, a mother tells him, "Son, do not go into the forest. A forest fire is there; ferocious animals are there." Why should the mother be blamed for the troubles which happen if he goes to the forest without listening to her warning?

Student: What is the cause of the sorrows which happen in life?

Mother: Desire is the cause of sorrow. The happiness that we get from worldly objects is only an infinitesimal fraction of the bliss that we get from within. The result will always be sorrow when we think that we are this body. This is only a rented body. We will be asked to leave at a certain time, and then we must depart. Before that, while we still reside in this body, that which is eternal should be gained . If we have a house of our own, we can happily move out when we are asked to vacate this rented one. Then we can live in the eternal house of God.

Student: Mother, there are many people who still experience sorrow even after crying to God.

Mother: We call God with many desires in our mind. The mind is filled with desires, not with God's Form. This means that we see God as a laborer, which should not be so. Even though God is the servant of His devotees, it is not proper for us to treat Him as a servant. Dedicate everything at His Feet. We must have the attitude of surrender, then

He will definitely protect us. After getting into the boat or bus, you won't still carry the luggage, will you? You will set it down. Likewise, surrender everything to God. He will protect you. Have the thought that God is near you. If there is a resting place nearby, the mere thought that the luggage which you are carrying on your head can soon be unloaded lightens the burden. But the thought that the resting place is still far away increases the weight. In the same way, when we think that God is near, all our burdens will diminish.

Many of the householder devotees tell Mother, "However much we householders meditate or do *mantra japa*, not much benefit is gained." Devotedly we go to the temple to pray to the Lord. But finishing the circumambulation and standing before the inner sanctum, our mood will change if somebody comes and stands in front of us. We will get angry at him. Even if God Himself comes in disguise, assuming a different form, we will get angry. This is our character. How, then, are you children going to get the benefit of meditation?

Student: If God is omniscient and omnipotent, then why am I not realizing the God-consciousness in me?

Mother: Son, He is very close to you; that is why you cannot see Him. Is it possible to see our own face without the aid of a mirror? And will it be possible to see our image in a mirror which is completely covered with dust? Look after wiping away the dust particles and cleaning the mirror; then certainly you can see.

Student: How is it possible to remove this ignorance?

Mother: Through devotion, through worship with pure, divine love and knowledge.

Student: Mother, I have seen a disturbing sight while leaving the house. Two crows were pecking and injuring an owl's fledgling. It was fluttering and crying in pain. What injustice is this? You say that God is compassionate. Then why does He allow such cruelties in Nature? Innocent deer become prey to lions. Human beings slaughter cows and eat their flesh. Is there no end to this?

Mother: Children, nothing is in excess in this world. Everything is accurately weighed and measured and noted down. It is according to their *vasanas* (latent tendencies) that beings take birth as a bird, cow or lion. Is God going to be responsible for that? Higher births are gained by exhausting each *vasana*. If this human birth, which we have finally attained, is spent living like an animal without using it for God-Realization, then again we might take birth in this world as birds or animals. Therefore, God is not cruel. Each creature is only experiencing the fruit of its actions.

Question: Mother, why is it necessary to worship God through a form when He is, in truth, formless?

Mother: Children, it is our present habit to share our sorrows with our friends in order to get peace. Instead, the sharing of sorrows should be with the Universal Being. This is the aim of worshipping God with a form.

Once Shiva and Parvati were sitting together. Suddenly, Shiva got up and started running but returned immediately. Parvati asked Him, "Why did You return so quickly?" Shiva replied, "One of My devotees used to tell his sorrows, big and small, to Me only; he never used to tell others. Today while returning to his house, he was mistaken for a thief and beaten up. Seeing this, I went to rescue him but on My way I saw him telling his sorrow to some other man, 'They beat me up for no reason! You should help me take revenge.' Since My help was not needed, I came back."

Do not increase your sorrows by sharing them with others. Tell them to God and try to solve them. If we share our sorrows with the Universal Being, we will get Eternal Peace.

An ordinary man may not develop love as easily for the formless aspect of God as he would if he worshipped God with form. Following the Path of Knowledge without devotion is like eating stones. The formless and omnipotent God can easily assume form for the sake of His devotees. If one has full faith and confidence in the form of one's Beloved Deity, one can reach the goal. We should think that God is our own Self and worship Him, seeing all forms as different aspects of the same God.

Question: If God is one and non-dual, why should we worship Shiva, Vishnu and other such gods?

Mother: An actor takes many roles, but he remains the same. God is like this. Truth is one; different are the names and forms. Men have different natures and characters. The different forms of God were described by the ancient sages to enable us to realize Him by selecting names and forms according to our mental constitution. It is not that these are different gods. The sages have portrayed the non-dual God in different ways at different times according to the taste and temperament of the people.

Question: If God is one, what then is the need for separate places of worship for each religion?

Mother: Will an object change just because it is known by different names? For example, water may be called '*vellom*' in Malayalam and '*pani*' in Hindi, but does the color and taste change? No. Is there any difference between the electric current which passes through the fridge, the lamp and the fan? No, only the object differs. Christians say Christ is God and Muslims call Him 'Allah.' Each person understands God according to his culture and worships Him accordingly.

Question: Mother, a lot of money is offered to God in temples for ritualistic worship and other purposes. Why does God require money?

Mother: God does not require anything from us. An electric lamp does not require the help of a kerosene lamp. God is like the sun. He sheds light equally on all things in the world. It is to this all-illuminating God that we offer a lamp and oil. This is due to our ignorance. It is like holding a burning candle in the daytime and saying, "O Sun God, here is light for You so that You can see the path clearly and walk." The offerings in temples are made for our benefit. God is the Giver of everything. He does not need or want anything from us.

TEMPLES

Question: What are the temples for? Is it not the sculptor who chiselled the beautiful statue who deserves to be adored?

Mother: Just as we remember our father when we see his portrait, we are reminded of God, the Creator of the world, when we see the statue. When a devotee of Krishna sees the image of Sri Krishna, he remembers the real Lord Krishna and not the stone image. Temples and images are needed for those of us who are drowned in ignorance.

Question: Are temples necessary for remembering God?

Mother: Small children learn about animals by looking at their pictures in books. These pictures will help them in their studies. Through them they get an idea of what a camel, lizard, or tiger is. At a later stage they will understand that it is only a picture, but at a young age these pictures facilitate development of intellect.

Question: It is said that if the daily worship is stopped in temples adverse reactions will occur. Is this true?

Mother: As a result of man's resolve, the power of the temple gods will increase. If the worship is stopped, that power will diminish. The power of the image depends on the attitude of the person who installs it. Don't stop the daily worship performed in temples or to the family deity. If these rites are stopped, great misfortunes may result.

Suppose we feed a crow for ten days. On the eleventh day, if we don't feed it, it will follow us cawing. Due to its cries, we will be unable to work attentively. In the same way, if we stop the daily worship of the gods, they will always trouble us in their subtle forms. This will affect weak-minded people a great deal, although a spiritual aspirant will not be affected much.

It is not enough that we build a boat; we should also learn how to row it. If we get into a boat without knowing how to row, it will move hither and thither. Is it proper to blame the boat if we have not learned how to row? Similarly, it is not enough that we construct temples. They must be properly looked after as well. Daily worship should be performed. If not, misfortune may result. It is meaningless to blame the temples at that time.

Question: Are gods and God different?

Mother: The gods are created and installed by man's resolve. Man's resolve has limitations, and therefore, his creations will reflect this fact. God, on the other hand, is all-powerful. His power neither decreases nor increases, but remains eternally the same. The difference between the many gods and God is like the difference between animals and man. Even though everything is one Reality, a dog does not have the discrimination that man has. A dog loves only those who love it; it may bite others.

Question: If so, then won't temples become harmful to human beings?

Mother: Never. This applies only to the temples where gods are worshipped. The installation of gods is done by priests who are incapable of controlling their own life force (*prana shakti*) and therefore we should be a bit careful. Never stop the daily worship in such temples. If worship is performed every day and in a proper way, material prosperity will result. Have you seen fish living in aquariums? The water must be changed frequently or it will become harmful to the fish. Similarly, temple worship must be done regularly.

The greatness of temples where *Mahatmas* have installed the images is something unique. By their mere will, they give divine power to the images which they install. They make the resolve that the images should be identified with the Undivided Existence, Awareness and Bliss. Such temples and their statues will be full of divine power. They are not like fish living in aquariums, but like fish that live in the river. In such temples the daily *puja* will never stop. Yet even if the *puja* is stopped, there will be no loss of power. These temples will be centres of great attraction and will have eternally auspicious attributes. Tirupathi, Guruvayur and Chottanikara temples are examples such places.

Question: Why were human sacrifices conducted in temples?

Mother: The ignorance of people of olden times prompted them to do this. They believed that such sacrifices would please God. Misunderstanding the words of the scriptures, they performed these sacrifices. Look at our present day world. In the name of politics there is so much bloodshed – killing a man who changes political parties or the members of different political parties, shootings and stabbings – these are all commonplace atrocities. Does any party's by-laws sanction murder or similar atrocities? The Manifesto and ideologies are very good, but what is carried out is entirely different. Similarly, there were fools in those days whose blind devotion and erroneous beliefs prompted them to kill in the name of sacrifice.

Question: Do such people incur sin?

Mother: If sacrifice is for a universal cause, there is no sin; but if it is for a selfish end, it is a sin. Once there were two *brahmins* in a village. Both became afflicted with the same disease. When they consulted a doctor he told them that if they ate fish they would be cured. As both were strict vegetarians, they were at their wits' end. The first man, yielding to the demand of his wife and children, ate fish and was cured. The second man, being afraid of sin, refused to take fish and as a result, died. His family was orphaned and subjected to many troubles.

The first man, by eating the comparatively insignificant fish, protected his whole family. This is not cruelty. The second man refused to eat fish and died, leaving his whole family to suffer. A family is of far greater importance than one or two fish. Don't we cut down trees to build a house? Such things are not selfish. When we act with vengeance or out of hatred or passion, this is a sin.

Question: Mother, what is the reason for the loss of sanctity in the temples?

Mother: In the name of festivals, people collect money and conduct worldly programs in temples. This makes the surroundings of temples impure. Instead of inculcating devotion and good thoughts in people, such programs create vulgar thoughts and passions. What nonsense is done in the name of festivals! People get drunk and fight; in the temple surroundings they conduct dance and drama programs which arouse worldliness in the minds of the audience.

Young children will be affected by this. At the tender age when good thoughts should be developed, these programs will make them stray from the right path. These kinds of thought waves will make the temple atmosphere unholy.

Children, we alone destroy ourselves. First we should become good. We should see that the temples are kept pure. Only arts of divine nature which increase devotion and faith should be held in temples. The daily *puja* should be done properly. Having ourselves made the temple surroundings impure, there is no use in accusing the deities. In olden days meditation, reading of the ancient scriptures, yogic postures and other spiritual activities were practiced in temples. Only stories connected with God would be presented as dramas during festivals.

The money collected from the public for holding festivals should be utilized for humanitarian purposes. There are so many people in our villages who are struggling without even a house. We can build houses for them. Clothes and food can be given in charity to the poor. Help can be offered to those who are unable to conduct a marriage ceremony for lack of money. Religious books can be printed, distributed free of charge, and used for teaching children. Orphanages can be built and the children therein can be brought up with culture and good character. If this is done, there will not be any orphans in the future. All this will help create unity among people.

Children, look at the Christians and Muslims and all the good things that they do. They build orphanages and schools where they teach the orphans religion and look after their everyday requirements. Have you seen any churches in a dilapidated condition? No. But look at the plight of Hindu temples. So many temples remain uncared for and unattended. The Devaswom Board (government agency for the maintenance of temples) will take over the management of big temples because there they can make money, but smaller temples are ignored.

We should take special care to renovate temples and to conduct divine arts during festival seasons. Unitedly we ourselves should take care of temples in the proper way. Their holiness should be preserved. If this is not done, our culture will continue to degenerate.

Question: Is it possible to attain Liberation through temple worship?

Mother: It is possible, but one must worship with understanding of the inner significance of the temples. God resides in temples, but don't think that He is limited by their four walls. Have firm belief that God is omnipresent. A bus will take us to the stop nearest to our house, and from there we can easily walk the remaining distance. Similarly, the correct way of temple worship will take us to the threshold of *Satchidananda* (Pure Being-Knowledge-Bliss); from there only a short distance remains to Perfection. You can take birth in a temple, but don't die there. That is to say that in the beginning a seeker can use temple worship as a stepping stone; but his final and real goal is beyond these things.

MANTRA

Question: Do words have the power to change the character of a person?

Mother: Definitely. In a temple once, a *brahmin* was teaching spiritual matters to his students. At that time the king of the country arrived. The *brahmin*, engrossed in his teaching, was unaware of the king's arrival. The king became angry and berated the *brahmin* for not noticing him. The *brahmin*

explained that as he was deeply involved with teaching, he
was unaware of the king's arrival. The king then asked what
the *brahmin* was teaching so earnestly that he was not aware
of the king's presence. He replied, "I was teaching the children things which will purify their characters. There is no
use in this if it is not taught with full attention and sincerity." The king mockingly asked, "Can mere words change
character?" The *brahmin* replied, "Certainly they can!" The
king retorted, "It will not change just like that." At that moment one of the *brahmin's* students, a small boy, told the
king to get out. Hearing this, he was enraged and roared,
"How dare you say that! I will kill you and your Guru, and
destroy this Ashram as well!" Thus said, the king caught
hold of the *brahmin* by the neck. "Please forgive me," the
brahmin pleaded. "You just now said that mere words cannot change the character of a person. Yet when a small boy
said a few words to you, how much you changed. You were
even ready to kill me and destroy everything."

Children, through words character can be changed. And
if ordinary words can change the character, then what to say
of the power of a mantra which emanated from the *rishis*
(ancient sages) and contains powerful *bijaksharas* (seed letters like 'om', 'hrim', 'klim').

Question: Mother, if a *mantra* is chanted will one get the
benefit?

Mother: Definitely. But one thing, *mantras* should be
chanted with concentration. Depending on one's attitude
one will get power. All depends on one's mental attitude. A
doctor will prescribe medicine and tell the patient to take
rest and to avoid certain foods. If the patient follows these
instructions, the disease will be cured. Like doctors, the
rishis have taught that if a *mantra* is chanted in a prescribed

way, certain benefitss will accrue. If we follow their instructions meticulously, we will definitely reap the fruits.

RITUALS

Question: Mother, do the rituals performed during *pitrukarma* (ancestral ceremonies) have any effect?

Mother: Children, pure *sankalpa* (resolve) has great power, but only when *sankalpa* is pure will rituals bear fruit. When *pitrukarma* is performed, the name, birth star, physical form and character of the dead person is remembered, and mantras chanted. Each ritual has its respective *devata* (deity). Just as a letter sent by a son to his parents in a distant place will reach them if properly addressed, the effect of rituals will reach the intended person if *sankalpa* is pure. When the *sankalpa* is pure, the *devata* pertaining to that ritual will make its results reach the intended soul.

RISHIS (SAGES)

Question: What is the guarantee that the *rishis'* predictions will come true?

Mother: The ancient *rishis* were *mantradrishtas* (visionaries); whatever they expressed has come true. Everything written in the *Srimad Bhagavatam*[1] about *Kaliyuga*[2] has been accurate. "The father will eat the son; the son will eat the father. All the forests will become houses; all the houses will become shops." Are these things not happening? We cut down the trees and build houses and shops in their place. Truth and *dharma* have no place at all. Is there mutual, trust, love, sin-

---

[1] An ancient scripture describing the deeds of Lord Vishnu's Incarnations.
[2] The present Dark Age of Materialism.

cerity, patience and sacrifice for higher ideals? Weather in
both the rainy season and the sunny season is extreme, and
during the growing season, due to a lack of rain, crops dry
up. All these things were predicted by the sages.

Eating only leaves and fruits, the ancient *rishis* did *tapas*
(severe austerities) and realized the secret of the universe.
The whole creation was like a mustard seed in the palm of
their hand. Even inanimate objects would obey their com-
mand. The *rishis* made many discoveries in ancient times.
Even present day inventions, which we consider to be very
great, were brought forth effortlessly by them. Today's scientists have produced test tube babies, but the sage Vyasa
brought forth the hundred and one Kauravas from clay pots.
Thousands of years ago, he imparted life to mere hunks of
flesh. When compared with this, the test tube baby is nothing. In the *Ramayana*[3] reference is made to "*pushpaka
vimana*" (airplane made of flowers), yet the modern airplane
was invented only recently. There are many examples like
this.

Mother does not consider present day scientists and
their inventions to be insignificant. Rather, she is telling this
to show that there is nothing that cannot be gained by *tapas*.
For the *rishis* all these things were quite simple; through
their *sankalpa*, they were able to create anything.

THE PATH TO LIBERATION

18 September 1976

Sitting in front of the temple, the Mother was conversing
with a few devotees. Unnikrishnan, one of the first Ashram

[3]A scripture describing the birth and life of Sri Rama, an Incarnation of Lord
Vishnu.

residents, was also present. He listened keenly to the conversation that Mother was having with the other devotees.

Devotee: Mother, what is the path to Liberation?

Mother: Children, what does Mother know? Mother is crazy. She will simply say some crazy things. Shiva! Shiva! Children, accept what you think is correct.

Permanent happiness will not be gained from the world which is changing every moment. If we depend on the Eternal Reality, Eternal Bliss will be gained. So much the better if the effort begins from a young age.

Devotee: Why does man commit errors?

Mother: We are caught in the illusion that we will get happiness from the world. So we madly run here and there trying to acquire it. Because of unfulfilled desires, frustration and anger result. Without discriminating between the necessary and the unnecessary, we do things as we like. Can we say that this is life? Whose fault is it that we are frustrated and angry?

Devotee: It is said that without God, even a blade of grass won't move. Can human beings be blamed for the errors if God is making them do everything?

Mother: For a person who has the conviction that "the real doer is not me, but God," it is impossible to commit any mistakes. He sees everything as permeated by God. It is impossible for that devotee even to think about making mistakes. To say it in another way, only one who has transcended all errors will have the faith that "God alone is the doer; even a blade of grass will not move without Him." There is no error or sin for one who has the conviction that God is the doer. But the consequences of the mistakes committed by a person who thinks, "I am the doer," must be accepted by himself alone. If he is without the awareness that God is the doer and thinks, "I am doing everything," he alone is responsible for his good and bad actions. Having committed a murder, it is not right to say that God is the doer. One whose thought is, "God is the doer," would not commit a murder, would he?

Devotee: We would not commit murder or mistakes if God didn't give us ignorance.

Mother: In Creation there is ignorance and knowledge, discrimination and indiscrimination - everything is there. God's Will is that we should proceed, using the discriminative power given by Him in order to do actions which will bring only goodness to the world. A student may make mistakes while studying in school, but why should he persist making mistakes? He can progress towards goodness by using the circumstances in the proper way, can't he? There is right and wrong in the Creation just as there is night and day. God has given discrimination to human beings in order to keep them from committing any errors. We must make use of it. The field is there and the seed is also there. Cultivate carefully and reap the fruit. Having acted without discrimination, do not say that God is the mischief-maker. If you say, "It is God who made me commit the murder," console yourself that, "It is God who is hanging me." Do not complain. Just when we were about to commit a murder or other evil deed, how many times has God prevented us saying from within, "Don't, don't."? Why do we not consider that? Afterwards, are you putting the burden of the responsibility of your errors on God's head? If it is spiritual progress that you children want, what you need is to take refuge in God with a pure heart without blaming God for your troubles or indulging in unnecessary disputes.

The effect should merge in the cause some day. The effects are the sense organs, mind, intellect, and vital forces. The world itself is an effect. Real life is a dispassionate, constant effort to merge the effects into the Supreme Self (*Paramatma*) which is the Cause. There is nothing that cannot be gained through a human birth. But if one feels that something should be gained, one's life is not full. That State should come where nothing needs to be gained. We must become eternally satisfied. That is Perfection. There will be no sorrow if and when the sense organs are withdrawn from sense objects.

Devotee: In what shape does God's radiant Power assume a form?

Mother: That cannot be told. Everything is God's Will. He will assume forms according to the need. None of them are without fruit.

Devotee: Can there be more than one *Avatar* (Incarnation) at a time?

Mother: It can happen. Why doubt it? Did not Parasurama, Sri Rama and Sita all exist at one time? What about Krishna, His brother Balarama and His wife Rukmini? There should be no doubt that more than one Incarnation of God can exist at once when it is the same God who has become all these worlds of diversity simultaneously.

Devotee: Mother, can *sankalpa* (resolve) come true?

Mother: When the world is true, *sankalpa* is also true. If the world is illusory, *sankalpa* is also illusory. If it is strong and sincere, *sankalpa* will come true.

ELIMINATION OF THE MIND

Devotee: Mother, I have been worshipping God for a long time, but there is no peace of mind. What can I do?

Mother: Is it not the mind which has no peace? Eliminate the mind. Thus the problem is solved, is it not?

Devotee: Is it possible to eradicate the mind?

Mother: Why not? Are not all paths for that only? Do not let the mind go towards sense objects. This is possible through *sadhana* (spiritual practice). Now and then the mind will go outward. Immediately make it turn inward saying, "No, I won't let you go."

Devotee: How do human beings become good or bad?

Mother: Due to *vasanas*, actions arise, and from actions, *vasanas* arise. From God alone we received the first *vasana*. And from that, action followed. According to the actions, good and bad come.

THE LAW OF KARMA

Devotee: If each one experiences the fruit of his actions, why should the suffering one be helped?

Mother: If what he is experiencing is the fruit of his actions, then can't it be the fruit of your actions to save him? If his *vasana* becomes a cause for experiencing sorrow, your *vasana* becomes a cause to help. Both are the continuation of past actions. Remember that if you do not help the ailing, you will have to enjoy the fruit of that evil action.

Devotee: No faith comes because God cannot be seen. The *Mahatmas* can be seen. Therefore, is it not better to worship them?

Mother: That is all right, but you should also understand the relationship between the *Mahatmas* and God. Just as electricity manifests through a light bulb, it is the Essence of God which manifests through the *Mahatmas*. *Mahatmas* should be approached with *iswara bhavana* (the attitude that they are equal to God). Only then is there benefit. Guru should be considered as God.

SARIRA TYAGA
Committing Suicide

Another devotee: Mother, I have no interest in sustaining the body, but there is the desire for God-Realization. What shall I do?

Mother: The body will exist as long as there is desire. When one body is given up, another will be gained. Body is the manifestation of desire. Desire is of different kinds. There is no harm in the desire to know God. In fact, that desire must be there. To attain God, spiritual practices should be done and the body is needed for that. Therefore, the thought to give up the body is wrong.

Your mind is always in the body; that is why you feel that the body is a burden and that it should be given up. It means nothing if one who always thinks of the body says that he is thinking of God. There will be no body-consciousness if the mind merges in God. Let the body exist or let it fall off. After realizing the Truth, it is not a problem either way. Therefore, son, think of God at all times. That is what is needed now.

Mother knows that this suicidal tendency in you is not based purely on your longing to realize God. Is not the basic cause the calamities which recently occurred in your family? Son, you feel frightened thinking that those calamities which have subsided for the time being are again waiting to burst out, don't you? You are fearful about the future, aren't you? Son, don't worry. Nothing will happen. Cast off this fear; Mother is with you.

The devotee was struck with wonder hearing Mother clearly and precisely reveal her knowledge of his most subtle thoughts. It was perfectly true that a calamity had happened in his family, instilling in him intense fear. Upon the death of his father a few weeks earlier, there occurred a verbal duel between the relatives who each wanted to seize the ancestral wealth. This culminated in a terrible fight. This unfortunate incident sowed the seeds of dread and terror in this young man, who was the youngest in the family and one who loved peace.

Now he wondered how the Mother came to know of all this. He tried to fathom the mystery but failed. The young man looked with wide-open eyes at Mother's face and then with eyes cast down, he shed silent tears.

While Mother lovingly stroked his back and comforted him, another devotee asked,

HOW TO KNOW THE TRUTH

Devotee: Mother, how can one know the Truth while living in this world of plurality?

Mother: It is difficult to know God while we live in this world, but both God and the world can be known if the world is seen as God. Suppose a white crane is sitting in the midst of many crows. When viewed from a distance, everything will seem all black. As we move closer, the crows can be distinguished. Coming a little closer still, we will see the crane and our attention will be drawn to that. Likewise, Pure Consciousness will not come into sight if we stand at a distance. Truth cannot be gained by searching outside. Truth is One. Search for It within. Truth is ever-existent, while all else lasts for a short period of time. In reality, the essence of the world is only God, but you must have the eye to see that this is so.

Devotee: It is said that God and the world are one. Then why are they seen as two?

Mother: Just as the sun is the same during sunrise and sunset, God and the world are one. If all our energy is wasted on trivial things, that which is the Essence cannot be known. Discrimination must be used. *Satsang* (companionship with the Great Ones) is necessary.

Devotee: I would like to know certain things from Mother.

Mother: That which is made known by another will not become knowledge. Then what can Mother make you know?

Devotee: With what attitude should we visualize God?

Mother: It can be imagined that "I am God's child." When one's resolve becomes stronger and stronger, God's existence will become more convincing.

Devotee: Whatever is seen is not Truth. The scriptures say that God alone is Truth. So how should one live in this world?

Mother: Live a detached life. Don't attach yourself to work or to its fruit. Perform it as a sacrifice. Then your actions will become beautiful and beneficial to others.

Devotee: I am worshipping God in an image. While travelling, I am not able to continue doing it. Is there any harm in this?

Mother: Harm may occur if you feel worried and think that the worship has been discontinued. But the worship will not be broken if the Beloved Deity is carried in your heart and worshipped mentally even when you go out. Actually, *manasa puja* (mental worship) is the greatest, but those who are unable to do it should worship by offering flowers.

Devotee: When will I be liberated from this cycle of birth and death?

Mother: To get liberated, the "I" should go. This present body is the result of *sanchita karma* (accumulated actions) performed in the previous births. The human body is something higher than other bodies, and God-Realization can be attained by doing *sadhana* with this body. It is due to the acquired merits in the previous birth that one feels interested to search for God in this birth. Your desire will be fulfilled in this birth itself if your resolve and effort are continued with the same interest. The tendency to enjoy sensual pleasures should completely leave the mind.

DO NOT BECOME A SLAVE
TO THE CIRCUMSTANCES

As the conversation continued, another devotee came to see the Holy Mother. He was a newcomer. Having prostrated before the Mother, he sat among the other devotees. When the opportunity came to clear some of his doubts, he asked,

Devotee: Mother, for a long time I have been thinking about coming to see you. I could finally come today. There is a time and circumstance for all things, is there not?
Mother: Son, time is always favorable, but we are not favoring time; that is all. Both favor and adversity are within us only. Not knowing this, human beings become slaves to their circumstances. Many good things will pass through your hands if you sit still, saying, "Let a good time come." Do not wait looking for a opportunity to do a good thing. Do it immediately if it is good.
Devotee: It is said that God dwells within yet why is it that nobody knows Him?

Mother: Ordinary people think that they are the body only. They are attached to their wives, children and other relatives. Unknowingly they persist in wrong actions. While drowned in ignorance, how can we know God who is dwelling in the heart? God not only dwells in the heart; He is all-pervading as well. But we should try to know Him. Instead of making the mind extroverted, make it turn inward towards God.

Devotee: Among fears ~ such as fear of enemies, of poverty, of starvation and of other calamities ~ the most terrifying is the fear of death. How can that be conquered?

Mother: Fear of death will be removed when we become convinced that we are deathless, will it not? We should understand the truth that "I am the Self, I am *Brahman*, I am deathless."

THE GLORY OF THE GURU

Devotee: How can that be understood?

Mother: A Guru who is established in that knowledge should be approached. It is impossible without a Guru. Suppose we are going to travel to a strange place. Somebody who knows the path must be there to protect us. *Satsang* is the easiest path. A scholar who has scriptural knowledge is not sufficient. A Guru who is a Knower of the Self must be present. Only one who has known the path can show the way.

19 September 1976

As usual, the sun god, the illuminator of the universe, emerged on the eastern horizon slowly sending forth brilliant rays to caress the earth and its creatures. Gazing at the beautiful rising sun, the Holy Mother lay in the front yard of the old temple. While looking at the sun, her mind soared to the heights of supreme bliss and, getting up in a semi-conscious mood, she walked into the shrine with faltering steps like one intoxicated. Having entered the temple, Mother started singing loudly, calling out now and then, "Amma! ...Amma!" After a couple of minutes, the Mother abruptly stopped singing, and placing her head on the *peetham* (the seat she sat on for the *Devi Bhava*), she started chanting the sacred syllable "AUM." She became totally lost to this world. Eventually, she began rolling on the ground from this side to that side.

One hour passed like this, then she suddenly got up and began dancing blissfully, having placed on her head the statue of Lord Krishna which was kept in the temple. Replacing the figure in its spot, the Holy Mother emerged from the temple still in the same blissful mood. It was then that she noticed that the milk brought for her by a devotee had been tipped over by the crows and had spilled on the floor. The Mother sat on the floor and drank some of the milk by scooping it from the floor with her cupped hands. Thus the Mother fulfilled the wish of the devotee who had brought the milk especially for her, even though it was no longer in the cup. The next moment, the Mother joined the children who were playing games in the front yard of the temple. Now she looked exactly like a small mischievous child making merry with her playmates.

Although seemingly strange, these crazy actions of the Mother were full of significance in the eyes of spiritually elevated people. Such childlike plays of the Holy Mother gave delight to the eyes of the devotees.

While the Holy Mother was playing with the children, some devotees came to see her. Having stopped her play, the

Mother approached the devotees smiling benignly at them. Now her mood again changed from that of a child to that of a compassionate mother. Followed by the devotees, the Mother went to the temple verandah and sat there with them. She lovingly asked, "Children, did you eat anything?" They replied, "Yes, we ate our lunch, Mother." "From where?" the Mother enquired. "From the shop," they replied. Mother smiled as the devotees sat looking at her, wondering at her compassion and love. They had many things to ask. It was often the experience of the devotees and aspirants who came to see the Mother that the Masterhood in her would be invoked by a person's thirst for knowledge. During such occasions one could see the unending flow of the Mother's profound wisdom streaming forth in all its beauty.

TRUE KNOWLEDGE

Devotee: Isn't it disappointing to see *bheda buddhi* (differentiating mind) even in famous *sannyasins*?
Mother: Children, true knowledge cannot be gained by merely studying the scriptures. *Bheda buddhi* will exist as long as there is no Self Knowledge. Scriptural knowledge is external; whereas knowledge of the Self is internal. *Bheda buddhi* will not be seen in one whose mind has merged in God. Book scholars will speak about renunciation, but they cannot withdraw their minds from sense objects. A real Master is a Knower of the Self. Such beings should work among people, giving guidance to them.

MONKS AND RENUNCIATION

Devotee: Shouldn't a monk keep away from the world? Isn't he someone who has renounced the world? Can he engage in material affairs again?

Mother: *Sannyasa* (formal renunciation, becoming a monk) is not the renunciation of the world and of action. *Tyaga* (renunciation) is renunciation of the fruits of action. It is the *dharma* (duty) of *sannyasins* to lead the world. *Sannyasins* are the ones who give peace to the world. Whoever may protest, there will always be a group of Knowers of the Self in this world. Even today there are people who can sanctify the world by their mere *sankalpa*. Not everyone will know about them. There are also many institutions which sincerely work for world peace.

Devotee: Can awareness of the Truth be gained through institutions?

Mother: What is meant by an institution is not an institution like a factory or a bank. It is a charitable institution. Many people would be working for each charitable institution. Several institutions like this should be formed; that is what Mother wants to say. Let at least ten people take the righteous path through each institution. Among them, at least in one person, awareness of the Truth might awaken. They, in turn, will protect many others.

Devotee: In this way, after how many years would the entire human race be turned into Knowers of the Self? Would such a thing be possible?

Mother: God's resolve is not there for this to happen. Everything must be there in the Creation. Otherwise, how could the *leela* (God's play) take place?

It is not Mother's intention to keep the children who are here inside the four walls of the Ashram. Tomorrow they have to do good things out in the world. Even though the world may not know the value of this now, in the future it will be known. Until then, the protests and abuses should be accepted happily.

Listening and getting absorbed in the ambrosial words and presence of the Holy Mother, the devotees were quite unaware of the passing of time. It was now one o'clock in the afternoon, yet no one wanted to get up and eat lunch. Hunger and thirst will disappear in the presence of a great Master. Presently some more devotees arrived. The Holy Mother was cheerful and compassionate as ever.

Question: Mother, I always want to come and see you, but I should get time, shouldn't I?
Mother: (Smiling) All those who come here say that there is no time. Then for whom is all this time? Each day some time should be kept apart for Godly matters.
Devotee: We are doing spiritual practices as instructed by Mother. Our children are also doing *japa*[4] and *dhyana*.[5]
Mother: Good, they will not swerve from the path in the future because they have begun doing this at such a young age.
Another devotee: (Pointing to his son) It is a school holiday. He came and told me that he wants to stay here for two or three days. I agreed.
Mother: Then let both the children stay. (Smilingly) Here I will play with the children. In the middle of the game I will play tricks on them. Afraid of me, the children will go along with all this.
Devotee: Mother, during meditation I feel headaches. Why is this happening?
Mother: It can happen if meditation is not done at the cor-

---

[4]Repetition of a mantra.
[5]Meditation.

rect time. A regular discipline is needed. Headaches may also occur if one meditates between the eyebrows. At that time stop meditation for two days and switch to *japa* and *kirtana*.⁶ If headaches return when you resume meditation then meditation should be done in the heart. Then there will be no problem.

Question: Mother, how can we think of God with our limited intellect?

Mother: It is possible if the intellect, limited in the individual, is expanded. The intellect should be fixed on the *atma bhava*⁷ giving up the *deha bhava*.⁸

Devotee: Is it possible for ordinary people?

Mother: Anyone can do so if they really have the desire. The only thing is that they have to do *sadhana*. They must understand that which stands as the Cause behind the perceptible non-eternal objects. The goal of human effort is to know that Divine Power which illumines even the sun, moon and stars.

BRAHMAN AND JAGAT
Absolute Consciousness and the World

Question: Mother, it is said that *Brahman* and *jagat* are one. How can that be?

Mother: Just as every object that exists has a name, the world exists in *Brahman.* . Name and form are inseparable. When there is the awareness of the world, there is no awareness of the Self. And when there is awareness of the Self, awareness of the world is no longer there . There is butter in milk, but it is not seen. When butter is obtained through

⁶Singing of God's Names and songs in praise of Him or Her.
⁷The attitude that "I am the Self."
⁸The attitude that "I am the body."

churning, it forms a ball. If heated, it melts, and the shape changes. In the same manner, *Brahman* is not seen in diversity. It can be found when *sadhana* is performed. When butter is heated, there is no form; when frozen it solidifies. God's form and formlessness is like this. There is no dross in either, no waste.

Question: The scriptures say that we are not the body but the Self. If one believes this, is it necessary to trouble oneself with *sadhana?*

Mother: Is it not a belief that is obtained through telling, hearing and reading? It will not last long. Whereas, the faith gained from experience will last forever. Suppose a person was travelling with his son. They felt very hungry and thirsty. Pointing out a rice paddy on the roadside, the father said, "Look, this is a rice paddy. After some time grain will be there. If the plants arehusked, rice will be obtained. Delicious food can be made by mixing rice flour, coconut and molasses which, when eaten, will stop hunger." But hunger will not be removed with this knowledge alone. You must eat the food if hunger is to be removed. Scriptures will tell about the *Atman*, but what is the use of these words if they are not experienced directly? What guarantee is there that we will reach a point when we think, "I will try for that,"? Without wasting time, we must start the effort immediately.

JIVATMA AND PARAMATMA
Individual Self and Supreme Self

Question: Mother, are *jivatman* and *Paramatma* two?
Mother: In *vyavahara*[9] there are two. When *samsara*[10] is

---

[9]The phenomenal world.
[10]The Ocean of Transmigration or birth, death and rebirth.

given up there is only one. There is a dam in the middle of a lake. When the dam is there, the lake is two; and if the dam is not there, then it is one. This dam is ignorance or *maya*. If that is removed, it becomes Non-dual Knowledge. Duality is only seemingly real. In truth, everything is strung together on one strand, the thread of *Atman*. We perceive duality when we are established in the pride of body-consciousness. Like air and movement, or fire and the power of burning, *Paramatma* and *jivatman* are one and the same. The perception of this Unity is called *Jnana*.[11] Perception of plurality is *ajnana*.[12] Those possessing a one-pointed mind understand that the same witness-consciousness exists within everything. But ordinary people do not know this. A powerful person is one who has known the unity of *jivatman* and *Paramatma*. He has neither fear, nor afflictions. *Jagat* (the world) is apparent; God is beyond the world. The goal is to reach the Non-dual State, abandoning all imaginings born of plurality.

EVOLUTION OF THE INDIVIDUAL SELF

Devotee: To where is the evolution of the *jiva* (individual self) leading?

Mother: The goal of this journey is to attain something great. Searching and roaming about the whole world, one becomes dissatisfied. One tries to think of a way to gain satisfaction, but thoughts and doubts arise in the mind. So next one looks to see whether peace can be gained if searched for in the mind itself. From then onwards the mind begins to turn inward. The enquiry continues, but at some point the path gets obstructed. We approach a Sat-

[11]Spiritual knowledge or wisdom.
[12]Spiritual ignorance.

guru, and again we move forward. At last, the goal of Self-Realization is reached. Such souls will later come forward to protect the world.

Devotee: Mother, will there be body-consciousness even after attaining Knowledge?

Mother: In Jnanis[13] the awareness of the Self is always there. A Jnani knows that the body is not real. Descending a little from the plane of the Real, the Jnani acts for the protection of the world, but he can give up the body whenever it is necessary. After going to your village and spreading news about the Ashram to many people, you can return here at any time. Like this, a Jnani will do many things while in the world, but he will always remain established in the awareness of the Truth. A Jnani has no body-consciousness. He has only awareness of the Self, but others will feel that he has a body.

All of a sudden the Holy Mother closed her eyes and sat motionless. Her face lit up with a blissful smile. All the devotees who were gathered around her began meditating. After a few minutes had passed, the Mother slowly opened her eyes and began singing rapturously,

> By which Power
> This world has been created,
> By which Power it is sustained,
> By which Power
> It returns to the unmanifest state,
> Let us offer our salutations
> To that Great Power...

---

[13]A Realized Soul.

Everyone joined her and went into an ecstatic mood.
The Holy Mother shed tears of bliss, now and then calling
out, "Amma, Amma" while continuing the singing. Her
poignant song and elevated spiritual mood filled the devotees' hearts with tremendous peace and tranquillity. Forgetting the world around them, they sang with great devotion.

THE SIGNS OF SELF REALIZATION

One of the resident *brahmacharins* had doubts as to
whether the Mother was a Realized Soul or not; but he was
a bit hesitant to open his heart to her. One day while talking
to some of the residents, Mother turned to the
doubting*brahmacharin* and said,

Mother: A Self Realized Soul is one who sees the Funda-
mental Principle in everything. He hasn't even an iota of
doubt. In him there is no place for the argument, "There is
or there is not," for he has the constant Vision of the Truth
alone, everywhere ~ in front, in back, above and below.
There is not even a hint of *prapancha bhavana*[1] in him. In
the plane of Real Awareness there is no place for the world.
The world merges in *Satta*.[15] Both within and without there
is the same Consciousness. It is beyond even the intellect.
Only such a person, none but a Self Realized Soul, can work
for the protection of the world. Renunciation, feeling of
equality, humility and simplicity are his characteristics.

The resident who was listening to the Mother's words
with great wonder shed tears, thinking of the compassion
that she had just shown him.

[14]Feeling of the existence of the apparent world.
[15]The Essence.

THE WAY A SATGURU DISCIPLINES

One of the residents was talking to the Mother about the things which made him sad.

Devotee: In the beginning stages Mother would show great affection to me, telling me stories and feeding me with her own hand. But now there is nothing. The only thing she says is to study the scriptures and do *sadhana* (spiritual practices).

Mother: (Affectionately) In those days that was necessary. Now this is what is needed. Fathers build playhouses with leaves and boughs of a palm tree for their young children. In those days you could not understand spiritual principles. Therefore, more external love was shown. Now Mother keeps that love within. What you need now is serious spiritual training. It is not that Mother has any less love for her children.

Mother looked most lovingly at him and his face lost its look of sadness. Later, a group of youths arrived. From their appearance it was clear that they were college students. They stood at a little distance from where Mother was seated. She smiled graciously at them and asked where they had come from. Perhaps it was the Mother's natural way of enquiring that made the students come closer to her. As they approached, she asked them to sit down which they did. Moments passed in silence while the Holy Mother sat in front of them, her smiling face radiating compassion and love. One of the students broke the silence, asking a question which made it clear that he was interested in spiritual life.

Question: Is there a God?

Mother: Why doubt it? What is, is only God.

Question: Why then is He not seen?

Mother: What then is all this that is seen? What we see in different forms is God alone.

Question: Then why don't I feel like that? What should be done to develop that feeling? Can it be said that everything of this diverse Nature is God?

Mother: Why not? Could there be diversity in God because you see Him as diverse? Diversity is felt because of the difference of each one's vision. Otherwise, there is no difference in God. God's real nature will be understood when the attitude of difference in us is removed. What is the difficulty in perceiving unity in diversity? We have hands, legs, eyes, nose, etc., but are these different organs not part of our own body? The limbs are not different from the body, are they? Like this, see everything as His limbs. The sun gets concealed by the clouds. In a like manner, God is concealed by our *vasanas*. He becomes visible when the dirt of latent tendencies is removed.

Question: How shall I do that, Mother?

Mother: The *vasanas* should be gotten rid of through *sadhana*. We are not the body; there is Truth within. That is what should be known. If we enquire outside, we won't get That. There is another thing: Just as He is within, He exists without as well. But searching for God outside is like trying to catch fish by emptying the ocean. Therefore, become introspective. Once God is seen within, He can be seen everywhere. The mind should be purified by getting rid of bad thoughts. God will shine in a pure mind.

MERITS AND DEMERITS, PRARABDHAM[16]

Question: Mother, what are *punya* and *papa?*[17]

Mother: The result of auspicious action is *punya*; the fruit of inauspicious action is *papa*. Action which brings *dosha*[18] to oneself and others is inauspicious, and that which brings prosperity and goodness is auspicious. *Punya* and *papa* can be transcended if *vasanas* are exhausted. For that, the mind should be cleansed through *sadhana*.

The *Atman* is not affected by merits and demerits, happiness and sorrow, and other opposites. They affect the mind only. The *Atman* is only a witness to everything.

Question: Mother, what is this *prarabdha karma?*

Mother: Children, *prarabdha karmas* are those *vasanas* which exist in subtle form in the *chitta*[19] alone. *Prabdha* will exist until Knowledge of the Self is gained; it will be there as long as body-consciousness remains. The body does not have to perish. If awareness of the body is overcome, *prarabdha* will cease. *Prarabdha* is related to the body, and will fall off when the knowledge that "I am not the body; I am the Self" is gained.

For a *Jnani*, there is no birth and death. Everything has only an apparent existence as far as he is concerned. For him, there is nothing different from *Brahman*. The body will exist for some time even after one becomes a Knower of the Self, but the feeling that one has a body will be in the eyes of others only. As far as a *Jnani* is concerned, what is called "body" is also *Brahman*. There are people who live peacefully even in the midst of all this confusion. Nobody is bound by

[16]The results of actions done in previous births which are now bearing fruit.
[17]Merit and demerit (virtue and sin).
[18]Evil.
[19]The mind.

samsara once even an iota of the principle of Stillness is experienced.

Question: Mother, what is *tyaga?*

Mother: *Tyaga* is abandoning the desire for the fruit of
one's actions. He is liberated who is desireless. The desire
rising up from the feeling "I" and "mine" is the cause of
bondage.

Question: There is only one God. Then isn't one path
enough? What are all these different methods of *sadhana*
for?

Mother: Different means can be chosen for travelling.
Travel can be done by water, air or land, but the destination
will be the same.

Question: Where is the best place to concentrate when doing *rupa dhyana?*[20]

Mother: Meditation in the heart is the best.

Question: Mother, when does the thought of God arise in a
person?

Mother: The thought of God can arise all of a sudden, due
to the accumulated merits of past births. If it is properly
nourished, we can make progress. But if we do nothing, we
will forget God, and go on living just as we were before. If
sadhana can be started at a very young age, that is the best.

Question: Why are most people not interested in Godly
matters?

Mother: Due to the lack of accumulated merits from previous births, the desire for sense objects will be predominant.

TIME NEEDED FOR GOD-REALIZATION

Some householders who were serious spiritual practitio-
ners came to see the Holy Mother. They sat among the other

[20]Meditation on a form of God.

devotees and listened keenly to the topic which she was discussing. One of them asked,

Devotee: Mother, I am a householder. All my time has been wasted. The *brahmacharins* who stay here with Mother have started doing *sadhana* at a very young age. Is it even possible for me to reach the goal now if I try?"

Mother: Why not? The mind should be firm. Not much time is needed for God-Realization. When one feels the interest, then and there one should start the effort. Quicker will be the effect if there is sincerity in the effort.

Question: For those of us who are ordinary people, is it possible to know God?

Mother: Children, God is also ordinary , and therefore He is not difficult to know. But there is one thing not to forget: the ignorant ones who are drowning themselves in worldliness cannot know the Truth. Whoever it may be, he who has sincere interest can know and see God.

THAT WHICH IS NEEDED FIRST

Question: What should a person who has become interested in spirituality do first?

Mother: Approach a real Master. *Sadhana* should be performed as instructed by the Master. Faith and devotion in the Guru should be there. A *Satguru* (a Self-Realized Master) alone is the refuge.

Question: How to search for and find such a person?

Mother: The Guru will come before one who has intense desire to Know. That omniscient Guru will gradually take the disciple to the goal. A *Satguru* is one who is capable of taking the disciple to the goal.

Question: Mother, I have saved a lot of money, but still there is no happiness anywhere. What is the way?

Mother: This thought will not be there in everyone. This is a good time for you children. These thoughts arise because of the merit of the good actions done in the previous birth. Happiness will not be gained if you go after sense objects. No one will wait for anyone in this world. Each one runs after his own happiness. God is of the nature of bliss. Therefore, we can live happily if we can live in God. Faith is needed. The thought that "I am the doer" should go. God is the doer. The mind should be always fixed in God. *Satsang* (association with sages) is necessary. *Sadhana* should be performed as instructed by the Guru. Meditation should be practiced. In the beginning stages, try to meditate for a short time. Later, it will be possible to meditate for a longer time. The Lord's Name should always be remembered without wasting time, associating with friends or making jokes.

Devotee: Mother, you should guide us.

Mother: Shiva! Shiva! This crazy one?! God will do all that.

The Holy Mother was talking with some of the residents sitting in the front yard of the temple. It was eleven o'clock in the morning.

Brahmacharin: Mother, how does one gain bliss?

Mother: Children, everything depends on the mind. All is well when the mind improves. Chanting, *japa*, meditation, etc., are to make the mind pure and one-pointed.

Another brahmacharin: Mother, what is fate?

Mother: There are people who take God's Will to be fate and who think that it is unchangeable. This is not correct. We perform actions according to our *vasanas*, the results of which will eventually come to us. The fruitof the actions which we have done in our previous births is known as our fate. Fate can be changed and transformed through self-effort – through sincere prayer and meditation.

Question: Mother, there are many religions. Of these, which one is the best?

Mother: All religions are good. All religions which help one realize God are good. The path which is not helpful for God-Realization should not be accepted as a religion. Religion is that which leads to Self-Realization. (Turning to the *brahmacharins*) You children are all lucky. At such a yong age, you have a mind to relinquish *samsara* , have you not? This is not possible with just one lifetime's merit. This is the fruit of many lifetimes' merit. Also, we might have met together before. If not, we would not be bonded together like this. Some of those who come here seem very familiar to Mother. It is impossible to be separated having been together before. The *brahmacharins* do not think about the opposition and difficulties from their families;   some do not even feel like going home.

At six o'clock in the evening, the sun set in all its glory into the Arabian Sea. The waves danced gleefully, singing the ever vibrant sound "AUM." The Holy Mother, accompanied by the residents and devotees, began singing devotional songs as they sat on the front verandah of the temple. Mother slowly became more and more absorbed in the singing.

> O Thou Who art meditated upon in
> thousands of hearts,
> Thou blazest forth forever in the minds
> of those who have realized God...

As the Mother sang these lines, she became overwhelmed with bliss and merged in a state of divine inebriation. She began crying like a small child, now and then calling out, "Amma, Amma!" Her cries and ecstatic laughter continued for a long time. The residents and devotees also were also filled with bliss as they sang, drinking in the nectar of the Divine Name. After some time, the Holy Mother rose from her seat and came to the front yard of the temple. She began a rapturous dance which she punctuated with blissful laughter. Some of the *brahmacharins* who were watching the scene became oblivious to the surroundings as they shed tears of joy. Some others sat quietly and merged into meditation.

Eventually, Mother's father came to the spot, caught hold of her, and made her lie down on a mat, for he thought that something very serious had happened to his daughter. But the Holy Mother remained in another world, her hands held in *amudra*[21], her face radiating like the rising sun. When she finally came down to a normal plane of consciousness, one of the devotees said,

Devotee: We were concerned that Mother would have gone on and on dancing if Sugunanandan had not caught hold of her.

Mother: He should not have done that. It was not good. It is unbearable if someone even touches the body on such occasions. Now the whole body is burning, due to being touched. In the future, be attentive and do not let anyone touch.

Without saying anything more about it, Mother walked away. It was almost eleven o'clock at night. Some of the

[21]A symbolic gesture done with the fingers.

brahmacharins went to meditate at the seashore; some went inside the temple and others went to their rooms.

PRAPANCHA AND VEDANTA

1 September 1977

A devotee from Quilon had come to see the Holy Mother. Prompted by what he had heard and read about spirituality, he began asking questions. When the Mother started to answer his questions, many devotees and a few residents came and listened keenly to the conversation. The time was ten o'clock in the morning. In a still and peaceful atmosphere the dialogue commenced.

Devotee: *Vedanta*[22] says that the *prapancha* (world) is an illusion, doesn't it? If it is so, then there is no relevance to worldly life, is there?
Mother: Son, *Vedanta* does not deny the material plane. *Vedanta* views the world in a slightly different way from the ordinary outlook, that is all. *Vedanta* says that all that is seen is not as we think it to be, but that it is *Brahman* (the Absolute) alone. Was it not because the *Vedantin* Sankara recognized the existence of the world that he worked hard his whole life for the upliftment of the world? Look at the life of Vivekananda who was also a *Vedantin*. *Vedanta* is saying that we should imbibe the correct awareness and remove the wrong understanding about ourselves and the world. If we do not, it will be difficult to surmount all sorrow and reach the shore of liberation.

In the beginning, the Guru will tell the disciple, "The world is an illusion. Rejecting it, become established in the

[22]The system of philosophy expounded in the Upanishads.

Self." This is to speed up the *sadhana*. The disciple will understand that this whole world is part of God when at last he reaches Realization. Then there will not be anything to reject; then he will love and serve all. The description of this state is not hypothetical; it is derived from experience.

VEDANTA AND IMAGE WORSHIP

Question: Mother, isn't *Vedanta* against image worship?

Mother: No, *Vedanta* denies nothing. Son, each and every one has a befitting path to make the mind concentrated on the Self. Hasn't Sankaracharya himself renovated temples, installed statues and composed poetry about gods and goddesses? Do not get entangled in image worship forever. At a certain stage of *sadhana*, all forms will merge and disappear, and one will reach the Formless State. Even though one or two may understand that the world is an illusion, for others the material world is real.

Scriptures and paths are to uplift those who are rambling in ignorance. They are not for the Knowers of Truth who have already attained the Goal.

Question: Can a devotee become a *Vedantin*?

Mother: *Para bhakti* (supreme devotion) is pure *Vedanta*. A true devotee sees everything as pervaded by God. He sees nothing but God everywhere. A devotee says, "Everything is pervaded by God," and the *Vedantin* says, "Everything is pervaded by *Brahman*." Both are one and the same.

Question: Who is the real "I"? When will I become aware that everything which is seen is "I"?

Mother: That "I" which fills the whole universe is the real "I." When the awareness that "I am not the body, I am the Self" awakens, we will understand that nothing is different from *Brahman*. At that time, we will know through experience that everything is "I" alone.

Question: Mother, everything is happening according to God's Will. Therefore, there is not much scope for our effort. It is not possible to prevent God's Will.

Mother: If you have that much conviction in God, can't you request Him to alter your fate? One who judges can also take back the judgement. Can you not just try and see?

If you accept what is not wanted and do not accept what is needed, there is no sense in blaming fate. Because of their pride, some people will not search for God. Sensual pleasures will not let go of others, and still others do not have time. What is the result? Sorrow.

Everyone sat gazing with wonder and amazement at the Holy Mother's radiant face.

PRANAYAMA[23]

After a few moments had passed, another devotee continued to ask questions,

Devotee: Mother, will *pranayama* help to attain Âtma Jñana (Knowledge of the Self)?

Mother: The mind will gain concentration through *pranayama*. It is easily possible to fix the one-pointed mind on the *Atman*, is it not? The mind fixed on the Self becomes liberated from *samsara* (*samsara vimuktam*).

Question: Mother, many come here for worldly purposes. Why?

Mother: Everyone will not come to spirituality at the same

[23]Control of the mind through control of the vital force, particularly the breath.

time. If they did, then one Sankaracharya or one Sri Ramakrishna would have been enough. According to their *samskara*· different people will reach the road to Liberation at
different times.

WHAT IS BONDAGE?

Devotee: Mother has entrapped me in the family; therefore,
I cannot come to see her often.
Mother: This is what all the children are saying. Having
glued themselves to sense objects, they complain that God
has bound them. God hears everything but keeps quiet.
Devotee: Then I am not going away from here anymore. Let
all the necessities be looked after by Him alone.
Mother: That is good! Once he has eaten the lentil curry
and buttermilk which we serve here, then he will not be
seen anymore! (All burst into laughter) It seems that until
now you alone have been looking after all the household
matters. Now you say, "I am not going from here. Let God
look after the necessities." It is God alone who is looking after you at all times. Son, bondage is nothing but the feeling
"I am doing."

Another devotee mockingly said to him, "Here, only wa-
tery lentil curry is available. If you are at home, you will have
thick curry and polished rice ." (All laugh)

Mother: None of you should mock him. This son only pro-
ceeds with caution.

---

[24]Tendencies inherited from past births.

That devotee, who was thoroughly convinced that although she teased him, Mother understood he was living as a *sadhak* in his daily life, turned to the others and said, "Mother is seeing each movement of mine. That is why she said that I am moving cautiously."

Question: Mother, I am having no peace of mind nowadays.
Mother: Son, can't you decrease a few of your outside affairs? Practice meditation for a few days in solitude. Otherwise, the strain on the mind will worsen.

WHAT IS FREEDOM?

13 September 1977

Some people arrived to see the Holy Mother in the afternoon. With them came a scholar. The Mother was sitting in the southern part of the old temple. Two elderly women devotees from the neighbourhood were trying to make the Mother eat something, but like an innocent and stubborn child, she refused to eat despite their affectionate pleading. Every time they requested her to eat something, the Mother would begin her playful antics and divert their attention from the food to herself. The devotees watched the charming sight from a distance, then eventually the Holy Mother saw them. With childlike innocence she said, "Look, these mothers are trying to feed me but I am not hungry!" One of the women said, "Dear sir, Amma has not eaten anything but some coconut water for the last three days. Please tell her to eat something."

Finally, due to their continuous persistence and prayers, the Mother ate just one ball of rice and then ran away like a child from its mother. She sat in front of the temple while the elderly ladies helplessly stood there, holding the plate of rice in their hands. The devotees followed the Mother and, after offering their prostrations, sat near her. A few moments passed and her *bala bhava* (childlike mood) slowly disappeared. She closed her eyes and sat motionless while the devotees gazed at her face in wonder and reverence. A few minutes passed in silence before the Mother opened her eye Withdrawing all other aspects within, she now looked like a great Master. Nobody would say that this was the same person who, like a child, had been making merry a few moments ago. The visiting scholar began the conversation, "Mother, we would like to know certain things."

Mother: Shiva! Shiva! From this crazy girl? She knows only one thing and that is that she does not know anything.

Despite the Mother's words, the devotees put forth their questions one by one.

Devotee: Mother, what is meant by freedom?
Mother: Freedom from worldly existence. Freedom from the cycle of birth and death. Total surrender to God alone is itself the easiest way. Either cultivate the attitude "I am *Brahman*, I am everything," or think "I am nothing, I am God's child, His servant."
Devotee: What shall I do to get purity of mind?
Mother: Mental purity will come through constant chanting of the Divine Name. This is the simplest way. But not everyone will have the faith to chant. Belief and disbelief are there at all times. Even this world is the result of disbelief. Then how can disbelief be completely eliminated? Disbelief will go

if belief becomes firm. Once faith comes, enquiry is no longer needed. Enquiry ends in faith. The faith that you children have now is not full. Therefore, try for perfect faith. Full faith means Realization.

THE GRACE OF LOVE

Scholar: It seems as if Mother has practiced yoga and other disciplines very well.
Mother: Shiva, Shiva! I have not practiced anything. But there is one thing which is natural to me, the nature to love. Love constantly flows from me to the Creation.
Scholar: How many people can love everyone equally like this?
Mother: Do not worry about the number of people who can love. Those who imbibe love are not lowly. Blessed are their lives.

MOTHER'S KNOWLEDGE AND THE PURPOSE OF HER BIRTH

Scholar: What are Mother's future programmes?
Mother: *Bhagavan* (the Lord) will look after all those things.
Scholar: Mother must have come down with that same knowledge, isn't that so?
Mother: After coming here I have returned that knowledge to Him also. Otherwise, who could keep all this knowledge? It will sit safely there in the hands of God, will it not? He will hand it over, little by little, to us when necessary.
Scholar: I have wandered a lot, but nowhere did I get peace. Mother, please bless me.

Mother smiled and then all of a sudden entered into deep *samadhi*. Her body became stiff like a log of wood. Everyone silently watched her. Regaining partial consciousness, she requested the scholar to sing a song.

> O Lord, if the blue mountain be ink,
> The ocean the inkstand,
> The branch of the Heavenly Tree be the pen,
> The earth the writing leaf,
> And by taking these, if the
> Goddess of Learning writes for eternity,
> Even then, the limit of Thy virtues
> Will not be reached...

He sang with great devotion and all the others sat in deep meditation. When the song was over Mother went on uttering, "Shiva! Shiva!" One among the devotees again asked a question: "Mother, what should be done to quiet the mind?"

Mother: *Japa, dhyana* and other spiritual disciplines should be practiced.
Devotee: How long will it take to attain the goal?
Mother: That depends upon each one's inner disposition.
Devotee: Mother's gracious look should always be there on this one.
Mother: Certainly. Is it not children like you to whom Mother should pay special attention? (Pointing to herself) Look here, this life itself is for that.

Usually, Mother did not speak so directly as this. Rarely would she give such hints which, even indirectly, would let

people understand that she had come down with that awareness, with the Realization of God.

14 September 1977

One devotee from Trivandrum came and prostrated before the Holy Mother. He was a doctor, a dermatologist, and
an ardent devotee of Lord Krishna. Mother smilingly asked
him,

Mother: Son, where do you come from?
Doctor: Do you know me, Mother? Your question was so
natural. It seems as if you are seeing your son again after a
long absence.
Mother: Do you think you would come here if we had no
prior acquaintance? Many people are familiar. Old acquain-
tances may be forgotten; but some people can refresh their
memories.
Doctor: When I was in Guruvayoor[25] one man told me
about Mother. He said that she is an embodiment of love.
Mother: Mother knows only, love. (Looking at the book
which the doctor was holding) What is that book, son?
Doctor: The Bhagavad-Gita. In Mother I see everything that
Bhagavan tells Arjuna about a *Jivanmukta*.[26]
Mother: (Like a small child) What does it say in there?
Doctor: Did Mother ever read it?
Mother: (Shaking her hands) No, it is not possible for me.
Should I know reading? Even if I manage to read, after three
or four lines, I lose control.
Doctor: What a fool I am! What is a book for Mother? Is

---

[25]A famous Krishna temple in Kerala.
[26]A Liberated Soul.

not Mother beyond all this? That is why so many people like me come here.

Mother: Let that be. What does it say in the Gita?

Doctor:

atmanyevatmana tushtaha
sthita prajñasta dôchyte

Sthitaprajña is one who is content
in the Atman, by the Atman.

GITA, CHAP.II, VERSE 55

Having heard these lines, the Mother became totally self-absorbed. In a semi-conscious mood she chanted, "Aum, Aum," lifting her hands up in the air and shaking her head sideways. This continued for a few minutes and slowly coming down to a normal plane of consciousness she said,

Mother: Always remember one thing. Studying the scriptures is good, but a shortage of devotion should not occur. You can read the books, but mere reading is not enough. Practice is also necessary. Mother cannot read or hear such books without her mind suddenly going to another world.

Doctor: And Mother again comes down for something.

Mother: It is enough if you learn just once to fix the mind in God. After that the mind will not leave at all.

MANTRA DIKSHA
The Necessity of Initiation

A few more devotees came and saluted the Mother.

A doctor: Is initiation necessary? Can't Perfection be attained without that?

Mother: Without initiation, partial progress can be attained. In Kashmir apples will grow abundantly. Apple trees will grow in our village as well, but here they will not bear much fruit. There will not be any taste either. Apples need to be grown very carefully and in favourable circumstances. For a *sadhak*, the Guru's presence is the favourable circumstance. If there is no Guru, one should be very careful, for then there are possibilities of falling.

God's Presence cannot be felt without purity of heart. The purpose of initiation is to gain mental purity. Because milk will spoil in a dirty vessel, first the vessel should be cleaned. Only then can milk be poured into it. Initiation will also help awaken the inner divine power. The *mantra*, itself a form of divine power, enters the heart of the disciple from within the Guru, a knower of *Brahman*. Just as water is used for external cleanliness, internal purity is gained through initiation. When a spark of fire is blown upon and ignites, it becomes a great power.

There is a natural way of making yogurt by adding a little buttermilk to warm milk. If this is kept still for a day, it will turn into yogurt. In a similar manner, initiation ~ the process of transmitting a portion of the Guru's power to the disciple ~ will enable the disciple to fully develop this same power if he works on it sincerely, applying self-effort. Great power can also be created if *mantras* are chanted repeatedly.

Devotee: Is it ineffective if *mantra diksha* is given without the customary rites?

Mother: The Guru's initiation will never be fruitless. It is to get rid of the vacillation of the disciple's mind that the initiation is given with established customs and pomp. The disciple might have doubts about the *mantra* if it is not given according to ritual. If the disciple has doubts, his practice will not be correct. Not only that, If *achara*[27] is transgressed, the sanctity of the initiation might be gradually lost.

Another devotee: Mother, I am a devotee of Devi (the Divine Mother). Having seen my enthusiasm, one *sannyasin* said, "Child, there is no doubt that you will soon gain a perfect teacher." Shortly after the swami said this, I happened to see Mother.

Mother: Everything is God's Will. His Grace is always there for His devotees. That Embodiment of Compassion is gazing at us. What do we have with which we can repay that mercy?

Devotee: Are God's Grace and Guru's Grace one?

Mother: Yes. What is received through the Guru's Grace is God's Grace.

Devotee: Mother, when will we be liberated?

Mother: Children, unload the burden from your head. At that time you will become liberated. It is not enough if it is simply turned over. It should be surrendered to God. Then happily continue doing what He makes you do.

Devotee: It is said that pure food should be taken, is it not? How should that be done?

Mother: Before taking food, it should be offered to God. If poor people come, give them food, seeing them as God. Then the food we eat will become pure.

---

[27]Customary observances.

As she was talking, the Mother's attention turned to the pictures of gods and goddesses hanging on the wall. Looking at the portrait of Lord Shiva, Mother said, "Oh...You?...Ancient One. Is it enough to sit like that? Who is going to look after the responsibility of all these people? I cannot be here for a long time."

Devotee: Don't say like that, Mother! Who is there for us if you go?

Mother: Do not be sad, son. Mother was simply saying that. Is it possible to simply go away like that? Are there not certain things to be done?

BHAVA DARSHAN
The Divine Mood

Devotee: Mother, are you always aware of your divine moods or are you aware of them only during *Devi* and *Krishna Bhava?*

Mother: These things cannot be said in that way. Different people's faiths are seen in different ways. Mother's intention is that each person somehow gets closer to God. Some people like it only if they see the dress of Devi and Krishna. Not only that; many do not know anything about spirituality. Some people can understand certain things about spirituality because these *Bhavas* are perpetuated. It is a little difficult for some people to believe if Mother tells something now. If told during *Devi Bhava*, they will believe.

A devotee who was sitting at a little distance asked, "Mother, why don't you inform the people about the real facts of your coming?"

Mother: Shiva! Shiva! What shall Mother make them understand? What does Mother know? Everything is Devi's
leela (play). Humility and simplicity are the characteristics of
greatness, the attitude that "I am nothing." Instead, we walk
around trying to exhibit our abilities. The coconut feels, "Because of me, the dish was tasty." The cook will say, "It was
because of my skill that it was good." The fire would say,
"Because of me the dish was well-cooked." But all ability is
God's.

Question: Is it good to meditate sitting on the seashore? I
am interested in doing so.

Mother: Certainly. The sea shore is holy. You should sit
there having prayed to the goddess of the ocean. After some
time, the roaring sound of the waves will not be heard.
Then, only a slight sound, *pranava*[28] will be there. If the
mind is fixed on that, then you will not feel like getting up.
Very loud sound and silence are equal. In both places, the
mind will become concentrated by itself. *Omkara* (Aum) can
be heard on the seashore.

THE IMPORTANCE OF ACHARAS
Traditional Customs and Observances

15 September 1977

The Holy Mother was sitting in front of the temple. One
person was distributing Mother's *prasada*[29] to the other devotees. A little bit of *prasada* fell to the floor from the hands of
the person who was passing it out. Another devotee took it
and threw it outside. Seeing this, Mother said,

[28]The sound "Aum."
[29]Consecrated offering.

Mother: What is that, son? Contempt for *prasada?* Lovers of God must not do like that. *Prasada* has no impurity even if it falls down. You can give it to birds if it has become dirty and you cannot eat it.

The devotee: Forgive me, Mother, for the mistake.

Mother: It is alright. Do not worry. It is enough if you touch that place where it dropped and salute. All Godly actions should be done with devotion. After we apply the sandal paste which we get from the temple, the remaining portion should not be put on the ground. It should be wiped on a tree or some other object.

Devotee: Isn't this all just external etiquette? Who can observe all these things? If they aren't observed, will *Brahman* be displeased?

Mother: *Acharas* should be observed as long as we live in the world. A person who has reached the Non-dual State and is beyond purity and impurity or do's and don't's, will not ignore*achara* even though nothing affects him. Ordinary people cannot progress without *achara.* Whether or not we observe *achara, Brahman* has nothing to gain. But for our own growth we need to observe *achara.* Nothing affects those who have reached the Non-dual State, but *Dharma* will decay if *achara* is not honoured by those who are still in a world of duality. *Acharas* will be useful for mental purity.

Another devotee: It is because of our merits accumulated in our previous birth that we could see Mother. Bless us, Mother.

Mother: All of you children came here because you have all been blessed by those who can bless. Hereafter, it will happen again.

Devotee: Mother, will I get God-Realization in this birth itself?

Mother: It is possible, if you try.

Another devotee: Here is God in front of us. What more is needed? What is Mother but an Incarnation of God?

Mother: Shiva! Shiva! What are you saying, son! Mother does not know about all these things. Look, Mother is crying for God. Your birth will also be fulfilled if you call for God.

26 September 1977

Some people who were very interested in spiritual matters came to see the Mother. They began talking to her.

Question: With our limited knowledge, can the truth behind this world be known?

Mother: It is not possible to know the truth of the world if you dwell on your limitations. The world can be perceived as the gross form of God. It is His Divine Play alone that is happening here. There is not a single place in this world which is not holy. Purity and impurity are superimposed by us.

Question: Oh, but even in *Bharata* (India) what *anacharas*[30] there are.

Mother: Do not judge things without knowing their different aspects. The volition of the Eternal God might be there, even behind those things which we consider to be *anachara*.

Devotee: I am convinced that Mother can save me. Hereafter I am not going anywhere else. I will come here frequently.

Mother: That is good. If all the commodities on your list are available from one shop, then you need not wander all

[30]Bad customs and habits

around the marketplace. But know that money is needed to buy the goods. Likewise, faith and dispassion are needed to gain spiritual knowledge. The means of Liberation can be bought with the money of dispassion in the vessel of *sraddha* (faith).

TYAGA AND BHOGA
Renunciation and Enjoyment

At eight o'clock Sunday morning already many devotees were sitting around the Mother. Some of them had a misconception that her highest spiritual moods were only during *Devi* and *Krishna Bhava*. They considered the Mother to be an ordinary girl at other times. All of a sudden, the Mother said (not to anyone in particular),

Mother: Not everyone will understand when God's actions are in operation in individuals. Ordinary people will misunderstand it as something else. Otherwise, what a benefit they would have by seeing God's greatness! For ordinary people, they want their household affairs to go smoothly. Towards that goal, they might go to certain temples and do worship. Or they may go and see some *Mahatmas*. Then they will ask, "My son appeared for the B.A. exam. Make him pass," or "I have planned to purchase some land but there are several obstacles. please remove them." How trivial they are!

Those who have faith will not tell such things to the *Mahatmas*. They will search for the path of Eternal Bliss. They will renounce anything for that. Some people relinquish everything for God. Some others accumulate everything for themselves. Those who accumulate will suffer. Those who relinquish will be joyful.

Question: Is it possible to give up all wealth?

Mother: It is not necessary. But the mental attitude that wealth is "mine" can be given up, can't it? Do not be attached.

Question: Is it enough to think that our wealth is God's, that it is God-given?

Mother: More than enough. But it must not remain as a thought; it should be there in action also. What if we eat plenty and the neighbouring families are starving? If the wealth which is in our hands is God's, then why can we not give some to the poor? If it is not given, that money will become the cause of troubles.

Having stopped the conversation at this point, the Holy Mother got up. While stepping from the temple verandah, she moved her right hand in a circular motion several times, lifting it in the air and showing a divine gesture while chanting, "Shiva! Shiva!" Some of the devotees who had been listening to the Mother's conversation talked softly among themselves. One said, "See, Mother has understood everything. The whole talk was surely intended for us. Wasn't it you who said that Mother does not know anything at any time other than *Devi* and *Krishna Bhava*? Did you hear what Mother said just now? There is nothing that she does not know!"

Another man who was an engineer said, "Although I have been here several times, I never understood the Mother's greatness because I never had a chance to talk to her." Another man who had just arrived asked, "Did you talk with Mother?" "Yes, we did," replied the engineer. The latecomer had no spiritual leanings at all, and referred to the Mother's often repeated words that she is just a "crazy girl" who makes some crazy utterances. Except during the *Bha-*

vas., he believed this to be true. He said, "Mother just bursts out with some crazy things." The other devotee said to him, "What the Mother told us is not crazy. To tell you the truth, we are the ones who are crazy."

20 September 1977

A *sannyasin* had come to see the Holy Mother. She was in an abstracted mood and was walking around the temple. The *sannyasin* observed her closely, neither blinking his eyes nor noticing anything else. A few more minutes passed and while going around the temple, the Mother stopped at a certain point in front of the temple, her body slowly swaying from side to side. All the time the *sannyasin* was gazing at her, and when she stopped in front of the temple he slowly approached her and offered his salutations. The Holy Mother looked at him compassionately and enquired, "Swami mon (monk son),[31] where do you come from? Have you had any food?"

Sannyasin: We heard about Mother when we came to the Oachira[32] temple and an urge arose to come see you. Different people said different things about you. Finally, I decided to come and see you myself, and now it is clear to me that you are not as I had heard.

Mother: There are two opinions for everything. One person is interested in one thing and another person in another thing. Not everyone will recognize the value and the truth in things. Some people will deny things out of jealousy. Yet all

[31]Mother would often address some of her children by adding son or daughter to the name of their profession.
[32]A famous temple dedicated to the formless aspect of the Supreme, unique in Kerala and perhaps in all of India.

is His Will. Because of His Will, millions and millions of planets and stars exist in the sky.

Sannyasin: Is it not because of gravity?

Mother: Gravity itself is God. What if gravity were not there? It would be a total disaster, wouldn't it? Again, look at the order and harmony in Nature. Seeing and observing all these things, can't an intelligent person easily guess that there is a Controller who systematically controls everything? Look at the millions of living beings! God's greatness cannot be expressed. Think of all the animals which live on the land, in the water and in the sky; some live both on land and in water. There are also people who live in God while existing in *samsara*, but they are very few.

Sannyasin: We have now reached a stage when even the people with ochre clothes don't need God.

Mother: That is not God's fault. Whoever calls, He will hear. Especially if it is a selfless call. Compassionately, *Bhagavan* will give everything to His devotee.

DUALITY AND NON-DUALITY

Sannyasin: All this will seem primitive to a non-dualist.

Mother: Does it seem like that? If so, it is the non-dualist who is primitive. It is also by His Grace that one gets Non-dual Knowledge. Nobody can acquire Knowledge without the Grace of Guru and God. Therefore, a real non-dualist will not reproach all this. For him, everything will be experienced as different aspects of the same Truth. Those who walk the path of duality also ultimately reach Non-duality. The non-dualist goes by himself and catches hold of God, while it is *Bhagavan* who catches hold of the dualist and takes him closer to God. This is the only difference. Why scuffle over this? Is it not enough to reach the goal? One person travels by water, another one by land; but both reach the same place.

Sannyasin: This is quite true. Various paths, one goal.

Two new visitors arrived and sat near Mother after offering their salutations. Mother asked,

Mother: What are you doing, children?

Devotee: We have no jobs, Mother.

Mother: Devotion is needed; and so is a job. The detached one does not need a job, but others will to need work. Obstacles will crop up for *japa* and *dhyana* if one is starving. Food is important when one is hungry. And for this, one needs a job.

Devotee: I have no interest in anything. Everything is kind of humdrum...

Mother: You are disgusted with the world? If it is caused by a detachment from sensual pleasures, it is good. But you do not have that much dispassion. For the time being, do some kind of worldly job, always keeping the remembrance of God.

Devotee: But won't *vasanas* increase if we continue to work in the world?

Mother: This is no problem if the work is performed while dedicating it to God. *Satsang* is also necessary now and then.

TO HOUSEHOLDERS

21 September 1977

Some householder devotees were sitting around the Holy Mother while she kept a baby on her lap. She asked the

child's mother, "Will you give him to me?" The mother of
the child replied, "Even now he is Mother's." Mother
laughed and said, "It is enough if you give him when he
grows up."

At this time more devotees arrived to see the Holy
Mother. Having offered the fruit which they brought to her,
they joined the other devotees. Looking at one of the women
who had just come, Mother said, "Daughter, my son has
just been employed with the bus company again, hasn't he?"
Hearing the Holy Mother's words, the woman fell at her feet
crying, "O my Mother, O my Mother!" Her husband, who
was a bus driver, had been without employment for many
days. That same morning he had been appointed as a driver
in another bus. The devotee was astounded that Mother already knew about her husband without having been informed. Overwhelmed with joy, she went on crying. Fondly
patting her back, Mother said, "Do not be sad, children.
God will look after everything." She turned to the devotees
and said, "See, you householder children should always
have Godly thoughts while living in this world.

An elderly man: Where is the time for householders?
Mother: Sorrow alone is yours if you run here and there always thinking "my" house, "my" wealth, "my" children. Live
your life surrendering everything to God. Protect your family and those in your care, knowing, "God has entrusted
them to me." After all, when did this wealth and these children come to you? Where were your kids when you came
into this world? You say now that they are yours. But when
you die, whose will they be? Your landed properties belonged to somebody else before. And in the future they will
again be in someone else's hands. There is nothing here

that can be considered ours. Changing hands, things come to us for some time; that is all. Understanding this, we should live in the house while taking refuge in God. Whatever work we may do, God can be remembered if we have the mind to do it.

It was now lunchtime. Calling everyone, Mother went to the dining hall. When everybody was seated, the Holy Mother herself served the food. While all were eating, she went to her hut. "Mother will be back soon," she said as she left the dining hall. "Eat your food, children." After lunch some devotees sat quietly, reading books while others discussed spiritual matters. Some simply sat alone in contemplation, enjoying their solitude.

At three o'clock Mother again came to sit with the devotees . She remarked, "Today is an auspicious day." "Why is that?" a devotee asked.

Mother: All the children who came today are interested in spirituality. Mother is happy to see people like you. So Mother will tell you some crazy things. People say that they like that.

Devotee: Again and again we come here because Mother will say what is necessary for us. Mother knows everything. Mother is just playing tricks when she says, "Mother does not know anything. Mother is crazy." It is not possible to tell us this anymore. We have begun to understand Mother's tricks. (All laugh)

Another devotee: People like Mother come to show us the path, don't they? Mother, is it possible for us to get Liberation in this birth?

Mother: Do not say "for us." There is no group Liberation.

Liberation is attained by different people in different births, according to each one's *karma*.

Devotee: Alright, Mother. Do I have a chance to attain Liberation in this birth?

Mother: Very many chances. Only you have to try.

Question: Everything is in God's hands. Nothing can be done through mere strength

Mother: Not so. Strength and enthusiastic effort are necessary. The result is according to *karma*. Nothing can be gained by those lacking in strong determination. The ego must be destroyed. Otherwise, nothing can be achieved spiritually. The ego can be removed through *bhakti* (devotion). Through *bhakti*, the attitude "I am God's servant" will come. If not through devotion, the ego can be removed through knowledge. Oh! How much devotion I had previously! Now not that much is there. (All laugh) Once I asked the Divine Mother to show Her true devotees to me. Having asked this, when I came from the temple, two real seekers were standing outside waiting for me. From then onwards true devotees of the Mother started coming and the number of worldly people who came only to fulfill worldly desires began decreasing.

One devotee remarked, "It was the same in Sri Ramakrishna's life." All of a sudden, the Holy Mother again became oblivious of the external surroundings, being transported to another world. Another devotee quietly said, "Whenever I come here I am reminded of Dakshineswara. But there are not many who can understand this." A second man said, "The people who come here are those who, as a result of their *karma* , are allowed to know about the Mother. How could anyone come here without having acquired merits in previous births!"

The Mother got up from her seat. She went to the back-waters and lay down under a coconut tree. Now five o'clock in the evening, two more devotees arrived to see the Holy Mother. After a few minutes, she got up from where she had been lying and came to greet them. When she began to speak, the others also joined them. At this moment, a woman devotee brought a glass of tea and offered it to the Mother. "You should give it to Mother only after giving to all the children." Having said this, Mother made the woman put the glass down. Mother asked the newcomers, "Children, where do you come from?" One man replied, "I am coming from Chenganoor and he is from Tiruvalla." Mother exclaimed like a small child, "I know where Chenganoor is, I have been there! But where is Tiruvalla? Is it in Quilon?" Everyone laughed and one devotee replied, "No, Mother, Quilon is south of Chenganoor. Tiruvalla is to the north."

Mother: What does it matter, wherever it is? Everybody comes here; so why should Mother ask, "Where do you come from? How many cows do you have? How many jack-fruit trees are there? (All laugh) Even when told, Mother will forget all this. One day I asked a *brahmacharin* son, "Are you returning from your house?" The *brahmacharin* asked, "Which house?" "My son's house," I said. Then the *brahmacharin* replied, "I don't know where that is. If Mother can tell where that is, I will go there. Once gone, I will not return." When he said that, I understood what he meant, but even then I did not give up foolish talking. (Everyone burst into laughter)

Tea was brought for everyone. Someone made a joke and Mother declared, "Children, do not laugh and joke while eating."

LIFE AFTER DEATH

Question: Mother, is there really life after death ?
Mother: Yes. If this life is real, then life after death is also real. Because we are alive now, we were also alive before. And hereafter we will also live. When one dies, *vasanas* will be there in the subtle body. But without a gross body, it is not possible to act according to the *vasanas* ; therefore, the *jiva* enters a body suitable for it. The case of a liberated soul is different. He does not have to live in the same manner. There is no birth and death from the point of view of a *Jñani*. Therefore, he does not have a life after death.

JNANA & VIJNANA,
THE PLANE OF PURE CONSCIOUSNESS

Devotee: Mother, *jñana* is the destruction of ignorance. Then what is *vijñana* the destruction of?
Mother: (After laughing) It seems that you are going to go beyond death immediately. (All laugh)
Devotee: No, Mother, I was just expressing my doubts.
Mother: If *jñana* is the destruction of *ajñana* (ignorance) it can be understood that *vijñana* is the destruction of *jñana*. If hearing and reading about Delhi is *jnana*, *vijñana* is like visiting Delhi. *Jñana* is intellectual knowledge, while *vijñana* transcends the intellect, and shows that even it is untrue. *Vijñana* affirms pure experience alone as the Supreme Truth. Is this not so, children?

Devotee: Only Mother knows all this.

Mother: There was once a man who would go and sit in a big academy of scholars. When the scholars discussed matters, he would stick his nose in and express his opinions even without knowing the subject matter. The people would tease him, but he did not care. Due to his association with them, eventually he also became a scholar. Looking back he would say, "No harm came to me from my *ajñana*. Because there was some discrimination, *jñana* dawned from *ajñana*. But even then, I did not let go of discrimination, and therefore, out of *jñana*, *vijñana* ensued."

There was a young man who used to visit a potter. In due course, he also learned to make pots. Even though at first he had no idea how to make pots, through close association and companionship with the potter he learned this skill. Children, suppose we visit an incense factory. Having spent some time there, when we return home we will smell the fragrance of the incense on our body. In a like manner, even weak-minded people or dullards will gradually evolve along the spiritual path through the constant association and companionship of spiritual people.

Once I said, "God is all-pervading; He is within us." Whereas now I see everything as God alone. God exists both inside and outside the veil of "I". The veil of "I" is also God. This veil is the body. When it is not a problem anymore, that is *vijñana*. There is another thing. Once you reach the plane of consciousness of *jñana* and *vijñana*, everything will flee. There is not even *vijñana* in the plane of Pure Consciousness. Pure Consciousness alone is. This cannot be expressed.

NAME AND LIBERATION

Devotee: Is there any hope for me?

Mother: You should pray with great yearning. Then it is possible to realize God. It is enough to call; He will come before you without delay. *Bhagavan* is always there, ready to come running when the devotees call. (Mother laughs) Because of this readiness, even *Bhagavan* can make mistakes. Sometimes He will come running even if He is not called. Ajamila called to his son, "Narayana," and, upon hearing this, *Bhagavan* started running. He did not even care whether or not it was He who was being called. So if you call His Name, then He will come running. (All laugh blissfully)

A great saint named Bharata thought about a deer at the time of his death. Even though he was a saint, *Bhagavan* did not come running. The reason is that "deer" is not *Bhagavan's* Name. Nobody had ever called *Bhagavan* "O Deer." So because His Name was not called, God did not come, and Bharata had to take birth again as a deer. However, because he had been a sage, in this next life he was saved. Only if the screen dividing two rooms is thin, can the other side be seen. In Bharata's mind there was only a thin screen of being a deer. Therefore, he could know who he was even when he took this birth. Because Bharata, a Knower of the Self, did not chant the Lord's Name, he took birth as a deer. Yet Ajamila, an ignorant man, became liberated through the name "Narayana." That much is the greatness of the Lord's Name.

In this birth, in this moment itself, he who fixes his mind on the Lord is liberated.

ENDLESS BEGINNING

Mother: What Mother has prayed to the Divine Mother for is for Devi to bring to her those who have some real stuff in them. Some come for temporary peace. Others come once and, whether or not their desires get fulfilled, they do not feel it necessary to come again, and so they do not return.

Devotee: How can they know unless Mother makes them know?

Mother: What is the benefit if something is made known to those without interest to know? There are very many (sincere seekers) yet to come and join. This is just the beginning, the endless beginning.

Another devotee: Are we included in your list, Mother?

Mother: All are there in God's accounts. But our birth will be fulfilled only if we abandon this kind of calculatingand estimating.

MOVEMENT-STILLNESS

Mother: (Pointing to one person) When this son started coming here, some people asked him, "Why do you go there? She is possessed, isn't she?" But without caring about their remarks he came here. Then what? He understood that it was they who were possessed. (All laugh) Some people call the *Bhava Darshan* a "possession." That is incorrect. It shows a lack of proper understanding. Both movement and stillness are different aspects of the same Truth. Really they are one. To reach the state of stillness, it is necessary to hold onto something, which, inevitably, is changing. Whatever it is, the means must be a name or form, and thus it is bound to change. Nobody can conceive of *Brahman* which has no form or attributes. The majority of people need name and form. Mother has to consider them as well. Is it possible for Mother to discard the thousands who are in need of name, form and attributes in order to progress spiritually, for the sake of one or two *jñanis* who do not need it? Stillness and movement are one and the same. If one is omitted, the other cannot be known. Enquiry is motion; the place where enquiry ends is stillness. Creating motion, God abides in stillness.

Twilight fell and the residents were about to begin the devotional singing. The Holy Mother got up from her seat and walked towards the temple verandah calling, "Come, children." Everyone got up and followed the Mother. One devotee commented to his friend, "How long we have been coming here but never have we heard Mother talk like this. The fact is that we have never stayed to hear it. We would come late in the evening to see the *Bhava Darshan* and after entering the temple we would leave the place immediately." The friend replied, "Did you hear what Mother said about the *Bhava?* It is to uplift ordinary people. To bring them closer to God and to develop faith in them, such things are needed. For those who come in search of pure spirituality, Mother will reveal her real greatness." The singing had begun and the heart-gripping songs of the Holy Mother filled the atmosphere with a divine fervour. She sang,

> There is nothing to tell
> To the all-knowing Mother...
> Walking beside us, She is seeing
> And understanding everything...
> The Primordial Being who is

Greater than the greatest,
Sees all the thoughts of the innermost self...

The Mother's *bhajans* were always a source of tremendous inspiration for the devotees. While singing, she would
soar to the highest planes of supreme devotion, elevating the
listeners as well. Some of the devotees took leave of the Holy
Mother after the bhajans and *arati*.[33]

PRABHAKARA SIDDHA YOGI

14 January 1978

As it was Sunday afternoon, devotees had already started
coming for the *Bhava Darshan*. Some of them were talking
about Prabhakara Siddha Yogi, an *avadhuta*[34] who had many
followers. Those devotees who were talking about him had
met him in Oachira on their way to the Mother's Ashram.
Some of Mother's devotees cherished a desire to see him
and expressed their wish to her. Mother replied, "If your desire is strong, Mother will make him come here." The conversation ended there. At ten o'clock at night. *Devi Bhava*
had already begun. To the wonder of the devotees who had
expressed their wish to see Prabhakara Siddha Yogi, he came
to the Ashram that night accompanied by three other
people. It was very difficult to understand the strange
behaviour of the yogi. Sometimes he spoke in a strange language and acted as if mad. His peculiar ways were incomprehensible to the devotees gathered there.

---

[33]The waving of burning camphor before the Deity signifying the offering of the
ego to God.

[34]A Realised Soul who does not observe any norms in his external behaviour,
sometimes acting like a sage but at other times acting like a child, madman or
ghoul.

It was nearly dawn by the time the *Bhava* was over. The Holy Mother came out of the temple and sat near the visiting yogi. When he saw the Mother he started saying, "Kali...Kali." He asked the Mother, "Why did you call me here?" The Mother replied, "I did not call, did I?" "No, you called," was his reply. "For the last few days I was being attracted here."

Mother: The children here felt like seeing you. That is the reason. (Pointing to a resident) That son wanted very much to meet you. Give what is needed.
Yogi: What am I to give? (Turning to the resident) The person to give what is to be given is here. I am not needed for that.

The yogi pretended to be angry and pointed to the Mother saying, "Do you know this person who is sitting here? No, you don't know anything! This is a place where many things will arise. Many are yet to come. Many will come by air and water. Everything is here." The yogi then turned to the Holy Mother's father, Sugunanandan. "You must be very careful. This is not your house, it belongs to the devotees. You have to become a little better. Do not make the devotees sad. All this is theirs."

After roaming around the Ashram for some time, the yogi left. Later, Mother told the devotees and *brahmacharins,*

Mother: The yogi was brought here because the children said that they wanted to see him. But you will not understand or approve of his ways. Children, now you go and do your *sadhana.* Everything that you want will come. Children, learn to know yourself. There is not much use in trying to understand people like this yogi. For different people there are different paths. Everyone cannot assimilate everything. What you need is Self-Realization, not *siddhis*.[35] Nothing else is needed by those who get Realization.

TAKING DISEASE

15 January 1978

Today the Holy Mother was not well. It was later than usual when she came from the hut where she resides. The number of visitors was not less, however, and having offered their salutations, the devotees came and stood around her.

Mother: Mother is not well today.
Devotee: Perhaps Mother has taken somebody's disease.
Mother: Oh, does Mother have the power to do it?
Devotee: Of course! How quickly Mother once removed my sickness. In just a few moments my symptoms were seen in Mother. Yet in her they lasted only a few minutes.
Mother: On certain occasions such things are necessary. If not to Mother, to whom will the children call? When Mother's children have pain she will say, "Devi, give it to me." Whether it is in your body or in this body (pointing to her own), it is enough to suffer, is it not? All is God's grace. Only if we get that will there be some benefit. Whoever else may help us, no benefit will come. One look, one word or a touch from God is enough to get rid of all the impurities in a person. Because you are believers, Mother speaks in this manner. Mother does not know rationalism and such things. At the time of death, all reason will run away and

[35]Psychic powers.

hide. The inadequacy of those who pretend to be courageous will be proven then.

Devotee: Not only for a skeptic, but for a devotee also there is death, isn't there?

Mother: All those who have taken birth will die. But the death of Knowers of God, that is something different. They are not afraid of death. Instead, they will welcome death. They enter not the world of death, but the world of God.

Another devotee: I have heard that Mother has not eaten for several days. Why is that?

Mother: There is no particular reason, son. Look, Mother has no problem. Very many times Mother has done this. So what? Did this body become weak? No. Good vigour is there.

Devotee: (Laughing) Mother should teach us that trick.

Mother: It is not something which is possible through trickery. Yet it cannot be explained. Such a nature is there during certain times, that is all.

By this time a group of women devotees had come to see the Holy Mother. They were members of a women's cultural centre and began by asking about the *dharma* of women.

Mother: There is only one *dharma*, the *dharma* to know God. There is no separate *dharma* especially for women; but they do have their own way to attain God. Women like yourselves should observe the scriptural statements and follow in the footsteps of Sita, Savitri and Satyavati, who were embodiments of *sthri dharma* (women's *dharma*). Living in it is greater than simply talking about it. Set an example for other women by living it. Take the case of Sita. The whole *Ramayana* depends entirely on her purity and virtuous character.

What would have happened had Sita had obstinately said, "It is not possible to go to the forest; the country is rightfully ours"? But Sita did not do that. This shows her detachment towards worldly possessions. And her love for Rama shows attachment to God. Sita epitomizes a courageous woman who has acquired enough mental strength to confront the challenges of life. This strength is seen in the form of her one-pointed devotion to her husband Rama. She is also an example of the infinite power of chastity. During her stay in Lanka, a symbol of material wealth, she was surrounded by demonesses (negative tendencies). Yet Sita would constantly remember Rama and shed tears due to the excruciating pain of separation. It was because of that power that Rama could come to Lanka and kill the demon Ravana. It is impossible for *Bhagavan* not to respond to a devotee's grief-stricken call. Where there is love, there *Bhagavan* is.

1 January 1980

A householder devotee and four young men came to see Mother. Several of them had heard about Mother but this was the first time they had come to see her in person. All four of them were humble and devoted. One of them was studying for his Master's degree and the other three for B.A. degrees. It was their inquisitive nature and desire to know more about spirituality which brought them to Mother.

Mother came out of her hut and sat in front of the temple. All five of the visitors prostrated before the Mother and stood by the side of the temple verandah. She affectionately asked them to sit down. The Mother closed her eyes and absorbed herself in meditation. After some time, she opened her eyes and, turning to the students she enquired smilingly, "Children, do all of you like spirituality?" One of the students replied, "Yes, we go to temples and holy places." Mother remarked, "It is a wonder that children who study in college have interest in such things." The student replied, "We are interested to learn about spiritual things. Mother, please give us some advice."

Mother: Children, Mother is crazy. She will just burst out with some crazy things. All of you children call her "Mother," and because of that she calls you "children". But other than that, Mother does not know anything. Children, you should live with the remembrance of God. Do not waste time. Repeat your *mantra* while doing each action, and every day practice meditation for some time.

MEDITATION

Student: Mother, how should we meditate?
Mother: Place a small picture of a god or goddess that you like in front of you. Sit gazing at the picture for some time. Then, while closing your eyes, try to fix the form within. When the inner form fades away, look again at the external picture . Again, close the eyes. Imagine that you are talking to the Beloved Deity, "Mother, do not go away abandoning me. Come into my heart. Let me always see Your beautiful form," and so on. Cry, embracing your Beloved Deity. That which we meditate on will appear in front of us if constantly repeated like this with faith.

Meditation is good even for small children. Their intelligence will become clear; memory will increase and they will learn well. Mother does not say that all children must become *sannyasins*. Children, seek a blissful life. You can understand the secret of bliss when you think of the nature of the Self. The waves of the mind will subside. Everything is there in you alone. If there is faith, you can find it. The happiness that we get from the objects of the world is only an infinitesimal fraction of the bliss that we get from within.

Just as the filter fixed on the water tap absorbs the impurities in the water, so should we absorb our own impurities with the filter of meditation. In the olden days there were forests outside. Now since all those forests have been cleared away, they have come inside every one of us. In the olden times animals were outside. Now they too are within us. It is the dirt within the mind that should be removed. Give up selfishness and thereby be rid of sorrow.

Student: What should be done to remove this dirt?

Mother: If the mind is to become pure, love for God should prevail. Virtues should prevail. The main obstacle to becoming closer to God is our selfishness; it will automatically fall off when we feel compassion for others. Just as the saline taste disappears when fresh water is added to salt water, the bad will leave us when we constantly think of the good. See how many poor people are suffering around us without shelter, clothes, food or proper medical care. We will lose our selfishness when we have compassion for them.

Suppose we smoke ten rupees worth of cigarettes a day. In one month, that is three hundred rupees. How much money will that be if added up month after month? A small hut can be built for a poor man to sleep in with the amount spent for one year's smoking. Presently, we do not understand that bliss is not in the cigarettes, but in us.

You children might ask, "Then what about the cigarette manufacturers?" They themselves are saying that cigarette smoking is bad for health and that it will destroy the body and mind. Those who have discrimination will withdraw from it.

Children, find satisfaction in the happiness of others. For example, suppose we are comfortably seated in a bus. An elderly person gets in at the next stop and there is no vacant seat. Immediately getting up from your seat, you should make room for him to sit. We will become worthy of God's Grace when each one of our little selfish actions is given up, for negative qualities thus get destroyed.

We are all children of one Mother. The same eagerness with which we apply medicine to our own burnt hand we must show towards the sufferings of others. If the left arm is burnt, does the right arm refuse to apply medicine, saying, "It is not I who has the burn?" "I" permeates the whole body. That "I" feels the pain in any part of the body. Likewise, we unknowingly experience the pain of even a small creature because the same Consciousness pervades everywhere. Children, understanding this, always act with compassion . We should not expect the fruit of our actions. It is enough to dedicate this to God, knowing that He will give us what we need.

Question: Mother, how do we get rid of sorrow?

Mother: We do not know what is eternal and what is not. Our desire is not for the eternal. Because of this, we become sorrowful. The mind burns and burns due to this sorrow and we become sick, thus decreasing our life span. To counter-act this, we should improve: Our mind becomes restless because wherever we go, we find the faults and defects of others. This is not the point of view that we want. Look carefully at what is of value in others and respect that. Forget what we think is lacking. When we go to a new place or meet someone new, instead of being critical and trying to find faults, we should try to see what is good and appreciate that. You should only look at those qualities in which you are lacking. In this way, we should always see the good. Thus we get rid of sorrow.

Student: Mother, parents expect a lot from their children, don't they? Is it right to stay in an Ashram without serving them?

Mother: Children, parents say "my" son, "my" daughter. But we are only their step-children. It is true that the parents have many expectations regarding their children; but think for a while. Do they perform their own duty properly? Mother would say, "No," because the real duty of a parent is to give their children a good spiritual education, and this they are not doing at all. If any one son or daughter of any parents takes to spirituality, Mother will consider it as a great blessing not only to that family, but also a blessing for the whole world. By turning to spirituality, a child renders a great service to his family as well as to the entire human race. Children, tell Mother which is better: to ruin one's life for just one or two people, or to sacrifice it for the good of the world?

Anyhow, it can be said without a doubt that only true *sannyasins* have served the world selflessly. Even today this is so. They never expect anything from the world. Whereas worldly people have only expectations and desires which will eventually steal away all of their human qualities and make them behave like animals.

If we are truly our parents' own children, they should be able to save us from death as well. We are God's children. What use are we if His power is not there? Everyone might seem to be our relative while we are riding in a bus. But each one will go away when he reaches his stop. This is life. We alone will remain. Father, mother and everyone else are like these 'relatives' in the bus. Only the Lord is always with us.

At this time, *brahmachari* Sreekumar came and sat near Mother and she continued,

Mother: Children, however much wealth we have, if its place and use in life is not understood, sorrow will result. Even if there is immeasurable wealth, momentary is the happiness that we get from it. Money cannot give Eternal Bliss. Didn't Kamsa, Hiranyakasipu and others all possess vast wealth? Did they ever have mental peace and tranquillity? He possessed fabulous wealth, but what peace did Ravana have ? They all lived egotistically, swerving from the path of Truth. They did many actions which they should not have done, and thus they lost peace and tranquillity.

Eternal bliss is not gained from wealth. Only non-eternal happiness can be gained in this way. You might ask, "How do we live without riches? Do we have to abandon the wealth that we have?" Mother does not say to abandon anything. Bliss and peace will become our wealth if we understand to use properly what we have. For those who have turned towards God, wealth is like the rice in which sand has fallen. It is of little use.

Seeing that the students were listening with interest, the Holy Mother continued,

Mother: In the olden days, spiritual aspirants stayed at the residence of the Guru throughout the period of their education. As a result, they came to know what life is, how to live and how to behave in the world. Because of that, they were blissful. They became strong-minded and could overcome any obstacle. Without fearing death, they were ready to dedicate their life to Truth. They were like good lion cubs — perfectly healthy, endowed with a long life span, magnificent in stature and full of vigour. They were not like today's people, who are short-lived and weak like lambs. They were not afraid of anything. In those days, people lit the oil lamps at twilight, and would then sing the Names of God. After that, they would think of the mistakes they had committed that day and would repent. They also tried not to repeat such mistakes again. All this gave them consolation. But what about today? Times have changed. At dusk, people sit in front of the television watching videos. People plot how to seize other people's money through fraudulent means or even by killing them. People would not hesitate to kill even their own mother for money. This is today's world. Is there peace? There is no peace anywhere.

Ganja (marijuana), sleeping pills, intoxicants, liquor ~ these are the present-day "gods" for people. If these are not available, they cannot live. Becoming slaves to all these things, people ruin their own lives and destroy the lives of others as well. Nowadays, three year old children are shouting slogans, "Hail revolution!" If somebody does not belong to his own (political) party even a child will say, "I will kill him." Going to school, he incites strikes. My children, do not be ruined like this.

Having said this, Mother closed her eyes and sat in an abstracted mood. After some time she got up from her seat uttering "Shiva...Shiva!" while showing a divine gesture with her fingers. As she walked out, Mother told Sreekumar, "Sit and talk about something to these children. Mother will come back after some time."

Student: As I was thinking to ask some questions, Mother went on giving the answers to them!

Sreekumar: Such experiences are not unusual for us.

Student: What inspired you people to come to the Ashram?

Sreekumar: Mother's pure love and unconditional mother-hood. These kindled in us the love for God and for ailing humanity. This must be known through direct experience. One cannot even dream of such love from even one's own parents.

Mother's love comes from having known the Eternal. There is no selfishness in it. It is untainted love. Mother clears and cleans the path in front of us. It is enough to walk upon it. At present, we are just like a pond with stagnant water. Mother connects the pond with the river by making furrows. Unknowingly, we come closer to God because Mother cuts off our selfishness with love. Mother acts selflessly; that is why she can do this. It is not possible for those who have worldly desires to do this. This is the true relationship. This is not available anywhere else.

All of a sudden Sreekumar became disconsolate. His eyes were fixed on a distant point and he sat motionless. His eyes became wet with tears.

Student: What happened, Sreekumar?

Sreekumar: Oh . . . nothing . . . I just remembered some-thing which happened on the *Thiruonam*[36] day after I first saw Mother.

Student: We would like to hear about it.

Sreekumar: It was the day before *Thiruonam*. I was talking with Mother after *Darshan* and she said, "*Thiruonam* is tomorrow, is it not? Children, please come." I and some of

---

[36]The most important annual festival in Kerala.

her other children were sitting nearby when she said this. When I returned home, my family would not let me go without first having food since it was *Thiruonam*. In those days, my family was not so close to Mother. Mother wanted us to eat lunch with her on that day which is why she had called us, but how could I escape from the house? It was nearly eleven-thirty when the cooking was over. Soon after eating lunch, I started for Vallickavu. All the buses were very crowded and none of them stopped. I waited for a long time at the bus stop. Although it was late, I was fortunate to get a direct bus to Vallickavu. It was three-thirty when I arrived. Crossing the river on the ferry, I quickly walked towards the Ashram. I can never forget the sight which I saw there, such a heart-breaking sight it was. Mother was lying on the bare ground full of sand all over her body. A temporary oven was seen near her. Crows were pecking and eating cooked roots from the pot and some pieces were lying scattered in the sand. Later, when Mother awoke, she related what had happened:

"Mother asked the children to come, didn't she? What can I give the children, Mother thought. Mother does not like to tell anything to the family members. Mother herself made a stove in the yard. Going to the garden, Mother plucked some roots and kept them on the stove to cook. When it was fully cooked, the pot was kept closed without removing it from the stove. Having extinguished the fire, Mother waited for the children to come. Several times Mother went to the jetty and looked to see whether the children were coming. Mother also did not eat anything. When it became late, Mother laid down in the sand thinking, 'It was wrong to call the children. Since it is *Thiruonam*, will their families let them leave their homes?' At that moment a

crow flew by, pecking one piece of cooked root. Mother got
up hurriedly. Some pieces fromthe pot had been scattered
on the ground. Some more crows came and tried to eat.
What will Mother give her children? Mother felt sad and
was about to drive away the crows, but the next moment
Mother thought, 'They are also my children. Let them eat.'
Mother again laid down in the sand."

    After a few moments some of the children arrived. Every-
one had brought something for Mother. She asked them all
to sit around her as she unwrapped the packages and distributed the banana chips and other edibles to each one. She
smiled with tears in her eyes. This innocent smile of a small
child made everyone cry also. Since that incident, all of us
would only eat with Mother during the *Onam* festival. By
this time the Mother returned and called everyone for lunch.
All followed the Mother to the dining hall.

5 December 1981

    The Mother was sitting on a cot in the hut. All four
sides as well as the roof were thatched with coconut leaves.
The entrance, being on the western side, faced the backwaters and the Arabian Sea. The roaring sound of the breaking
ocean waves could be clearly heard from this side of the
Ashram, although a full view of the sea could not be seen.
Big fish, diving through the backwaters while gleefully moving their tails and fins, could be seen as we were sitting in
the hut. Different varieties of flowering plants grew on the
raised ridge of the backwaters. On the walls of the hut hung
pictures of great saints and sages and different gods and goddesses. The cot was situated along the southern side of the
hut adjoining the wall. Grass mats were spread on the floor.

Some young men had come to see the Holy Mother. They entered the hut and sat on the floor, having offered their salutations to the Mother. She also sat down on a mat and smilingly asked, "Children, when did you come?" One man replied, "Some time before." Mother asked if they had eaten anything to which they replied in the affirmative. One of the young men said, "Mother, we have certain questions."

Mother: Mother is crazy. Mother does not know anything. She just babbles something or other.

Question: Mother, how can one lead the world?

Mother: Only one who has studied can teach. Only one who has acquired can give. Only one who is completely free from sorrow can free others from sorrow completely.

Question: Mother, what is meant by death?

Mother: Son, death is only a change like all other changes. Each being takes birth on earth according to the fruit of its actions. Coming to this earth, each one lives, proudly thinking "my" wealth, "my" wife, etc. Each one of us dies as we are trying to fulfill our desires. Eventually, we are forced to go, leaving behind everything that we considered our own. While travelling in a bus, we have to get off at a certain stop. When we sat in the bus we proudly thought "my" seat, and even claimed it to be so. But when leaving the bus, we do not take the seat with us. Only God knows how long we will be here. The existence of all of us is in God. The *jiva* which makes the body act departs, leaving behind the corpse. This is what we call death. But death is not the complete destruction of the body. It is the beginning of the decomposition of the five elements of which the body is made, so they can merge with their original principles. This change

of the body has nothing to do with the soul, which will remain unchanged forever.

EASY PATH

Devotee: What is the easy way to attain God's Vision?

Mother: An easy path is sought due to lack of surrender.
God's Vision cannot be gained simply by torturing the
body. Whatever the path, the mind should merge in God -
that is important. Regularly performing *sadhana*, we should
wait with patience. There is no shortcut. Having put rock
candy in one's mouth, no one will swallow it quickly just because it is sweet. If the candy is swallowed quickly, the
throat will get cut. Let it dissolve and then swallow. *Sadhana*
is the same. The path of devotion is simple.

Devotee: Mother, what should be done to develop devotion?

Mother: *Satsang, kirtan, mantra japa, dhyana,* all these are
helpful.

Devotee: Mother, how can those who are involved in
worldly affairs sustain devotion?

Mother: Children, remember God while doing actions.
(Mother points to a man who is leading ducks through the
backwaters). There is hardly any room in the boat even for
him to stand properly. It is such a small boat. Standing in
the boat, he will row with a long oar and lead the ducks as
well. Making noise by slapping the oar on the water, the
man will guide the ducks if they stray. At intervals, he will
smoke a cigarette. With his feet, he will scoop out any water
that enters the boat. He will also converse with the people
standing on the bank. Even while doing all these things, his
mind will always be on the boat. If his attention wavers even

for a moment and he loses his balance, the boat will capsize and he will fall in. Children, like this we should live in this world. Whatever work we are doing, our mind should be centered on God. This is easily possible with practice.

It was now time for lunch and one *brahmacharin* came to call the young men. Mother affectionately said, "Yes, my children, go and eat your lunch. It is Ashram food. There will not be many spices to add flavour. It is good to have some training!" All moved towards the dining hall.

PURPOSE OF BIRTH

A few *brahmacharins* sat nearby while Mother was eating. She also fed them with small balls of rice. One *brahmacharin* asked, "Mother, what is the purpose of your birth?"

Mother: Mother's birth is for the good of the world. Some people dig wells only for their own use. There are others who dig wells for the use of the whole village. Their intention is that all should quench their thirst by drinking water from the well. Mother dug at a place and there was water there. Gradually it flowed as a river. Some bathed in it and others quenched their thirst. Each one does as he requires.

Was not Sri Krishna the Supreme Self? The Lord had no attachment to anything. Even then, the Lord incarnated on the earth and acted ideally for the good of the world. It was not for Himself. He is not in need of anything. It is not for the Knowers of the Self that God takes birth. God assumes a body to bring the ignorant to the path of goodness. What defamations Sri Krishna heard! Was He not killed by an arrow? Jesus Christ was crucified. Had they chosen to, they could have reduced their enemies to ashes in an instant. Yet to show the world what renunciation is, they did not destroy their enemies.

All of us should learn to live with equal vision, to love one another with a brotherly attitude. Different kinds of people come to see Mother during *Bhava Darshan*, for devotion, for fulfilling worldly desires, for curing diseases and for many other things. Mother discards no one. Could Mother discard them? Are they different from me? Are we not all beads strung on the one thread of the vital force? Each one understands Mother according to his own way of thinking. Those who criticize me and those who love me are the same to me. A continuous stream of love flows from me towards all beings in the cosmos. That is Mother's inborn nature.

Lifting both hands in the air and looking upwards, the Holy Mother called loudly, "Shivane . . . Shivane . . . (O Shiva, O Shiva)."

KUNDALINI

Brahmacharin: Mother, yesterday I read certain things about *kundalini shakti* but it was so confusing that I finally put the book down. What is *kundalini shakti?* How does it work? What is meant by "awakening of *kundalini?*" Mother, please could you say something about it?

Mother: Son, first of all, a serious seeker should not think about and go on asking each and everyone about the workings of *kundalini*, whether it is awakened or whethers it is going to awaken soon. Mother does not say that you should stop reading and gathering knowledge about such things. That is good. But too much reading is dangerous; mere reading without practice is harmful. Do your *sadhana* regularly, with utmost sincerity and faith, supported by self-surrender. All other developments will happen automatically. You do not have to worry about it. They must take place provided that your effort is sincere.

Because you asked, Mother will say something about *kundalini*. Mother does not want to disappoint you. Son, *kundalini*, or the serpent power, is the vital force which flows in and through all living beings. This power is situated below the spine in the form of a coiled, sleeping female snake. It is awakened through incessant meditation and through the Guru's Grace. When it is awakened, it ascends through the *sushumna*[37] which lies in the spine, yearning to see the male serpent which is residing in the *sahasrara*.[38]

Mother paused for a moment and the *brahmacharin* took this opportunity to clear his questions about *kundalini* by asking, "Does all this exist on the gross level or on the subtle level?"

Mother: This is subtler than the subtlest. As you know, there are six *chakras*.[39] *Sahasrara* is the last and the most subtle. Each one of them is a storehouse of spiritual power which can be experienced only through yogic intuition. As the serpent power reaches each *chakra*, it makes that particular region blossom fully and mature before it passes to the next one. As the *kundalini* reaches each plexus, the seeker will get different kinds of visions, both tempting and divine. The *sadhak* who is not under the strict control of a *Satguru* might misunderstand these lower states as something very great, or as equal to Self-Realization, and become prey to a

[37]A vital nerve.
[38]The mystic thousand-petalled lotus at the crown of the head.
[39]Mystic centres along the spine.

fall. That is why it is strictly said that a *Satguru* is absolutely necessary to guide the aspirant during the course of his *sadhana*.

Several changes occur in the body when this power moves from one plexus to another. One feels a burning sensation all over the body, as if hot chillies have been rubbed on the body. The body also experiences tremendous heat and horripilates now and then. Water may ooze from the pores like sweat. In certain stages blood may come out through the pores, and the body may become gaunt like a skeleton.

Brahmacharin: Isn't this a frightening situation, Mother?

Mother: Yes, it is. The *sadhak* who undergoes these experiences for the first time may get frightened. Not only that, sometimes he might also become mentally abnormal or perverted due to fear and lack of inner strength. That is why it is strictly prescribed that *kundalini dhyana* should be performed only in the presence of a Realized Soul.

Brahmacharin: What things should an aspirant be careful about during this period?

Mother: During this state the aspirant should be very careful and alert. He should be looked after with as much care as a pregnant woman would be. The body should not be moved unnecessarily. He should not even lie down on a mattress because the smallest folds will be unbearable to him. He should lie on a straight, smooth wooden plank. The spine should not receive any knocks, as the after-effects will be great. When the *kundalini* wakes up, the aspirant becomes a tremendous centre of attraction and being deluded by this, women and others may flock around him. In such a state, the absence of a *Satguru* to impart proper instructions may tempt him to indulge in sensual pleasures, thus draining away all his accumulated spiritual energy.

Brahmacharin: Mother, what happens when the *kundalini shakti* finally reaches the *sahasrara?*

Mother: Transcending all six *adharas,*[40] including the *muladhara,*[41] it finally reaches the head which is its real abode. The body experiences a rejuvenating coolness and there follows a showering of ambrosia throughout the body. The old body gets transformed into a new vessel of tremendous spiritual power.

Roots absorb water and manure from the soil and carry these to the leaves. Thereupon the leaves do their part of the process by dividing and distributing the substances to all parts of the organism, including the roots. This refined energy sustains the tree. Similarly, the spiritual energy which reaches the *sahasradala padma*[42] from the *muladhara* transforms itself into ambrosia and, flowing through the nerves, pervades the whole body and nourishes it, imparting a rich glow and splendour, marvelous energy and vitality.

Another brahmacharin: Mother, the mind is not getting any concentration during meditation. Why is it so?

Mother: Children, the mind is naturally one-pointed and pure, but until yesterday we have made room there for many impure worldly emotions. Thus it is difficult to make the mind concentrated while sitting for meditation. The worldly thoughts and emotions are like tenants to whom we have given a small plot on our un-used land to build a hut. When we ask them to leave, not only do they not care , but they come to fight against us. We have to fight to kick them out.

---

[40]The chakras.
[41]Chakra situated at the bottom of the spine.
[42]Thousand-petalled lotus.

We have to argue in court as well. Likewise, to kick out the
tenants of the mind we have to file a case in God's court. It
is a constant fight. We must continue fighting until we come
out victorious.

It will be experienced that more *vasanas* come up as you
do more *sadhana*. While sweeping a room, we can remove
only the superficial dirt. Whereas, if the room is wiped with
a wet cloth, more dirt will come out. In a similar way, more
dirt will rise up when we do more *sadhana*. It is only for the
purpose of being destroyed that they will rise up like that.

Brahmacharin: Mother, is it not necessary to fight against
the injustice in the world?

Mother: That is work for worldly people who are endowed
with *rajasic*[43] qualities, not for a seeker of Truth. Do not see
the faults and defects of the world. God-Realization is our
goal. After attaining that, we can make the world good in accordance with God's instructions. Is it practical to worship
God only after wiping out all the injustice in the world?

SATGURU
Self-Realized Master

Question: How does one know whether one's spiritual experiences are valid, invalid, or just fascination or imagination?

Mother: Son, for that a *Satguru* is needed. A *Satguru* is one
who has gained God-Realization. He will guide the disciple
along the correct path and take him to the goal. Those who
are sincere will get a Guru. It is not necessary to wander
here and there.

---

[43]One of the three gunas or qualities of Nature, the quality of activity.

Question: Mother, which is better, meditation on God with or without attributes?

Mother: That depends on the seeker. Usually, it is best to begin by meditating on God with attributes and to end with the Attributeless.

Question: It is a little difficult to clearly get the form of the Beloved Deity in meditation. Why is this so, Mother?

Mother: It will be like that. There is no other way but to continue the *sadhana* correctly. The mind which runs here and there in the beginning will later become fixed on the Beloved Deity. Then the form will become unclouded.

Question: Why does the mind run like that?

Mother: Because of the *vasanas*.

Question: Can a householder attain God?

Mother: Why such a question, son? Do you want to lead a householder's life just because your meditation is not becoming firm? (Everyone laughs) A *grahastashrami*[44] will attain God but not a *grahasta*.[45] There is no problem for a *grahasta* who leads an Ashram life, understanding the eternal and non-eternal. One can reach the goal if selfless action is performed with an attitude of dedicating everything to God. A seeker should stay firmly fixed on the goal. Do not stop the *sadhana* out of disappointment and frustration. The intent to reach the goal should predominate.

Question: Can't the Guru remove the shortcomings of the disciple?

Mother: A passenger can be dropped off at the station, but it is he who must first get into the bus and travel. The Guru will show the path. All the rest depends on the mind and effort of the disciple.

---

[44]One who makes his house into an ashram, i.e. leads a spiritual life.
[45]An ordinary worldly soul leading a married life.

Question: What is the difference between worshipping God with form and the formless aspect of God?

Mother: What is gained through meditation upon God with form is *savikalpa samadhi*, the perception of Reality while retaining the state of duality. Owing to the vision of one's Beloved Deity, the attitude of "I" is there. The feeling of duality is still there.

In meditation upon the Formless, the ego-sense is completely removed. There is only One. What is gained is *sahaja nirvikalpa samadhi*, the natural state of abidance in the Absolute.

Question: Mother, how will the disciples be who take birth to do good for the world?

Mother: They are *nitya siddhas*.[46] They are detached from the very moment of their birth.

Question: Why does the world slip into error?

Mother: Due to *kama* (lust) and *krôdha* (anger) human beings commit errors and become unrighteous. What is necessary is the control of desires.

6 December 1981

Since it was a *Darshan* day, there was a big crowd to see the Mother as Devi and Krishna and to receive her blessings. At four in the morning when the *Bhava* was completed, a moving incident took place which made this an unforgettable day.

A black cow which was living at the Ashram had given birth to a calf one year before. It was a beautiful sight to see the gleeful calf running here and there around the Ashram premises. That night the calf suddenly became afflicted with

[46]Ever-perfect.

an acute illness. Unable to bear the pain it cried aloud, "Ma...Ma!" as if it were calling the Holy Mother. Although many people tried to relieve the calf of its pain, it was to no avail and its condition became worse and worse. The poor creature was struggling for life.

Coming out of the temple after the *Bhava Darshan*, Mother went straight to the calf and, with great love and affection, placed its head in her lap. She carressed it and asked everyone to chant the Divine Name. After some time, the Mother asked everyone to chant the sacred *mantra* "Om Nama Shivaya". As the chanting was going on, the Mother asked for some *tulasi* (basil) leaves and sacred water to be brought in a *kindi*.[47] When the water was brought, she poured some into the calf's mouth, which it drank. She then took some in her palm and sprinkled it on its body along with the sacred *tulasi* leaves. The calf was lying down, gazing at the Holy Mother's face. After a couple of minutes the Mother again carressed its face and body and said, "All right, you go." A few seconds later, the calf breathed its last breath, its head still on the Mother's lap.

The Mother, later relating this incident, said,

Mother: That calf was a *sannyasin* in its previous birth. Due to its *karma* it took birth as a cow. Because of the merits accumulated from its previous birth, it happened to be born in this Ashram. The *brahmacharins* raised it. It grew up hearing the Divine Names. And in this way it left its body.

10 December 1981

At ten o'clock in the morning the Mother came into the kitchen. One *brahmacharin* was cooking tamarind seed for

---

[47]A metal pot with a fluted rim.

the cow on the gas stove. Mother commented, "Cooking gas is very expensive. This can be cooked using firewood. The stove will be ruined if you keep big vessels like this on it." The *brahmacharin* did not heed the Mother's words. She continued, "If you cannot do this, Mother will cook it." He replied, "Where is the time to do *sadhana* if I must sit here doing this kind of work?" Hearing this, the Mother became a bit serious and told him, "From now on you don't have to look after anything to do with the cows." Having said this, she entrusted the work to another resident. Then the *brahmacharin* became sad, but Mother would not agree to his request to continue doing the work. What followed was a beautiful piece of spiritual instruction.

Mother: One should learn to do every action with utter dedication to God, shouldn't one? What kind of spirituality is this? Spirituality is not sitting in a corner with closed eyes. We should be ready to become everyone's servant and to see all equally. Going out into the world tomorrow, you should serve everyone without selfishness. Serving the cow is an especially meritorious action. It is said in the *Bhagavatam* that Sri Krishna Himself used to graze the cows.

Once a sage who was sitting underwater in meditation got caught in a fisherman's net. As instructed by the sage, the fisherman took him to the king's palace to be sold. Although large sums were offered, the sage did not agree to be sold to the king. At last, as suggested by a clever minister, the king offered a cow as payment. Only then did the sage consent to be purchased by the king. The cow is that sacred an animal. Serving a cow should be considered a good fortune. It is a *sadhana*. Son; do not do this work half-heartedly.

One who simultaneously does *karma yoga* and remembers God is the noblest. Son, can you not repeat your *mantra* while cooking the tamarind seed? Otherwise, can you not read spiritual books?

The sage Narada thought that he was a great devotee. Once Lord Krishna said, "Narada, there is one farmer on earth who is a greater devotee than you." Narada doubted this and came down to earth to see the peasant in person. He found that the farmer would chant the Lord's Name only three times a day. "How could he be a greater devotee than I?" thought Narada. Upon returning he questioned the Lord. The Lord gave him a small vessel filled to the brim with oil and asked Narada to keep it on his head and go around a particular hill without spilling even a drop of it. When Narada returned after finishing the round, the Lord asked, "How many times did you chant My Name in between?" Narada thought and was surprised to discover that he had not remembered the Lord's name even once because his attention had been fully concentrated on keeping the vessel of oil steady so as not to spill it. *Bhagavan* smilingly said, "Now do you understand what a great devotee that farmer is? Even in the midst of his toilsome work, thrice he is remembering Me, is he not?"

The *brahmacharin* who had tried to say that cooking tamarind seed was an obstacle for his *sadhana* understood his mistake and apologized for his lack of discrimination. Still Mother did not allow him to resume that work. She said, "When you are able to do this work with faith and without selfishness, then Mother will ask you to do it. Until then, meditate." Out of remorse, the *brahmacharin* fasted that day. Learning that he had not eaten, the Holy Mother, out of her affection, also did not eat anything. Greatly pained at heart to hear that she was not eating because of him, the *brahmacharin* had his supper. Thereupon the Mother also ate.

19 December 1981

At eight o'clock in the morning the *brahmacharins* were getting ready to chant the *Lalitasahasranama* (The Thousand Names of the Divine Mother) as instructed by the Holy Mother. It was the first day of the *Laksharchana* when they would chant it one *lakh* (one hundred thousand) times. Everyone came into the temple and, ready to begin the worship, they sat around the sacred seat. When all preparations were complete, *brahmacharin* Unnikrishnan commenced the formal worship which would be followed by the chanting. Each one had kept flower petals before himself on a piece of banana leaf. All sat with closed eyes as the verse for meditation was chanted. Unnikrishnan led the worship in the presence of the Holy Mother. He chanted the Names one by one and the *brahmacharins* repeated them, each offering their flower petals on the holy seat. Noticing one *brahmacharin* who offered the flowers carelessly, Mother spoke,

Mother: Do not perform the offering disgustedly and drearily. If you feel disinterested, take some rest, and then continue. Children, do not force the body to do the worship. It is not a problem if the *puja* finishes a little late. While taking each flower petal, visualize Devi's form on the *peetham* (seat) . Offer the flowers at Her feet. Then you will get good attention. External attentiveness results in internal attentiveness.

SAHAJA SAMADHI
The Natural State

It was three o'clock in the afternoon. *Brahmacharin* Nealu was conversing with the Holy Mother in the hut. Sitting nearby, *brahmacharin* Balu was keenly listening to the Holy Mother's words.

Nealu: Mother, what is meant by *sahaja samadhi?*
Mother: Son, imagine that there is a rubber ball and a ring within us. The ball is always moving up and down. This ball is the mind. At times it gets caught in the ring and remains motionless. This can be called *samadhi.* But the ball does not rest there permanently. It will again move up and down as before. Eventually, a state will come when the ball rests permanently in the ring, and there will be nofurther motion. This is called *sahaja samadhi.*

Merging of the mind is experienced by the *sadhak* (aspirant) in an advanced state of meditation, but the mind starts functioning as before when he gets up from meditation. *Sahaja samadhi* is the state wherein the mind completely merges in the Reality. After this, the mind does not have any power to function independently. The person who has entered *sahaja samadhi* will be blissful, perceiving his Real Nature in whatever object he sees.

22 December 1981

At nine in the morning Mother was sitting under a coconut tree in front of the temple. Some *brahmacharins* came and sat around her. She said,

Mother: There is a lot of benefit in doing group meditation. The atmosphere gets permeated with the concentrated air of everyone and it becomes more conducive for doing meditation. Since everyone's thought vibrations are of a similar pattern at that time, good concentration can be attained.

One *brahmacharin* liked to spend most of his time only in the presence of Mother. He asked, "Is my feeling correct?"

Mother: In the beginning stages attachment to the Guru's external form is good, but the disciple should not observe the Guru's actions and try to judge him or her. In most cases the disciple becomes too attached to the Guru's external form and forgets about his all-pervasive nature. Attachment to the Guru's form, supported by the awareness of his omniscience and all-pervasiveness is the perfect attitude. In the former case, which is more common, the disciple gets deluded due to lack of knowledge about the Guru's infinite nature and thus becomes an easy victim to all kinds of negative tendencies. Devotion to the Guru backed by the understanding of his higher nature is real devotion.

Mother paused for a while and then, fixing her eyes on the blue sky, she said, "Balumon, sing a song." He sang,

> O Thou Who appears as
> This illusory Universe filling it throughout,
> O Radiant One, won't Thou dawn
> In my mind and stay forever
> Shedding Thy brilliance?
> I will surfeit myself, drinking
> Thy motherly affection...

As the song went on, Mother sat motionless, her eyes still fixed on the expansive sky. Tears rolled down her cheeks. As the song was coming to an end, she laughed blissfully and pointed her index finger to the sky, all the while uttering unintelligible words, and again and again bursting into rapturous laughter. It was as if she was asking something of an unseen being. In a semi-conscious mood she turned to the *brahmacharins* and said,

Mother: Look here (pointing to her own body), this one's will has no separate existence from that One's Will. They are one and the same. If you take Mother as the body, then you cannot grow spiritually. Mother is not this body. She is her children's Self. Mother is ready to give all that she has to her children, but you should become deserving of it. Mother is always serving what her children need, but you children are not yet ready to accept it.

Children, always think of the goal. Only if you have strength of your own can you serve others selflessly. What will you say when others ask you about spirituality? For this reason, the scriptures should be studied. Do not torture the body unnecessarily. Control of food should be gradual. You should meditate during the night time. Yogis will not sleep in the night, they will meditate. All of Nature becomes still at night. The vibrations of worldly activities diminish. Therefore, at night good concentration can be gained.

TO THE HOUSEHOLDERS

It was a *Darshan* day and the householder devotees started coming one by one and in groups. Having saluted the Holy Mother, they all sat down. *Brahmacharin* Venu was

sitting near Mother, fanning her while she distributed some
sweets that had been brought by a householder devotee.
While distributing the *prasada*, she sang:

> Hey Shiva who takes everyone,
> Take me also, hey Shiva...

(All laughed, hearing Mother's song)

One devotee asked Mother if he could ask a question.
She replied, "Shiva . . . yes, yes, . . . ask, ask."

Question: Mother, is it possible to lead a spiritual and
worldly life side by side?
Mother: Certainly it is possible, son. But one should be
able to act selflessly. Sorrow comes when we think, "I am
doing this. I must have the fruit of it." A certain amount of
detachment is needed. Never think "my" wife, "my" child.
When you consider everything as God's, then it is not possible to be attached. When you die, the wife and children
will not come with you, will they? God alone is Truth. A
householder should also go to temples and ashrams.
Devotee: To say all these things is easy; but to practice them
is difficult. How can we do that? Can Mother please say
something about this?
Mother: Children, it is not impossible. Nothing is impossible in this world, especially for human beings. Strong determination and unshakable faith are the two things needed
for success in anything and everything. Mother clearly
knows that as far as a *grahasta* is concerned, it is not so easy
to practice these things because of the pull from all direc-
tions. His mind is much too involved in worldly affairs. Do

your duty but do not get entangled in it. This is difficult. Suppose you will live in this world for eighty or ninety years. Why should you waste your entire energy only for enjoying worldly pleasures and fulfilling your desires? Think about what you are doing your whole life. Just repeating the same things over and over again, or jumping from one type of enjoyment to the next. Therefore, my children, slowly try to change your lives. Out of thirty days in a month, spend at least two for your spiritual development. Try to change your bad habits by gradually replacing them with good thoughts and actions. Every day before going to bed, recollect the day's activities and try to discriminate between the good and bad. Repent for the bad thoughts and actions. Make a strong determination to abstain from them the following day. The next day also do the same. Before going to bed, make a comparative study of the actions which you did that day and the previous day and see the differences. Pray to the Lord to bestow on you the mental strength needed to fight your negative tendencies. Surrender everything at His Feet. Have compassion for ailing humanity. Do charity for righteous purposes. Real charity or renunciation means giving up your dearest things. Actually, it is said that the mind itself should be offered to the Supreme. But the mind is immersed in money and other worldy things. So offering money for righteous things is equal to offering our mind. Such actions will make your mind more and more expansive. Expansiveness is God. Let not your wealth be used only to fulfill your desires and those of your family members. Let at least a small portion of it be used for the benefit of the world. This in turn will purify you.

Another devotee: Mother, you told us that householders should go to temples and ashrams, but there are many people who scoff at image worship. Why is this so?

Mother: They criticize because they are ignorant about temples and the science behind image worship. To put it in one sentence, the temple structure represents the body and the image symbolizes *Atman* ~the soul, which is situated in the sanctum sanctorum of the heart. The temple represents the seeker's body in full prostration with all the *adharas* including *sahasrara*. Ordinary people with gross intellects cannot conceive of a formless or nameless God, though this is His real nature. They need something to hold onto and someone with whom to share their heart. Being limited individuals, human beings are not satisfied with another limited being. Knowingly or unknowingly, one is always in search of an infinite, Universal Being to whom one can unburden one's sorrow and thereby find peace. The *rishis* knew that the people of the forthcoming ages would be unable to grasp these subtle truths unless they were put in a different way. Thus the idea of temples dawned in their hearts as a way to make Truth available to even the most gross-minded. But misinterpreting the significance of the temples , we make a mess. Whose fault is this? Who is to blame? Neither God nor the great forefathers, but we, only we.

In any case, son, why do you care if out of utter ignorance, a person says something insulting about God or image worship? Let him babble. This shows his lack of understanding. Let us pray and work for his upliftment as well. And let our faith be unshakable.

Devotee: What Mother says is perfectly true. If we can correct ourselves, then everything will be all right.

Another devotee: Mother, it is believed and said that one will get mental peace if one goes to temples and prays sincerely. How does this happen?

Mother: This is true; but as you have said, sincerity should be there. We call on God, having looked at the statue once and then we close our eyes. Even then, we are looking within ourselves only. The case of meditation on God with form is also the same. We are meditating on our own Self. This means that all other thoughts will be restrained and our mind will become concentrated on the image of God. This again means that there are no other thoughts, which cause all our external and internal problems and conflicts, except that one thought of God. Fewer thoughts means more peace of mind. More thoughts means less peace of mind. When we go to a temple, the atmosphere is calm because everyone goes there with one thought only. All minds will become one-pointed while waiting for the sanctum sanctorum to be opened and to behold God's image. The atmosphere there becomes peaceful because of that concentrated thought. This is why we get peace when we go to temples.

Mother stopped speaking and became absorbed in meditation. Opening her eyes, she called aloud, "Sreemon, come with the harmonium." Looking smilingly at the devotees, Mother said, "Talk alone is not sufficient. Let us sing His glories. " By that time Sreekumar had come with the harmonium. He was followed by Pai. "Pai mon, sing some verses," Mother said. Having prostrated before the Mother, Pai sang,

> O Mother, I know neither the divine mantras nor the yantras which embody Thy Power; nor do I know any verses which praise Thy glories.

O Mother, please tell me, there may be sons
who are sinners on this earth, but is there a
cruel mother?

Hearing the Sanskrit verses, the Mother became totally
drawn inwards. Her body was motionless. With half-closed
eyes she sat there like a statue. Tears born of supreme bliss
rolled down her cheeks and her face became most brilliant.
Pai went on singing until he also burst into tears. Sreekumar
who was playing the harmonium also slowly slid into a
meditative mood. Except the sobbings of Pai, all was silent
for a few minutes.

At this time, one *brahmacharin* burst into tears while embracing the Mother's feet. He was thinking how fortunate
he was to have Mother, the embodiment of innocent love
and selflessness, as his Guru. How many devotees have wet
those feet with their teardrops? How many are taking refuge
at those holy feet? How many ailing people's tears have been
wiped by those hands? She does everything for others, and
nothing for herself.

When the Holy Mother emerged from her ecstatic
mood, Krishna Shenoy, an ardent devotee arrived. He offered his salutations to the Mother and sat near her. With a
mischievious smile on her face, the Mother exclaimed,
"Hey, Krishna, little thief, you got your job back, didn't
you?"

Krishna Shenoy was left speechless for a moment; he
looked amazed. Gazing at the Mother, he shed tears. He
then fell at her feet and cried like a small child. The Holy
Mother caressed and consoled him with great affection and
love. The devotees who were standing around could not understand the meaning of all this. When Shenoy became nor-

mal, one of the devotees who was sitting near him asked, "What happened?" Full of emotion, Shenoy said,

Shenoy: How can I tell you? Everything is Mother's grace. After the last darshan, when I reached the factory where I work, the first thing I learned was that a suspension order had been made against me. It was for taking more holidays than were alloted without having officially informed the management. Those holidays had been taken in order to come and see Mother, for I became crazy for her after meeting her. What is amazing is that everything was straightened up within three hours and the suspension was withdrawn. How it happened, I don't know. It is still a mystery. As far as I know, nobody supported me or recommended the withdrawal of the suspension order.

One devotee: Who told you that nobody made a recommendation for you?

Shenoy: What do you mean?

Devotee: Don't you know that Mother was there to recommend you? (All laugh)

The first devotee: But how did Mother know all about this?

Shenoy: That is a good question. Is there anything which Mother doesn't know?

Mother: Children, Mother knows one thing ~ that she doesn't know anything.

Question: Mother, can you please tell us what we householders need?

Mother: In the olden days *grahastashrama* (householder life) and spiritual life were led simultaneously. Parents would chant *mantras* into the ears of their baby from the time of birth onwards. Thus, the child would grow up hearing godly *mantras*. Later, the child would be sent to a *Gurukula*.[48] There he or she would learn all the *Vedas* and *Sastras* (scriptures), while observing perfect celibacy and practicing what he learned. Later, having married a girl who had been raised in the same way, a man would become a *grahastashrami* and would lead a righteous life. He would serve others selflessly and feed those who came to him hungry. He would not hesitate even to worship their feet.

Only to sustain the family line would a couple procreate. The child born of such a couple was considered to be a portion of the husband which came through the wife. When the child was in the womb, the mother would observe different kinds of religious vows. Because of that,her child would be noble-hearted and wise, and would become a benefactor of the world. The quality of the woman's thoughts during the period of pregnancy influences the character of her child. The child born to a woman who maintains the remembrance of God will become a devotee. There is no doubt about that.

In those days both the husband and wife had perfect control over their minds and never allowed themselves to be influenced by petty emotions. From the day their child was born, the husband would see his wife as mother. Later, having raised the child and made him self-reliant, both the husband and wife would go to the forest and do *tapas* (penance).

Because human beings have given up their *swadharma* (intrinsic nature), today everything is out of order. Great sages have written that in this *Kali Yuga* (Dark Age of materialism) people will be blind, deformed and have many other weaknesses.

---

[48]Residential school of a Guru.

Forests will become houses...
Houses will become shops...
The temple will be sold,
Betel nuts will be eaten...
The father will be eaten by the son
And son by the father...

There will be no rain. There will not be any agricultural yield. Then there will be only excessive sunshine. The cause for all this is the selfishness and lack of mental purity of human beings.

Her discourse finished, some more devotees came and prostrated before the Mother. Having made some light talk with them, the Mother went near the huts where the *brahmacharins* were staying. It was time for their meditation; Mother went to observe them.

THE MOTHER HEN AND HER CHICKS

23 December 1981

Sitting in his room, Brahmacharin Venu was loudly singing Sri Sankara's *Nirvana Shatkam* :

I am neither the mind, intellect,
Ego nor memory;
Neither ears nor tongue
Nor the senses of smell and sight;
Nor am I ether, earth, fire, water, or air;
I am Pure Awareness-Bliss,
I am Shiva! I am Shiva!

In those days Venu's nature was that of a child, and this created a lot of problems for him. Constantly repeating the Divine Name, he would do all the work entrusted to him. One could always see his lips moving. Because of this, sometimes his mind would lose its contact with the external world and he would knock over or break things that happened to be near him. One day, the Mother scolded him for his lack of external attention. She said,

Mother: Son, constant remembrance of God is good, but if you cannot concentrate your mind on the work that you are doing, then don't do it. Go and meditate sitting somewhere. If God is everything, then work also is Him. Do your work as if it were worship. You cannot be careless while doing worship.

Hearing Mother's words, Venu felt a little sad and went to his hut. It was then that he sang the above mentioned song. Having heard his singing, the Mother again came to his hut and said,

Mother: Son, nothing can be gained if in the beginning of our *sadhana* we walk around saying "Shivoham," (I am Shiva). If an egg is to be hatched, it must incubate. An egg hatches because of the mother hen who patiently sits on it for many days. A *sadhak* should perform *sadhana* according to the Guru's instruction. It is not possible to be 'hatched' if you sit chanting, "Shivoham." Would a chick say, "I am a hen," before it is hatched? Pure devotion is the best. It is the easiest path. In the beginning, one should say, "Dasoham, Dasoham," (I am your servant). "Shivoham" is not something to be said. It is something to be known through direct experience. If somebody beats you, is it possible for you to sit there patiently, thinking that he is Lord Shiva? If so, chant "*Shivoham.*" Otherwise, chant "*Dasoham*" alone.

As the Mother went out of Venu's hut she sang the following refrain of one song:

> If Thou givest me another birth,
> Then bestow the boon of taking birth
> As the servant of Thy servants forever.

24 December 1981

It was a *Bhava Darshan* day and there were many people to receive the Holy Mother's blessings. All of them were sitting in front of her. As she called the devotees one by one, she listened keenly to their woeful stories, bestowing peace and tranquillity. To each of them she gave instructions in accordance with their mental nature and reassured them that she would always be with them. It was two p.m. when the daytime *Darshan* was over. Getting up, the Mother went to the hut of a *brahmacharin*. Having seen several things scattered here and there in the room, she said,

Mother: There should be order and discipline. In the olden days when a bridegroom first went to see the bride to make the marriage proposal, he would judge the girl's character by observing the cleanliness of the house and its surroundings . Likewise, it is by seeing the character and orderliness of the children who come to stay with Mother in the Ashram to do *sadhana*, that others learn.

Another *brahmacharin* came to the room where the
Mother was standing. He was angry about something which
somebody had said.

Mother: Son, imagine that we are the servants of everyone.
Children, suppose you become angry if somebody who
comes here gets angry with you. If that happens, the mind
should be immediately controlled through the understanding that the ego in you is the cause of your anger.

Children, when you see a person for the first time, greet
him respectfully. If he is an uncultured person, he may not
return your greeting. Butthe next time you see him, greet
him again. That day also he may not return it. The next day
also you should him greet him in the same manner, without
hesitation or hatred. Then he will think, "This man has
been greeting me for the last two days and I haven't greeted
him back. Again today he is doing the same. It is not correct
that I don't greet him." Automatically he will offer his greet-
ings. In a like manner, if there is virtue in us, we can make
everyone good.

The *brahmacharin* listened to everything silently and, full
of remorse, he prostrated at the Mother's feet.

The Mother walked towards her hut followed by Gayatri.
At five in the evening, the *bhajan* before *Bhava Darshan* began. The Holy Mother sang,

> The sound "AUM" is ringing everywhere
> As an echo in every atom.
> With a peaceful mind,
> Let us chant "Aum Shakti."

O Noble One who is adored
By the Universe,
We come to know Thee well
When this Universe is understood to be
Worthless which so far was felt as great...

Sreekumar played the harmonium and Venu the drums. Balu, the other *brahmacharins* and the devotees sang along with the Holy Mother. The Mother's songs were poignant with the love for God, and filled the atmosphere with waves of supreme devotion which penetrated the hearts of the *brahmacharins* and devotees. All were led into a meditative mood. It could be seen that some were silently shedding tears of inner joy.

DIFFICULT IS THE PATH OF KNOWLEDGE

25 December 1981

At ten in the morning the Mother was giving darshan to the many devotees who were present. Some Westerners from Kanvashram in Varkala had just arrived. Most of them were newcomers. One among them named James was highly intellectual and did not believe in a God with form. His strong conviction was that there is no truth beyond intelligence.

James: There is a Cosmic Intelligence. I believe in that, not in Rama or Krishna or Christ. What I want is peace of mind which I don't have at all.
Mother: Son, if this is your belief, let it be so; but it is not correct to say that other paths are wrong and that your path

alone is true. You believe in a Cosmic Intelligence, do you not? It is that same Cosmic Intelligence that we call Rama or Krishna or Christ. Whatever the path, *sadhana* should be performed and truth should be known through experience.

When we worship Rama, Krishna or Christ, we adore the eternal ideals which manifest through Them. If They were mere individuals, nobody would have worshipped Them. When They are worshipped, a true seeker is not adoring a limited individual, but that same all-pervading Cosmic Intelligence which you believe to be the one Truth. To climb a tree, we need a ladder or something else as a means. Nobody can simply reach the top of the tree in one leap. If somebody tries to do that, it is certain that he will fall down and break his arm or leg. (All laugh) These names and forms will serve as ladders so that we can attain the Supreme without struggling too much. Anyhow, self-effort is implied in all paths. Self-effort and Grace are interdependent. Without one, the other is impossible.

The Path of Knowledge is suitable only for a few who accumulated the necessary mental disposition in the previous birth. Whatever the path, there is no problem if there is a real Guru. In meditation with form, we also meditate on our own Self. During the midday when the sun is directly overhead, no shadow will be seen at all. The same is the case with meditation on a form. We become That. When you reach Perfection there is no shadow. No two. No illusion. Son, once you understand that from your own experience, Mother will not object. Anyhow, though your path is a difficult one, anything can be gained, attained, or accomplished if there is faith. When you say, "My way alone is true," think that the Intelligence in which you believe is the same Truth that makes others set out to work on their own paths.

Son, you yourself have said that you don't have mental peace. What is the use in saying, "Intelligence, Intelligence," if there is no mental calm?

Balu translated the Mother's words to James, who seemed very satisfied with her advice.

All the while, Ganga was sitting near the Mother. It was obvious from the expression on his face that he had something on his mind. Before meeting the Mother, he had been practising *atma dhyana* ,or meditation on one's Real Self. After seeing the Mother, he had changed his meditation to *rupa dhyana* ,or meditation on a form. Yet, he could not persist with the same enthusiasm and inspiration that he had had in the beginning and thus felt a bit confused. He wanted Mother to clear his difficulty, and was therefore waiting for her to finish her conversation with James. Before Ganga could say anything, the Mother turned towards him and said,

Mother: Son, do *atma vichara* (self-enquiry) if you find it difficult to meditate on a form. You have more attraction to that; but in that path, more attention is needed. Do not waste even a moment, but continue to ask yourself, "Who am I?" or think "I am none of this" even while working. Ramana Maharshi (Ganga's previous ideal) was a supreme devotee who had the attitude that "I am nothing." Now no one is applying that teaching of his. He did not want fame, yet that and everything else came of its own.

Ganga was happy to hear the Mother's advice, and at the same time, astonished to find that she had understood what was on his mind even though he had not said anything about it to her. He became convinced that she was closely observing both his internal and external activities.

In the evening the Mother went to a householder devotee's house in Quilon, some thirty-five kilometers away from the Ashram. Every month this family would invite the Mother and the *brahmacharins* to their house. Many people would gather there to see the Mother and to listen to her *bhajans* and words. The day of the Mother's visit was like a festival for them. This day the Mother also took the Westerners with her. There were two cars. The Holy Mother, Balu, Gayatri, the mother of the family, her daughter and her three year old son travelled in one car. Five or six people rode in the other car and the rest took a bus. The Holy Mother first enquired about their family affairs. Then slowly the subject turned to spiritual matters.

Mother: Children, don't think that you can start spiritual life after satisfying all your desires. The desires will go on and on. They form a never-ending circle. When one desire is satisfied, another one will occupy its place. If somebody thinks he can take up spiritual life after fulfilling all his desires, he is like a person on the seashore who waits for all the waves to subside before taking a bath.

The housewife's daughter: Mother, what is the way to overcome desires so that people like us can get closer to God?

Mother: Daughter, the only way to overcome desires is to understand that each and every object that you desire is riddled with pain. If they are not controlled now, later they will control you; and eventually desires will swallow you up. Mother doesn't say that you must give up all desires. You can enjoy them, but don't think that this life is only for that.

That is dangerous. Let us control our desires gradually, before their grip becomes too tight. For this, strong
determination is needed.

Try to lead a happy life, finding satisfaction in what you
have. If you have more than you need, give it to the poor
and needy. For example, if you have twenty saris, why can't
you give at least two of them to those who don't even have
one good sari? Often rich people will purchase a minimum
of two or three saris a day and arrange them nicely in their
closets. Every morning they will look at them and feel happy
about their great achievement. There is no giving up at all.
Children, just think for a moment. Is this the right way to
live? Thousands of people are thrown in the midst of poverty and starvation, yet we go on enjoying the objects that we
acquire.

If all are God's children, then the poor are also His children. They are our brothers and sisters who came from the
womb of the same Mother. Instead of adding more and
more to our existing negativities by creating more and more
desires and fulfilling them by any means, why can't we help
the poor? We can't take any of our so-called achievements
with us when we leave this world, except for the virtuous
deeds that we've done. These alone will be there in the list
of God. The final judgement depends entirely on that. By
helping others, we help ourselves to expand and be purified.
This will also help us a lot to gradually lessen the burden of
attachment and thus increase the amount of peace.

As the talk went on, the three year old boy started to
whimper. He caught hold of his mother's sari and asked for
something to eat. As there weren't any edibles in the car, his
mother said, "No, you can eat later, when we reach home."

The child kept quiet for a few moments, then again caught hold of her sari and repeated the same request. Now the mother became a bit angry and said, "Keep quiet. Let me listen to the Mother's words." But the child was hungry and could not keep quiet. After a few seconds he began crying out, "I want something to eat. I want something, I want something to eat." The mother this time became really angry and hit the child, pulling his hand from her sari. The child fell on his mother's lap bursting into tears, calling "Amma...Amma..." Now the mother's face blossomed with love and affection for her child. Embracing him tightly and kissing his cheeks several times, she consoled him uttering soothing words, "Mother's darling son...little thief, don't cry..." She asked the driver to stop the car and get some bananas for him.

Now the Holy Mother turned towards Balu and said,

Mother: Did you see that? This is the attitude that a true seeker or devotee should have towards the Guru or God. He may scold you or kick you out, but you musn't loosen your hold. Like this innocent child, go on calling Him with more and more intensity. Go on asking while catching hold of His Feet. The relationship of the child to his mother is so strong that he didn't feel any hatred or anger towards her. Instead, he tightened his hold and finally laid down on her lap when she hit him. This was enough for the mother's hidden compassion to overflow all its bounds. Son, this is the kind of attachment that a *sadhak* should have towards God. Whatever happens, hold on to His Feet without loosening the grip even slightly. Then He is bound to shower His grace. Love with attachment to God is good, but not love with attachment to the world.

By this time, the group had reached Quilon and every-one got out of the car. Having worshipped her feet and of-fered *purnakumbha*,[49]the family members led the Holy Mother into their house. The devotional singing started at seven p.m. and the Mother's ecstatic singing went on until ten. Sometimes she burst into a blissful laugh and at other times she shed tears of joy. Occasionally Mother became lost to this world and sat motionless. All the devotees who had gathered there were full of bliss and remained spellbound until the end. After the *bhajan*, Mother gave *darshan* to all present. It was twelve o'clock when everything was over.

The Mother returned to the Ashram at one-fifteen in the morning. She sat on the front verandah for some time and all the Westerners sat around her. Brahmacharin Madhu, who was a native of Reunion Island, was there. He didn't know Malayalam and was sad because he could neither un-derstand what the Mother said nor could he talk with her. Looking at Madhu, the Mother spoke to allthe Westerners,

Mother: Children, Mother is deaf and dumb in front of you; and you all are in the same situation, as well. Mother has seen your happiness when she speaks any English words. Mother doesn't speak your language and knows that you are very sad about that. But Mother can understand the language of the heart. (Like an innocent child) Have you ever heard Mother speaking English? Yes, Mother knows some. (Pointing to Balu) He taught me a few words like, "Open the door. Congratulations." (Mother recites, pausing after each word. All laugh; Mother also laughs and pointing to Sreekumar, she says,) He also taught me one or two words.

---

[49]A pot full of consecrated water offered to God or holy persons as a form of reception.

After a short pause the Mother continued,

Mother: Others should be loved without any desire or expectation. You need not love or respect me. I won't be bothered about it. Nor do I ask that any of you serve me. If you were to get involved in that you would become angry. For Mother is crazy, isn't she? Visualizing each and every atom of this world as the Truth, serve all with an attitude of equanimity. Equanimity is God.

Madhu: There is hope for us. It will be easy if Mother can learn English. She can do it. (Mother smiles)

Having spent a few more minutes with her Western children, the Mother went to her hut.

27 December 1981

The Holy Mother always observes both the external and internal actions of the *brahmacharins* and instructs each one according to his mental consitution. Sometimes the instructions are general, at other times personal. These instructions are spontaneous and soul-stirring; they spring forth irrespective of time and place. Sometimes they may come in the middle of some work, or while travelling, or in the middle of devotional singing.

Today, while sitting with the *brahmacharins*, the Mother said,

Mother: Either you should dedicate everything to Mother, whom you say is your all in all, considering everything as Mother's Will; or you should have faith in yourselves. Look within yourself with the thought, "I am the Self pervading the whole universe." The intent to reach the goal should always predominate. One should be attentive while doing anything and everything.

SUBTLE BEINGS

The Holy Mother next went to the Ashram library. A devotee who was sitting there reading told the Mother about an experience he had with subtle beings. He asked, "Mother, are such experiences valid? Do subtle beings really exist?"

Mother: Everything depends on the mind. If you believe in their existence then they exist. If not, then no. There are many beliefs which are not scientifically proven but still they remain as facts because they can be experienced or seen, not with these external eyes but with the inner eyes. We cannot simply deny them because we haven't seen them. After all, have we seen or experienced even a corner of this vast universe? Certainly not. Then how can we say that subtle beings do not exist? There are many things that we cannot perceive with the external eyes but they still exist. For example, look at that ray of sunlight which is entering the room through that hole in the roof. You can see numerous dust particles moving in it. But why don't we see them when that shaft of light is not there? Are they not there when the light is not coming? Yes, they are there. Likewise, subtle beings are always there, but our mind is not subtle enough to see them. When the mind becomes clear and subtle through *sadhana* , then one can see them. But a *sadhaka* should not give much importance to such experiences. He must simply ignore and transcend them. This is nothing compared to the experience that you are going to have. These silly experiences will create obstacles on your path and will distract your attention from the Real.

A REAL GURU AND DISCIPLE

Another devotee: Mother, what is the nature of a real *Guru-sishya* relationship?

Mother: In a real *Guru-sishya* relationship it will be difficult to recognise who is the Guru and who is the disciple. The Guru will be a person who has a more servant-like attitude than the disciple. The only aim of the Guru will be the advancement of the disciple. The Guru's sole intention is to somehow improve the disciple. The Guru will observe each and every action of the disciple. But the disciple will not know it. Do you know how a real disciple will be? He will be one who serves the Guru with the attitude that the Guru shouldn't even know about his service. *Seva* (service) means obedience. Spontaneously, the Guru will shower his grace on that disciple who moves with *sraddha* (faith). When the field is low, water will naturally flow into it. However high a mountain is, no water will get collect on the top. Rather, it will flow down into the stream. Son, humility and simplicity are the characteristics of a great soul.

At this time *brahmacharin* Venu approached the Mother to clear one of his problems.

Venu: Mother, I have a big problem. I feel aversion to some people. What should I do to remove this?

Mother: Son, are you not meditating on Lord Krishna's form? Son, you should ask Him, "Kanna! are You not the

one who shines in me? Do You have hatred towards anyone? Is it not Your mind, bereft of attachment and aversion,
that I should have?" We will not reach that Supreme Self if
there is even an iota of selfishness.

Venu: Mother, is it possible to completely remove likes and
dislikes through meditation?

Mother: Certainly! When the mind becomes pure through
meditation, each atom one can be seen as the form that one
meditates on. Then we feel love towards all creatures.

We do not know anything. Everything is controlled by
that Supreme Self. We are like a log of wood in the water.
Wherever the current carries it, there the wood goes. The
wood doesn't have any power of its own. This "I" should
become a corpse. Only then will knowledge dawn. If a
corpse is put in water, it will move according to the course
of the current. The corpse doesn't have the feeling of "I."
God can be seen only if we develop this attitude. Either proceed according to His Will, remaining convinced that
everything is God; or enquire "Who am I," having the
strong conviction that "Everything is in me."

One devotee who had been sent to a distant town for
scriptural studies was at the Ashram to spend a few days
with the Holy Mother. He came and sat near the Mother after offering his salutations.

Mother: (To the devotee) When you complete your scriptural studies, don't waste time saying "*Shivoham, Shivoham*"
without having experienced this. Don't become a caretaker
of someone else's wealth; become the owner. What is said
in the scriptures should be brought into experience through
sadhana. You will not get sweetness if you simply lick a piece

of paper with "molasses" written on it. Scriptures are point-ers.

It was four in the afternoon and many devotees had ar-rived for the *Bhava Darshan*. They were all sitting around the Holy Mother on the verandah of the old temple. One householder devotee's family who had come for the first time was also there. Their daughter could sing devotional songs beautifully. Mother asked her to sing a song. She sang "*Atmavin Dukham*" (Sorrow of the soul). That innocent girl's poignant song, full of love and devotion, stole the Mother's heart and she became lost to this world. Although there were about two hundred people sitting around the Mother, complete silence prevailed. All silently gazed at the Holy Mother's face which to them was an extraordinary sight.

The *Bhava Darshan* started at seven in the evening and was preceded by the usual devotional singing by the Holy Mother and the *brahmacharins*. The *Darshan* was over at three in the morning. Werner, who had been sent to Tiruvannamalai, had arrived that day to spend a few days with the Mother, so she talked with him for some time. He always had only one complaint – this was about the delay in attaining Self-Realization. The clock had rung five by the time the Mother returned to her hut. There wasn't much time for her to take a rest, for some devotees were waiting with a car to take the Holy Mother to Quilon to attend a pre-arranged program.

In the early morning the Mother went to their house ac-companied by some *brahmacharins* and Gayatri. During the daytime, the *brahmacharins* conducted the reading of *Srimad Bhagavatam* and chanted the Thousand Names of the Di-

vine Mother. In the evening many people came to participate in the *bhajan* and to receive the blessings of the
Mother. After the *bhajan,* the Mother herself distributed
prasada to everyone. With great enthusiasm, she went on
talking with the devotees, making jokes and enquiring about
their family affairs. Since the previous night had been the
Bhava Darshan, the Mother had not slept. Some of the close
devotees felt very sad about this. At their persistant request
the Mother finally went to bed at one o'clock. But, in a few
minutes she again came out and straightaway approached a
person who had just arrived. Upon arriving, he discovered
that the Mother had gone to bed. He felt very dejected, as he
was a poor man who had come from a far away place only to
see the Mother. He was cursing his own misfortune and
thinking, "I am a sinner; that is why I am not able to see the
Mother," when suddenly he saw the Mother walking towards him. He could not control his emotions. Bursting
into tears, he called aloud, "My compassionate Mother, it is
so kind of you to come and see this worthless son." The
Mother spent a few minutes with him, consoled him and
then went to her room at two thirty.

The next day the Mother and the *brahmacharins* returned to
the Ashram by three-thirty in the afternoon. During the return journey the Mother said,

Mother: God does not take a body for the sake of the
Knowers of the Self *(Vijnani).* They don't need anything.
God incarnates in order to bring the *ajnani* to the correct
path. It is not necessary to improve the noble.

If you *brahmacharins* go to any householder's house, you
should not go to rooms other than the *puja* room. Reply in
few words to the questions asked. And never forget the goal.

Be very careful. Though we cannot understand the mental attitude of worldly people, their thoughts will affect us. The presence of a lustful woman will create desire even in a person with no lust. Butter will melt if kept near the fire. Keep this in mind.

The car stopped at the Vallickavu boat jetty and everyone got out. As the sun slowly journeyed to the western horizon, everyone crossed the river and reached the Ashram premises. Hearing the pitiful cry of a goat, the Mother hurried to that spot. A goat which had been raised by the Mother's family was crying in great pain and lying on the ground. This goat had great love for the Holy Mother. The members of Mother's family and a few devotees were standing around, helplessly watching the goat. For a week it had been afflicted by a disease in its udder. None of the treatments had proved fruitful and the disease had continued to increase. By the time the Mother reached the goat it was nearing its end. Unable to watch the poor creature's struggle, the Holy Mother sat at a distance and got lost in meditation and prayer. As everyone looked on, the goat approached the Holy Mother, crawling on its knees. Having reached her side, the poor animal placed its head on her lap and breathed its last breath while gazing at her face. Seeing this extraordinary sight, all who were present started singing Divine Names and chanted the sacred mantra "Om Namah Shivaya" with great devotion. A blessed death it was. Who knows what the goat may become in its next birth?

DISEASE AND MEDICINE

1 January 1982

The Holy Mother was sitting in front of the dining hall. Ganga, Venu and some other devotees, all of them spiritual aspirants, sat nearby.

For the past few days, the Mother had been very sick. She was afflicted with a terrible cough and pain throughout the body. To express their love and concern, the devotees had brought different kinds of medicines. The Holy Mother, drank from each bottle everyday in order to fulfill their wishes. Out of his devotion and love for the Mother, Ganga became a little bit angry about her irregular and unsystematic way of taking medicines.

Ganga: Why does Mother take all the medicines they bring?
Mother: Son, they will bring medecine even if Mother says she doesn't want it. So what should Mother do? It is for their happiness and satisfaction that Mother takes all these. If it is not taken they will become sad. Mother's disease won't go simply because she takes these things. The diseases of others are affecting Mother. They should be exhausted through suffering alone. You need not get angry with the devotees. If you have faith in Mother, why should you fear? There is only one doctor to cure my disease — that doctor is the Supreme Self.
One devotee: Mother, can't you remove the devotees' diseases without undergoing suffering?
Mother: Yes, they can be burnt up in the Fire of Knowledge *(jñanagni).* But even then, a little suffering must be experienced in order to show that by its very nature, the body

must suffer. Whether it is the body of a saint or a sinner, Mother accepts its pain. *Mahatmas* suffer in order to teach us renunciation *(tyaga)*.

Another devotee: Mother, can yogis live without air?

Mother: Those who have reached a particular state can live without air. They can live merely by breathing air from within, without taking it from outside. They can live even if they go beyond the atmosphere.

INTENSE DISPASSION:
THE ATTITUDE OF A SERVANT

Devotee: Mother, no noticeable progress is seen even though *sadhana* has been performed for a long time.

Mother: Children, even if we sit all the twenty four hours with closed eyes, nothing will be gained if God's Grace is not there. God's Grace and the Guru's Grace are one and the same. Many people come to Mother and say that they haven't had any spiritual experience, though they have made efforts over the course of many years. Children, presently what we are doing is like filling a tank by drawing water from a well from morning till evening, and then putting a hole in it in the evening. What happens? All the water will flow out and the tank will be emptied. All our efforts will have been in vain. Likewise, children, we will do some kind of spiritual practice, but we will drain the energy which we acquire by indulging in worldly activities. This is like producing sugar on one side and creating ants on the other. The ants will eat all the sugar.

One who meditates can be understood by his character. His attitude will be "I am nothing." Humility will be there. We should have a mentality that will allow us to prostrate to anyone without shame. The ego can be removed only if we develop an attitude that "I am the servant of everyone." Only then is God's Vision possible. Even four years are not needed if *sadhana* can is performed with intensity. The goal can be attained within two or three years. Intense detachment should be there. Lying in the midst of a blazing fire, would we notscream out, "Save me, save me!" Forgetting body, mind and intellect, do we call out in complete surrender to God? When death approaches we act like this, do we not? God should be called just like that. Not much time is needed to attain the goal if we call to God in this way.

3 January 1982

Though various medicines were given by different devotees, the Mother's cough went on increasing. It was heartbreaking to see the Holy Mother coughing. This morning she again said to Balu, Nealu and Gayatri who were sitting near her,

Mother: Don't worry children. This is not bothering me as much as you think. It will only last for a couple of minutes, or sometimes for a few days. Anyhow, there is suffering even if it is only for a short period of time.
Nealu: Mother, why can't you stop taking different kinds of medicines? That is also harmful.
Mother: Mother wants to show that these medicines can do nothing unless "She" wills it. (Mother coughs for a long time and holds onto Gayatri's shoulder while Gayatri softly rubs her back).
Balu: Mother, it is already a week since this started. I can't bear to see Mother suffering like this. (His eyes become filled with tears).

Mother: Alright, no more medicines. This cough will go by
tomorrow evening.

It was ten o'clock. Although she was very weak, the Holy
Mother came out of her hut to see the devotees and spent
three hours with them. Nealu, Balu and Gayatri were struck
with wonder at the tremendous enthusiasm which manifested in the Mother while talking with the devotees.

Sundays are the most crowded days and on this day
many devotees had come. The Holy Mother received one
and all. But the cough troubled her several times, and the
devotees were greatly pained at heart. A young man who was
very devoted said, "Mother, it is unbearable to see you suffering. Give some of it to me."

Mother: (laughingly) This love is good; but son, you know,
it would be impossible for others to bear even an infinitesimal fraction of this weight. Son, Mother is not
suffering at all. The body is suffering a little. That is quite
natural. But Mother's mind is constantly reveling in the
Paramatma. Pain and pleasure are like the waves of the
ocean; they come and go. But they are only on the surface; it
is calm and peaceful underneath.

The daytime *Darshan* finished at two-thirty. At four-
thirty, the Holy Mother returned to begin the devotional
singing that preceeded the *Bhava Darshan.* She sang,

> O blue clouds, how did you get this blue
> colour, this beautiful blue colour which is the
> colour of Nanda Kumara (Krishna) who
> sported in Brindavan?

O my beloved Lord, is it Thy Will to make
me drown in this excruciating pang of separation?

O Lord of my life, O Beloved, my All in All,
I am unable to go away from Thee. Please
abandon me not.

The Mother was transported to another world. Her
songs created wave after wave of devotional bliss. The devotees also sang aloud, clapping their hands, forgetting all
about the surroundings. She again sang,

O Divine Mother, O Great Goddess, O
Thou Whose nature is Illusion, O Creatress
of the Universe, O Mother, I bow to Thee
again and again...

O Empress of the Universe, Blue sacred
One, O Great Illusion with beautiful limbs,
O Supreme Goddess, Thou art the Friend of
the devotees granting both Liberation and
bondage...

The Mother entered the shrine at six-thirty and the
Bhava Darshan started at seven, continuing until four
o'clock the next morning. At the end of the *Darshan*, the
Holy Mother sucked blood and pus from the wounds of the
leper, Dattan. Those on his forehead received special attention.

After the *Darshan* the Mother again spent some time
with the devotees. At the end of *Devi Bhava*, while the
Mother was still behind the closed doors of the temple,

people could hear her coughing. What was amazing was that she had not coughed even once during the entire *Bhava Darshan*. When she at last came out of the temple, she seemed like a mischievous and innocent child, so brilliant and full of cheer. She moved among the devotees, joking, sometimes sitting on the lap of an elderly woman or playfully hitting a devotee on the back. She played with her pet black and white dog for some time, riding on him and playfully fighting with him. While doing all this, the Mother coughed several times, but still she went on with her innocent play until five o'clock when finally she went to bed due to the insistence of some of the *brahmacharins* and devotees.

4 January 1982

The previous day the Mother had stopped taking medicines, but still the cough did not subside. Today, during lunch she said, "Don't worry about this body. Mother is not at all attached to it. (Pointing to her body) This is here to do service to others. It can be thrown away at any moment. Its existence depends on the people's need."

Today the Mother fed one ball of rice with her own hands to all those present. At two-thirty she went to her hut accompanied by Gayatri.

The evening *bhajan* started as usual at six-thirty. The singing reached its peak as the Holy Mother sang,

> O Beautiful One, please come,
> O Consort of Purandara (Lord Shiva),
> Please come, O Auspicious One,
> Please come...

O Giver of radiance,
Thou art the All in All of those
Who consider Thee as their dear relation...
O Mother, please remain as
The spring of my inspiration...

Becoming intoxicated with the love for God and standing up, the Mother began dancing ecstatically. The *brahmacharins* went on singing with overflowing devotion. From the temple verandah the Mother moved towards the coconut trees in the front yard where she went round and round completely lost to this world. She was showing a *mudra* (divine pose) with her right hand which was slightly raised. A beaming smile lit her face, which was clear even in the dim light. This ecstatic mood went on for more than half an hour and it seemed as though it would not end. Some people sat nearby and others at a distance, but all were watching the Mother. Some of the *brahmacharins* made a chain by holding hands to protect the Mother from hitting the coconut trees. Eventually Sugunanandan appeared on the scene, due to his usual fear that his daughter would soon leave her body if this state persisted. Without asking anybody's permission, he carried Mother into the hut and laid her on a cot. The Mother was totally lost to this world and her body now seemed like a corpse. Sugunanandan later related, "The little one's body was so light that it felt like I was lifting a basketful of flowers, but her face was glowing like the rising sun."

It was only after two hours that the Mother came out of this deep *samadhi*. She asked for something to eat. Gayatri served her rice and some curry, but she hardly ate two balls of rice. Then like a small child, she asked for some peanuts and some "mixture" (a combination of various tidbits). Finally, without eating anything, she got up and went away. Amazingly, as the Mother had told the previous day, her cough had mysteriously disappeared. No symptoms of it were seen from that evening onwards.

12 May 1982

After the evening *bhajan*, the Mother was sitting in front of the temple with *brahmacharin* sVenu and Werner.

Venu: Mother, should incense be lit during meditation?
Mother: Children, you shouldn't light incense. It will create a distraction in the mind. Your attention will be diverted to the smell. As far as a *sadhak* is concerned, incense is not necessary. It is simply a sensual pleasure; and it is impossible to control the mind without conquering the senses. Whether it is for food, fragrance, women, or anything else, do not think that you can satiate the desire by enjoying them. Each time that you enjoy the pleasures of the senses, the *vasanas* will only increase. (Pointing to her own head) Here there are all five sense organs. (Pointing to the place between the eyebrows) And here there is ambrosia as well. But human beings do not want that; they want only sensual pleasure which is equal to excreta.
Venu: Mother, how can desire be controlled?
Mother: No desires will rise up once the love for God is there, and attachment to other things will automatically decrease. If intense love for God arises, a person becomes like one who is suffering from fever. A feverish person will not feel any appetite at all. He will not feel anything if he sees food, however delicious it may be. At present, external con-

trol is necessary for you, due to the lack of intense love for God within. Because we are addicted to worldly pleasures, we should physically refrain from them in the beginning. Thereby the tendency of the mind to enjoy them will gradually decrease. Through physical abstinence, in due course the mind can be controlled. While seated in the midst of a hundred bottles of liquor, a drunkard cannot help but drink. At first, physical control is necessary.

Venu: Mother, how can the "I" sense be destroyed?

Mother: Either surrender everything to God or the Guru and become like a flute in His hands, or else have faith in "I" itself. It is good for a *sadhak* to sit gazing skywards. No movement is there at all; in the sky there is only attributeless, formless, undivided bliss. When looking down at the earth, we find ups and downs and other irregularities. But there is no diversity in the Real Thing. Always be convinced that you are the nature of *Satchidananda* (Pure Being-Awareness-Bliss). We can learn lessons from everything if *sraddha* (alertness) is there. Everything is our Guru. Having imbibed the essence of any object, throw away the rest.

4 July 1982

At this time, Werner was doing severe penance. For four days he had been meditating day and night without drinking even a glass of water. One *brahmacharin* told the Mother about this. She replied,

Mother: I will not ask him to eat. You should also get such *vairagya* (detachment). How much change has occured even in his complexion. It is a sign of getting closer to Truth. Let him continue his practice.

However, the Mother did insist that Werner drink some tender coconut water. After he had drunk she said,

Mother: Remember that in order to blossom, a tree sheds its leaves. The flower of love is blossoming within; that is why your desires are falling away. But it is not enough if alone, we attain Liberation through renunciation. Our *sadhana* should benefit all people. For that, the body should be taken care of. Not only that, we may have to take birth again if the body perishes before attaining Liberation, and then the work will again be there.

Realizing with all humility that what the Holy Mother said was true, Werner started taking food from that day onwards. The Mother said,

Mother: Ten *sadhaks* like him is enough. I will become your servant if you are ready to sit like that. I will bring food for you to the place where you are sitting. Mother does not ask the one who meditates all the twenty-four hours to work.

A group of young men had arrived to see the Holy Mother. Some were still studying in college while others had finished. Among them one was studying for his Master's degree in philosophy. Generally, such students would come only to ask some intricate questions of the Mother, hoping to make her speechless. Only a few really wanted to learn from her. The former always left disappointed or humbled, for the Mother was quick to reply and was never without a remarkable answer. The philosophy student asked, "Mother, have you taken sannyasa?"

Mother: Namah Shivaya! Mother is one gone crazy. Some children came here. Mother told them that such and such is Truth. Mother did not ask them to believe her. Mother has only told them, "Look within yourselves." They called me "Mother" and because of that I call them "children." But Mother does not know anything more than that.

Young man: Has Mother attained Perfection?

Mother: If Mother says, "I am perfect," then there is "I." Whereas, in the state of Perfection there is no sense of "I" at all. Not only that, such statements always imply a feeling of ego. *Mahatmas* set an example for the world through their humility and servant-like attitude, hoping that others will follow them. Therefore, Mother doesn't want to say such things. Everything depends above all upon the children's faith.

The young men, particularly the one who had questioned the Mother, appeared to be deeply contemplating the Mother's statement about perfection. The philosophy student stopped asking questions and kept silent. Later, when they were about to leave, they met Balu and the philosophy student remarked, "To be frank, we came to corner her but we failed in the face of her wisdom, humility and simplicity."

VASANAS
Tendencies

8 August 1982

At eight o'clock in the morning the atmosphere was calm and and all was quiet except for the reverberating sound of the ocean waves. The ringing of a bell indicated

that the morning worship was beginning. The chanting of
the Thousand Names of the Divine Mother was heard emanating from the temple. The Holy Mother was meditating
under a coconut tree near the backwaters. One *brahmacharin*
came with a glass of tea for her. After a while she opened
her eyes and gazed into the water for a long time, aimlessly
throwing stones into it, enjoying the dance of light and
shadow created by the ripples. There was a beautiful smile
on the Mother's face. Having offered the tea to the Mother,
the *brahmacharin* sat nearby and asked, "Mother, I am unable to cry and call to God."

Mother: Son, sorrow will come if you truly long to become
one with God. While abandoning all other desires, you
should have the attitude, "You alone, God, are enough for
me." There is no yearning now because renunciation is not
firm. The Vision of God will not be gained if one iota of
ego lies within. The mind must become expansive. Everything should be seen as One. Compassion should be felt for
the sorrow of others; their difficulties should be felt as if
they were our own.

Brahmacharin: Mother, do *vasanas* come from this birth or
from the previous births?

Mother: Child, the impressions created by the actions performed in the previous births manifest in this birth. These
inherited tendencies determine the course of action during
this lifetime. What we should do is exhaust them while doing spiritual practices, and avoid adding new ones. Take ten
eggs and keep them under a hen to hatch. Suppose that one
of them is that of a duck, but the rest of them are chicken
eggs. After being hatched, the duckling takes to water immediately. But what about the baby chicks? Not a single one

will go to the water. This is the nature of *vasana*. It is derived from previous births. Was it not a hen who sat on the eggs? If *vasanas* come from the present birth, the chicks and the duck would act the same. But the duckling does not show any traits of a hen.

The Mother's thoughts during her pregnancy play an important part in the child's character. That is why in the olden times a mother would always chant the Divine Name during pregnancy. If this is done, the child will also be one who remembers God.

As soon as a baby is born, he starts asking, "'Enge, enge?" He is asking "Who am I? Where have I reached?" But what do we do? Suddenly taking the child, we breast-feed it. The baby relishes the milk. Later, if we give fresh water it will not drink. It wants only sweetened milk, for in this it experiences the comfort of the mother's contact. After some time it feels sad if it does not get milk. When milk is stopped, we give biscuits, bread, rice, etc. Thus the mother binds the child.

The first *vasana* in a *jiva* is God-given. From that arises *karma* . From those actions new *vasanas* arise. All these *vasanas* accumulate as latent tendencies, and bring forth a new birth. This cycle will go on spinning like this. Liberation from *samsara* is possible only through attenuation of all the *vasanas*. All spiritual practices like chanting of the Divine Name, meditation, *japa* and *satsang* all help to weaken the *vasanas*.

At this time another *brahmacharin* came to the Mother and asked, "Mother, what should be said at this evening's speech?" At the request of some of the devotees, Mother had agreed to send one of the *brahmacharins* to give a spiritual talk at a temple. He wanted to know from the Mother the way in which he should present the subject.

Mother: Before talking about spiritual matters with anyone, you should first understand what sort of person they are. Many will not understand if you use complicated or subtle spiritual terms. Only bread and milk can be given to a small child. His stomach will be in trouble if you give him rice and sweet pudding. When you talk with today's youths who do not believe in God you can say, "Let there be no God; but do you believe in 'I'?" You can tell them to try to know that 'I'. As far as possible, try to instill *bhaya bhakti* (devotion with reverence) in them. The world is benefited only by that.

SADHANA AND SCRIPTURAL STUDY

10 August 1982

A discussion was going on about a syllabus for the *Vedanta* course which would be starting soon at the Ashram. Some scholars and philosophy professors were present. Each one was offering his opinion about which teaching-method and text should be used. Having listened to all their suggestions, the Holy Mother said,

Mother: Mother gives importance to *sadhana.* Scriptural knowledge is also necessary. But more time should be spent for *sadhana.* Meditation should be done for at least six hours each day. There is no benefit at all in merely studying. Having drawn the picture of a coconut tree, even if you think that you can quench your thirst by plucking a tender coconut from it, it is not possible. *Sadhana* and scriptural study should be maintained simultaneously. Together they will become a constant meditation. In any case, there must be innocence and sincerity in the work we are doing.

In the beginning stages, due to the power of the *vasanas*, it is difficult to fix the mind firmly in meditation. At this time companionship with Great Souls is most beneficial. Meditation is also a type of *satsang*. There, the companionship is with God. But it will take some time for that state to come. In the beginning *satsang* is more beneficial than meditation. *Satsang* can be a close association or companionship with a Self-Realized soul. It can also be the discussion or hearing of spiritual truths expressed by them, or study of the scriptures. But studies must not make one egoistic. Remember that everything is done to uproot the ego. The first type of *Satsang* is a direct physical, mental and intellectual relationship with a Great Soul. The second type is also the same kind of relationship, but it is established indirectly ~by studying, reflecting on and practicing their teachings. In both cases, the aspirant or devotee must have utter dedication and devotion, supported by knowledge. In the presence of a living *Satguru*, spiritual practice becomes smooth and less complicated. They are the souls with whom we must establish an unshakable relationship.

As the Mother spoke, her mood suddenly and completely changed. In a semi-conscious state she said, "Everything is nothing but that Supreme Self alone. There is no form, no name, neither Krishna nor Rama, nor Incarnations." Mother entered into an abstracted mood. Her body became still and her face shone with the light of perfect peace. Everyone gazed at the Mother with great devotion and wonder. One of the scholars sweetly sang:

Salutations to that all-pervading, all-knowing,
omniscient, pure, attributeless, unchangeable, formless Omkara, the Absolute Sound,
the Unmanifest, the non-dual Turiya, the Supreme Self. (*Turiya* is the Fourth State of Reality, which is beyond the three states of consciousness ~waking, dream and dreamless
sleep)

It took some time before the Mother came down to the
physical plane of consciousness. After a few more minutes
the lunch bell was heard. All saluted the Holy Mother and
moved to the dining hall. As they were walking, the scholar
who had chanted the Sanskrit verses said to his friend, "After hearing Mother's talk and seeing her state of *samadhi*, I
really feel sad to think how fruitless our long years of study
have been. Yes, my friend, it was a waste." As he finished
his sentence he turned around and, noticing a *brahmacharin*,
he remarked, "Lucky fellow." That evening during the devotional singing, the Mother became intoxicated with divine
love as she sang:

Aren't Thou my Mother, O aren't Thou the
Dear Mother Who wipes away one's tears?

Aren't Thou the Mother of
The fourteen worlds?
O Mother, aren't Thou
The Creator of this world?

For how many days am I calling Thee,
O Supreme Energy?
Won't Thou come? Won't Thou come?

Tears rolled down her cheeks. She laughed blissfully calling, "Amma...Amma...!" Her mood was that of a perfect devotee as she cried for God's Vision with an overflowing heart. There were many devotees present and all were spell-bound by the Mother's *bhajan*. Both her presence and her singing gave tremendous solace to the devotees. Some sat in contemplation and others clapped their hands, their bodies swaying to the ecstatic music. The *brahmacharins* were also totally absorbed. The ashram seemed like a kingdom of bliss.

16 August 1982

After the evening *bhajan*, the Mother sat with the *brahmacharins*. She called Gayatri and asked her to cut the apple offered by a devotee into small pieces. The Mother then distributed them to all. As she was serving it, she said,

Mother: Human beings can learn many things from Nature. Take an apple tree, for example. It gives all its fruits to others, taking nothing for itself. Its very existence is meant for other living beings. Likewise, a river. Everyone comes and bathes in it. It washes away everyone's dirt, expecting nothing. A river willingly accepts all impurities and gives purity in return. It sacrifices everything for others. Children, each and every object in this world can teach us sacrifice. If you look closely, you can find that all of life is a sacrifice. Each one's life is a story of sacrifice. The husband sacrifices his life for his wife, and the wife sacrifices hers for her husband; the mother for her children, and the children for their family. Each one of us is sacrificing our lives in one way or another. But each of us is limited to our own little world.

Without sacrifice, there is no world. Sacrificing everything for the good of the world is the greatest sacrifice. This little world of ours should evolve and expand until it becomes the whole universe. As it grows, we can see our problems slowly dissolving.

Brahmacharin: Mother, is it possible to reach the goal just by sitting in a place and meditating with the eyes closed?

Mother: Children, patience is *tapas*. Mental impurities will be removed if one meditates constantly, patiently sitting in one spot. If there is a Guru, the disciple has only to do *sadhana* ; the Guru will take care of the rest.

Brahmacharin: Mother, it is said that Sri Krishna was a perfect Incarnation. Is that true?

Mother: Children, if Sri Krishna is the ocean itself, then Sri Buddha, Jesus Christ and Sri Ramakrishna are each waves on the ocean. Sri Krishna is the physical embodiment of the Supreme Self.

Brahmacharin: Doesn't a *Jñani* attain Perfection when he gives up his body? Do such people come back to this earth?

Mother: Children, that depends on their will. Just as a rubber ball bounces back if it is aimed and thrown at a particular spot, having left his body, a *Jñani* can return according to the *sankalpa* which he made at the time of his physical death. He will never think, "If I come back, I will have to suffer." *Jñanis* are ready to take any number of births in order to uplift the world.

17 August 1982

The time was ten in the morning and the Mother was sitting with the devotees. *Brahmacharins* Venu, Balu and Unni were also present.

Mother: Always move with faith. One who has faith (*sraddha*) will never swerve from the path. Remember the form of meditation form while doing any work. When you first see somebody, chant "Hari Om" or "Nama Shivaya" . This will help to create Godly thoughts in both the other person and in yourself. When you talk with someone, imagine them as the form that you meditate on. Imagine this form in the atmosphere while you are travelling. Time will not be wasted if this is done.

Never become weak-minded. Do not see Mother only as this body. Sorrow will result if you children think that Mother is limited to this body. Always know that Mother is all-pervading. Have faith that Mother's Self and your Self are one. Have the conviction, "I have power, everything is in me."

All human beings say "I, I." That person is "I," this person is "I." Therefore know that "I" is the same in all. Everyday some time should be spent in solitude. Soon after getting up in the morning, meditate for some time while sitting on the bed. In this way you will get alertness. It is not necessary to be concerned with purity and impurity at that time. At night before going to bed, contemplate all the day's actions and thoughts. If you have committed any mistakes or hurt someone, repent as you recollect these things. This will help to keep you from repeating these mistakes tomorrow. Many trees joined together are known as a forest. Many thoughts joined together are said to be the mind. Thoughts should be diligently controlled. Instruction should be given to the mind, "O mind, think only of good things today. You should not run after the objects that you see here and there. Many people will come to attract you. You should not even look at them. Stand firm in thoughts of God alone."

Satsang should be done daily for some time. All of you children should gather together and discuss some spiritual subject. In this way, through various *sadhanas,* the mind should be concentrated on God.

The Mother turned to Balu. "Son, sing some songs," she asked.

> O man, wandering around in search of worldly pleasure, have you peace of mind even for a moment?
>
> Without knowing the principles of virtuous living, out of confusion you are groping in the darkness of Illusion.
>
> Like the moth that rushes into the flame, you are fruitlessly destroying yourself.

The Mother and the other devotees along.

18 August 1982

The previous evening the *Bhava Darshan* had ended by two a.m. Due to the infrequency of bus services at night, many of the devotees would leave the Ashram early the following morning, at which time the Mother would be in her hut resting. Because they would not see her in the morning, the devotees would stand outside the temple after the *Bhava Darshan* and wait for the Mother to come out, even though she had sat before them for nine or ten hours continuously. Emerging from the temple, the Mother would go to the waiting devotees, once more consoling each of them with some

words, a touch, or a look. Sometimes she would call someone who had wanted to speak privately with her. Finally, she
would walk around the grounds, making sure that all her
children had a place to sleep. Usually it would be at least
four or five o'clock in the morning before she went to her
hut to rest. This night was no different.

At four a.m. one devotee, Velayudhan Pillai, woke up
and called some other devotees. The Holy Mother had
agreed to visit his house that day and he was very happy.
Whether the Mother had taken any rest cannot be known;
she came from her hut at five a.m., ready to go. Some brahmacharins and householder devotees joined the Mother and
together they set out for Velayudhan's house in Haripad, a
village about twenty-five kilometres north of Vallickavu.

His house and front yard had been so beautifully decorated in anticipation of the Holy Mother's visit that it looked
as if there was a festival going on. Velayudhan's elderly
mother and other family members had come out to the front
gate to receive the Mother and lead her to the house.

It was a blissful day filled with the reading of the
Bhagavatam, satsang ,and devotional singing led by the
Mother. After the bhajan, she got up in a semi-conscious
mood and walked straight into the adjacent compound; but
she did not stop there. The Mother crossed that property
and entered the next yard. Gayatri, Velayudhan's mother
and several other devotees followed her. As she entered the
second plot of land she turned to them and said, "Do not
come."

There was an old, small but beautiful Devi temple in
that compound which belonged to the nieghbouring family.
The Mother entered the temple and sat there for a long
time, deep in meditation. Later, when she came out of the

temple, she walked around it in a bliss-intoxicated mood for
more than an hour. As she circumambulated the temple she
raised her hands to the sky and sang,

> O Mother, Supreme Goddess Kali,
> Today I will catch hold of You
> And devour You! Hear what I am saying!
> I was born under the star of death!

> A child born under such
> A planetary conjunction
> Devours it's own mother.
> So, either You eat me
> Or I will eat You today itself!

The family members were amazed as no one had mentioned a word about that temple to the Holy Mother. Later,
while talking about that particular incident, the Mother said,
"With concentration and devotion, many *pujas* (worship)
were performed that temple ." When inquiries were made
of the family who owned the temple, Mother's statement was
confirmed.

19 August 1982

In the morning the Holy Mother was about to return to
the Ashram. As there was not enough space for everyone in
the car, some were asked to go by bus.

One brahmacharin: I will also go by bus.
Mother: Mother will neither say that you should or
shouldn't go by bus because if she asks you to go, then you

will say that she has no love for you. Son, you are too sensitive and are seeing Mother with the same attitude that you see the mother that gave birth to you. This Mother should be seen as the Mother of all. Then only can you grow spiritually.

The *brahmacharin* was about to get up and go by bus when the Mother said, "Son, you don't have to go by bus. Come in the car." The Mother knew that even though he offered to go by bus, he didn't really want to.

By eleven-thirty in the morning everyone returned to Vallickavu. After lunch, while all the *brahmacharins* were still in the dining hall, the Mother came and told them,

Mother: Whatever Mother says, consider it to be for the good of the children. Sorrow arises because there is desire. There is no sorrow if you think, "Mother is my own." No one will make progress as long as there is selfish interest. You children should have adedicated attitude and think, "I have offered everything to my Mother; I have nothing of my own."

Today was a *Darshan* day and, as usual, the devotional singing began at five o'clock. The Mother sang,

Hare Kesava Govinda Vasudeva Jaganmaya
Siva Sankara Rudresa Nilakantha Trilochana

Gopala Mukunda Madhava
Gopa Rakshaka Damodara
Gauripati Siva Siva Hara
Deva Deva Gangadhara

Then,

> Parama Siva Mam Pahi Sada Siva Mam Pahi
> Sambho Siva Mam Pahi
> Parama Siva Mam Pahi
>
> Akshara Linga Mam Pahi
> Avyaya Linga Mam Pahi
> Akasa Linga Mam Pahi
> Atma Linga Mam Pahi

Everyone became absorbed in the ecstatic singing of the names of God.

20 August 1982

At nine o'clock in the morning, the Holy Mother was sat in her hut while Gayatri was served her tea . The previous night *Darshan* had ended at two-thirty a.m., but the Mother did not rest until four-thirty. Even if she didn't sleep for days on end, she was always fresh and full of enthusiasm. The Holy Mother took the glass of tea from Gayatri's hand and after one sip, she put it down. With a frown on her face she turned to Gayatri and said,

Mother: Daughter Gayatri, you have not chanted even a single *mantra* while making this tea. If it was a householder who did this I would have forgiven them; but you, a spiritual aspirant, should be chanting your *mantra* at all times — especially when preparing something for Mother. Even the householder devotees are careful in chanting their *mantra* while making something for Mother.

Having said this, the Mother set the tea aside without drinking it. Gayatri became dejected and stood there silently with her eyes downcast. It was true that she had forgotten to chant her*mantra* while preparing the tea, but that was only because she was in a hurry to make it while in the midst of taking care of numerous other urgent matters. Realizing the seriousness of her mistake, she felt repentant, and took the incident as a good lesson to remind her that the Mother was always watching her inner movements.

At that moment, Venu entered the Mother's hut and bowed before her. As she would do with everyone, she touched him and greeted him with joined palms.

Venu: Mother, when somebody prostrates to you, why do you touch their body and offer your salutations?

Mother: Son, is not everything one and the same Truth? Mother bows down to the Truth. I bow down to my own Self.

Venu: Didn't Mother tell me that the relationship between Mother and me has extended over a period of several births? If so, I should have known the Truth in my previous birth, shouldn't I? So why have I had to lead a life in the world all these years?

Mother: Light will be sought only if there is darkness. One can renounce something only if one understands the thing that is to be renounced. Mustn't untruth be known in order to understand that Truth is God? In order to see what is not true, you had to be in the world. *Jñana* (Wisdom) will not be attained by individual souls within only one birth.

Brahmacharin: Sometimes God will give everything to those who don't do any *sadhana*. Yet He does not turn around and look even once at one who strives hard.

Mother: God's nature is like that of a child. To some He will give. To some others He will not give. Goodness must be inherited from the previous in order for one to become worthy in this lifetime of what God can give. A Perfect Master is capable of seeing the subtle aspects of things which others cannot. God will become the servant of one who has innocence. No matter how much one pays attention, no further progress will be possible if one is not innocent. Since you have a Guru, you need not worry about Grace. It is enough if you do *sadhana.* Though many do not attain anything even after years of doing *sadhana,* you children can know the Truth if you do *sadhana* for four years as instructed by Mother.

Brahmacharin: Is God the servant of the devotee?

Mother: Yes, He is the servant of His true devotee. A true devotee is one who takes everything, both bad and good, as God's Will. For him nothing is bad. Everything is seen as good and beautiful for a true devotee. For him, all is God, so there is nothing to hate. Something is good and something else is bad only for a person who has likes and dislikes. But in the case of a real devotee, there are no likes and dislikes. He sees God's Divine hand behind every experience and every act. For such a person, is there anything that could be called "bad?" If he hates or dislikes something it is the same as hating God; this is unnatural to him. In his world there is only love. God is the servant of such a devotee.

The Mother suddenly entered an abstracted mood and as if from another world she said,

Mother: Children, Mother is the servant of every one of

you. I do not have a particular dwelling place. I dwell in your hearts.

Brahmacharin: Mother, now and then you say, "Mother does not know anything. Mother is nobody." Why do you destroy our *sankalpa* (attitude that Mother knows everything) like this?

Mother: Children, no matter what Mother says, will there be a decrease in your *sankalpa?* Do you know the attitude of those who have reached Perfection? It is "I am everyone's servant." To say "I am *Brahman*" indicates movement. But there is no movement in *Brahman*. There is nothing to say once you reach that state.

At this point, the Holy Mother got up and walked away towards the coconut grove, thus ending the conversation.

It was after lunch and the Mother was lying on the bare ground in the dining hall. Her behavior was often strange and incomprehensible. For her there was no such thing as "preference" or "choice". Most of the time she would do things as she felt. No one could insist that she do one thing or refrain from doing another, unless she was in the mood of an innocent child. On such occassions, she would sometimes beg, request or do as someone bid.

One who closely watched the Mother could observe the many different moods and aspects which she would manifest. Sometimes she appeared as the Master, the Mother, or the Father; sometimes she was like an innocent child; and at times she was a proficient administrator and organizer. This same all-powerful Mother could at times be found lying in the muddy back waters, at other times in the scorching sun or pouring rain, in the sand, or on the bare ground. Sometimes she would ask for a particular dish or edible and after it was brought, she would taste just a little bit and then not want any more. Sometimes she would eat a lot, at other times very little. Sometimes she would not eat any food at all for days.

Brahmacharin: Mother, why are you so loving to small children?

Mother: Previously, Mother would imagine childen to be Krishna; she would talk to them, keeping them close beside her. Mother used to call to them to come nearby saying that she would give them toffee. Playing with them, she would see them as Krishna and thereby get absorbed in meditation. Then Mother would completely forget about the children. After two or three hours would regain consciousnessand those children would still be sitting there. As soon as Mother opened her eyes they would ask, "Auntie, toffee..." They were waiting for that.

Spending some time with children is a *sadhana*. A child has all the signs of one who has reached Perfection. The innocence of children will reflect in us. Forgetting everything, we will sit looking at them. In them, *vasanas* are only in the seed form; they have not yet manifested. Children have the eyes of one who has attained Perfection.

Brahmacharin: Is it possible to verbally express the experience of *Brahma Pada* (the Absolute State)?

Mother: Son, if Mother were to give you a pinch, would it be possible to say how much your body hurt? Just as a dumb person cannot speak about the taste of molasses, similarly it cannot be said that such and such is the experience of the Absolute. Mother has the conviction that all her spiritual children will some day have that experience. Other than that, there is no reason to talk about these things now.

Brahmacharin: It is said that the mind of a Knower of the Self will always be fixed on the Truth. How is that possible?

Mother: Son, a Knower of the Self has dissolved his mind completely through constant and intense spiritual practices. As a result, his mind is fully fixed on the Supreme. Because he is one with That, he can see everything as That. As is the mind, so is the man. When he sees an object, what he perceives is not the external appearance, but that which illumines it. For a goldsmith, all ornaments, whatever their shape, are nothing but gold. Likewise, for a Knower of *Brahman*, everything is *Brahman* alone. Even if he talks to someone, that person is also *Brahman*. He talks only for others, that is all.

The sun slowly sank below the western horizon. The auspicious hour of twilight had arrived. The horizon glowed a brilliant red as if the fire of separation from her beloved, the sun, was burning within. The vibrations created by the poignant songs of the Holy Mother filled the atmosphere with divinity and bliss. Her piercing voice transcended everyone else's as she sang,

> O Blissful One, O Absolute One,
> Whose form is of unsurpassed beauty,
> Crossing the six mystic centers, the yogis
> Come to know Thee,
> The Invaluable Treasure.
> Thy Glory, O Infinite Power,
> Is however, only slightly known to them...

The singing ended by eight o'clock and was followed by the *arati*, the worship performed by waving burning cam-

phor before the deity in the shrine. Afterwards, some devotees sat inside the temple while others sat under the coconut
trees. Ganga and Madhu, two of the brahmacharins, went to
the sea. The Mother was lying in the sand on the southern
side of the temple. After supper the brahmacharins came and
sat around the Holy Mother. Gayatri was fanning her. The
sound of the splashing waves and the gentle flow of the
breeze from the sea made the atmosphere peaceful and calm.

Venu: Mother, what is the sleeping state like for one who
knows Brahman?

Mother: Full awareness will exist. He knows that he never
sleeps. He will be a witness to the sleeping state of his body.
If you children try sincerely, you will have all these experiences.

Brahmacharin: Mother, do Brahma, Vishnu and
Maheswara (Shiva) truly exist?

Mother: Due to the Primordial Resolve, vibration arose in
Brahman. From that arose the trigunas , or threefold qualities of Nature: sattva (goodness), rajas (activity) and tamas
(inertia). These three qualities are represented as the Trinity
of Brahma, Vishnu and Shiva. All these are also found
within. In fact, all that we see in this universe exists within.
For example, sometimes a man will have the cruel character
of a tiger, sometimes the calm nature of a deer. At other
times, he will have the forgetfulness of a lizard. Like a cha-
meleon, his colour is changing all the time. All these
existcharacteristics exist within. During a particular state of
meditation, we can grasp the essential principles of any object we see. It will be possible for us to know the mind of
whomever we see. Those who are not under the supervision
of a Satguru will waste their time and energy trying to mea-

sure the minds of others when they reach this state. This will obstruct their progress.

Brahmacharin: Mother, Vivekananda did not have the same amount of devotion to a personal God as Sri Ramakrishna had, did he?

Mother: Vivekananda had a *Satguru* in Sri Ramakrishna. He had firm devotion and faith in his Guru. He who has a *Satguru* does not need a particular God. For him, the *Satguru* himself is God.

Brahmacharin: Mother, it is said that when in order to test Sri Ramakrishna, money was put underneath his pillow, he got up trembling. Why did he tremble like that?

Mother: When he trembled like it may have seemed to others to be a weakness for it may have indicated to them that he saw money as different from God. But for one who has known *Brahman*, everything is *Brahman*. There are no differences like good and bad. If differences arise, there is duality. In reality there is no duality, is there? But that is not the question. By reacting like this, Sri Ramakrishna was setting an example to show how much distance a devotee or *sadhak* should keep from gold.

AVATAR AND JIVA
Incarnation and Individual Soul

Brahmacharin: What is the difference between an Incarnation and an individual soul?

Mother: From birth itself, spiritual tendencies exist in fully developed form in an *Avatar* ; whereas in others they must be developed through effort.

A great musician is born with the talent to sing. Within five minutes of first hearing it, he will be able to beautifully sing any song. An ordinary person cannot sing like that even if he works at it for five hours. *Avatars* come with this inborn ability; others have to develop it. Anyone can develop spiritual qualities through constant practice. *Sadhana* should be done properly. Never become lazy. Do not waste even a moment. In the olden days Mother would not sit idle even for a moment. She would always meditate. If someone came to talk, Mother would see them as the form of Devi. They could talk as much as they liked. Mother would not know anything. If one moment was lost, Mother would feel terrible distress and think, "O God, this much time was wasted." Then Mother would do twice as much *sadhana*. You will also get the fruit if you try with a sense of urgency like that. Being part of God, all are incarnations. Perfect Knowers of the Selfare known as *Purna Jñanis*, or Incarnations. Those whose knowledge is partial are called *jivas*.

Brahmacharin: It is said that *Atman* is the root cause of everything. Therefore, it is *Atman* which causes the senses to function, isn't it? If so, why shouldn't *Atman* itself enjoy *karma phala* (the fruit of its actions)?

Mother: In *vyavahara* (the phenomenal world) there are two kinds of souls ~ *Paramatma* andj *ivatma*. It is the *jivatma* which experiences *karma phala*. *Paramatma* is only a witness to everything. *Paramatma* is the platform or stage on which the drama of the world is enacted. Without the stage there can be no drama; but even without the drama, the stage still exists. The Self is the Substratum on which all activities take place, but It remains ever unaffected. The Self is inactive (*nishkriya*), it does nothing.

Brahmacharin: Does one take birth even after attaining *Atmajnana* (knowledge of the Self)?

Mother: By one's own will, one may do so for the protection of the world. Mother is ready to accept any number of births in order to serve the devotees and the suffering.

It was just past ten o'clock at night. The Mother told the *brahmacharins* to go to bed after meditating until eleven o'clock. She then went to her hut. One by one the *brahmacharins* got up and took their different places for meditation.

21 August 1982

At six o'clock in the morning the Mother and some of the *brahmacharins* were visiting a devotee's house in Quilon. About twenty-five people had come to see the Mother and to listen to the *bhajan*. Pai began by reading the *Devi Bhagavatam*. Now and then the Mother also read a few lines. It was melodious to hear her reading. Sometimes she would abruptly stop reading and exclaim, "Hey Mother! Everything is a play for You, but don't play your tricks with this one. Hey Kali, You can't fool me. I am Your daughter, little Kali!" The devotees enjoyed this tremendously and laughed at the Holy Mother's recitation and her seemingly light but significant utterances.

In the evening there was again devotional singing led by the Mother. It went on from seven until ten and was followed by the chanting of the *Sri Lalita Sahasranama* led by Ganga. The whole house was filled with the bliss of devotion. The Mother spent a great deal of time with the devotees after the *bhajan* had finished. The family members did all they could to serve the Mother and the *brahmacharins* through their hospitality and love and reverence.

KIRTANA IN THE KALI YUGA
Devotional Singing
In the Dark Age of Materialism

A group of devoted women were sitting around the Holy
Mother. A few of them had taken a course on *Vedanta*. The
Mother said to them,

Mother: *Jñana* is the goal and *bhakti* the means. Children,
bhakti is the path to *Jñana*. Devotion and love for God
should arise. In this age, more concentration is gained
through *kirtana* (devotional singing) than through *dhyana*
(meditation). Because at present the atmosphere is always
filled with different kinds of sound, *dhyana* will be difficult.
Concentration will not be gained. But this can be overcome
if *kirtana* is performed. Not only that, the atmosphere will
also become pure. Innocence will arise if one travels on the
bhakti marga (path of devotion). Through *bhakti,* all can be
seen with an attitude of brotherhood.

A woman devotee: Mother, isn't *jñana marga* good?

Mother: Daughter, *jnana marga* is good, but very few can
follow this path correctly. If a real Guru is present, then one
can travel the path of knowledge. If ego arises in the disciple, the Guru understands it and will immediately correct
him . Thus the disciple will not swerve from the path. But
if there is no Guru, the *sadhak* will think, "I am *Brahman*. I
can do anything. I have no attachments at all," and will be
prey to making mistakes.

A person who accepts the path of knowledge without
having a Guru is like one who studies for an M.A. degree
without having attended the first grade. Some, however, will
become followers of the *jñana marga* because of *samskara*

from the previous birth. From the beginning, they will have the vision of light within.

A devotee will have *dasatvam* (humility, servant-like attitude). The attitude that "I am nothing; everything is God" will come. Having this attitude, one will become a benefactor of the world.

22 August 1982

In the afternoon, the Mother started for Vallickavu from Quilon . On the way, she visited the homes of two devotees and blessed them. As the car proceeded to the Ashram, the Mother suddenly said, "Stop the car. One son is lying prostrate crying in his house. Mother had told him that she would come. Quickly drive the car there." Immediately the car headed for the house of this devotee. Only after arriving did everyone understand why the Mother was so intent on going to that house.

The head of the house was an ardent devotee of the Holy Mother. He was lying prostrate in the family shrine room, weeping like a small child. Totally dejected, his wife was standing near him. Seeing the Mother approach, he got up and burst into tears saying, "Mother, I thought that I must be a great sinner. Why should I live after coming to know that Mother had gone back to Vallickavu after telling me that she would visit?" The Mother replied, "How could Mother go back when you were weeping so much, thinking of her? My son, your innocence and love stopped Mother from proceeding."

With great affection, the Mother consoled the devotee and sang a few songs in the shrine room; afterwards she did the *arati*. Seeing all this, the devotee was very happy. After taking leave of the devotee and his family, the Mother again continued on her way to the Ashram.

It was four-thirty when she arrived. Because many devotees had gathered for the *Bhava Darshan* that evening, the Mother straight away sat for *bhajan* . It was amazing to see her full of energy, even after the journey and the two days of outside programmes. All the others were quite exhausted.

Krishna and *Devi Bhava* ended by three a.m. Afterwards, Mother came out of the temple, and herself began spreading sheets and mats out for the devotees. Some of the devotees prayed for her to go and take rest. The Mother replied, "How can Mother be inside the hut when all the children are lying outside exposed to the cold? You children say that Mother should sleep. Likewise, Mother thinks that you children should sleep comfortably as well."

CONTROL OF FOOD

23 August 1982

At five-thirty, the Mother was sitting in front of the temple with the *brahmacharins* . Venu asked, "Mother, what is the reason for dietary restrictions?"

Mother: In the beginning stages a *sadhak* should observe such rules closely. You should not eat much delicious food. As far as possible, avoid chillies and oil. Semen will increase if fat accumulates in the body. If the desire for tasty food increases, so will the passions in the body. Diluted milk and fruit can be taken moderately. It is better not to take food in the morning, and at night, only a little food should be taken. Half of the stomach should be for food, a quarter of the stomach for water, and the remaining portion for the movement of air. A little sweet can be taken. Salt should be decreased.

At a particular stage of meditation, one may feel a terrible hunger. There are different kinds of roots and leaves in Nature. If they are eaten, hunger will not be felt. In the highest state of meditation, food can be given up altogether. One can live for any length of time on the *prana* (vital force) taken from within. Tasty or otherwise, every food is the same for one who has attained Perfection. He can travel in any world without attachment to anything. He is beyond likes and dislikes.

EKAGRATA
One-pointedness

Brahmacharin: Mother, what is the goal of *sadhana?*
Mother: One-pointedness alone, son. Always practice sitting in one *asana* (posture). *Asana siddhi* (perfection in sitting unmoved) should be acquired. We should be able to sit three and a half hours at a stretch. The spine will be held correctly if we sit in *padmasana* (the lotus posture). One must attain concentration somehow. Wherever a man of one-pointedness may go, he will have no problems. He can travel in any world. He will never swerve. One who has concentration can bring others to spirituality with only one look. Other living creatures who touch even the spittle of a Realized Being will attain Liberation. Even the ants who creep along his path will attain Salvation. A *sadhak* should meditate at least six hours each day. External actions should be done during the remaining time. Sleep should be reduced. At a particular stage of meditation, the need for sleep will spontaneously diminish.

It was dusk and the soul-stirring songs of the Mother resonated in the atmosphere, sanctifying the whole village. In a God-intoxicated mood she sang,

> O Mother Divine, the Eternal Virgin,
> I bow to Thee for Thy gracious glance.
>
> O Maya, Mother of the Universe,
> O Pure Awareness-Bliss,
> O Beloved Great Goddess,
> I bow to Thee.
>
> O Mind of the mind,
> O Dearest Mother,
> I am a mere worm in Thy play...

As the song ended, she became totally absorbed in a transcendental state. In her own world, she got up from her seat, her right hand held in a divine pose (*mudra*). She gently swayed from side to side in that mood of inexpressible divine bliss.

Those who stand on the shore can see only the flag of a ship which passes in mid-ocean. The ship itself will not be seen. Likewise, we stand gazing at the moving image of the Holy Mother. But where is her real form? Her divine nature is concealed from us by the many layers of this ocean of ever-changing Illusion.

28 August 1982

It was nine-thirty in the morning and the devotees were preparing flower petals for the Devi *puja*. The Mother was also there and joined them in the preparations. She told the devotees,

Mother: Fixing the mind on each external action, we should proceed with *sraddha* (attention). *Sraddha* is most necessary. Every action should be done as an offering to God. Without external alertness, internal alertness is not possible. If there is *samatva buddhi* (equal-mindedness), *shanti* (peace) will arise. Everything should be seen as One. We will hate nobody if we see that others and oneself are one.

DHYANA AND BRAHMANUBHUTI
Meditation and the Experience of the Absolute

After the worship was completed, Venu came to sit near the Holy Mother and asked, "Mother, no matter much I try, I am not getting my *dhyana rupam* (one's form of meditation) clearly. Why is this?"

Mother: Son, a minimum of four years are needed for the form to become full within. In the beginning stages one should try to get concentration by sitting and looking at the form. If you sit with closed eyes for ten minutes, then the next ten minutes should be spent looking at the picture of one's form of meditation. At first external alertness is what is necessary. If there is no external alertness, it will not be possible to conquer the internal nature *(antarika prakriti)*. There is nothing else to know once one knows that one is *Brahman*. There everything is full.

Brahmacharin: Mother, what is the state of *Brahmanubhuti* (experience of the Absolute)?

Mother: *Anandam* (bliss). There is neither happiness nor sorrow. No "I" and "you." The state of *Brahmanubhuti* can be compared to deep sleep. But in this state there will be

complete awareness, while in deep sleep there is no awareness, is there? In sleep there is no "I" and "you." It's only
once we wake up that I, you, yesterday and today are there.
Sahaja samadhi (the natural state of abidance in the Absolute) is *purnam* (fullness, perfection). There the mind attains
complete absorption.

Brahmacharin: Sri Ramakrishna used to pray, "O Mother,
do not make me mad with *Brahmajñana* (the knowledge of
Brahman). It is enough for me to become Your child." Why
was that?

Mother: Form is a ladder on the path of devotion. Even after attaining *Brahmajñana*, the devotee loves to be God's
servant. A true devotee's wish is to continue as such even after attaining the supreme state of *Brahmajñana*. In order to
drink in the sweetness of devotion, a realized soul will again
come down and intentionally retain the devotional attitude.
No one will be satisfied with anything else once they have
enjoyed the *rasa* (essence or sweetness) of *bhakti*. Didn't Sri
Krishna Himself incarnate as Gauranga just to know the
rasa of *Radha bhava?*[50] Children, the sweetness of devotion is
something unique.

Brahman has no name or form. It is infinite like the sky.
Knowledge is eternal. When we are in the world of name
and form we are in the non-eternal. By his *sankalpa*, the
devotee can do *rupa dhyana* - meditation on the form of his
Beloved Deity - even after becoming one with the Absolute.

All the signs of *parabhakti* (supreme devotion) as described by the great sage Narada in his classic work on
devotion, the *Narada Bhakti Sutras*, are manifest in the the
Holy Mother. For instance, in the days when she was per-

[50]Gauranga or Chaitanya Mahaprabhu of Bengal had the attitude of Radha, Sri
Krishna's Beloved, His greatest devotee.

forming *sadhana* to realize the Divine Mother, she would suffer excruciating pain of separation from God. If she happened to forget the Divine Name even for a single moment, she would feel extremely dejected thinking of the lost time. To make up for that, she would chant or meditate with more intensity. At that time the Mother would see everything as Devi, and in that mood she would embrace the trees, actually feeling them to be the Divine Mother herself. Sometime she would sit for a long time on the banks of the backwaters, touching her nose on the surface of the water as if kissing the ripples. If she happened to see any women or girls dressed in saris at this time, the Mother would run to them and embrace them calling "Amma, Amma!" Now the Holy Mother was sharing her own experiences with her spiritual children and devotees. She said, "Even now I am struggling hard to keep my mind down. Epecially while singing *bhajans.*, it is always shooting up." The Mother continued by explaining,

Mother: While taking each flower into your hand to offer during *archana* , the Beloved Deity's form should be remembered. Then it should be imagined that the flower of the mind is being offered to God. *Sraddha* (alertness) is what is most necessary. It is enough if you have *sraddha, sahôdara buddhi* (brotherly attitude) and complete faith. Progress will occur by and by. If even one iota of ego arises in the *brahmacharin* children's hearts, Mother will rub it and remove it that moment itself. Mother is ready to take any number of births to serve the devotees, but Mother cannot become the servant of the ego.

The bell was rung for lunch. There were no visitors today, only *brahmacharins*. Mother came to the dining hall and lay down on the floor. Calling aloud, "Shiva...Shiva...Shiva...," she playfully pummeled those who were sitting nearby. Some of the children would purposely sit close to the Mother when she was in this mood simply to receive these playful jabs . They considered it a great blessing.

As the *brahmacharins* watched the Mother, her mood took a sudden change and she began rolling on the ground, her hands showing a divine *mudra*. Her mind soared to some unknown plane. In this absorbed state, she closed her eyes and her body became still. Gayatri fanned her. Some of the *brahmacharins* observed her closely, and others sat for meditation. It was almost one hour before the Mother returned to this world of appearances. When she opened her eyes, she said, "I am thirsty, bring some water." The Holy Mother would say, "If Mother expresses a desire it is only to give you a chance to serve. It will also help me to keep the mind down."

1 September 1982

Today the Mother was visiting *brahmacharini* Vimala's house in Vallickavu. From the very beginning of the Mother's divine moods, that family had been extremely devoted to her.

The Mother was sitting in the backyard of their house. It was five o'clock in the afternoon. The atmosphere was calm and quiet. Their family deity was the snake god and there were small shrines situated randomly in the yard. On the western side of the old style Kerala house, there were bushes, flowering plants and creepers. On the whole, the property looked like a hermitage. Pai, Ganga, Balu, Venu, Ramakrishna, Gayatri, Vimala and the elderly mother of the house were sitting near the Holy Mother. Venu asked about his Sanskrit studies.

Mother: Venu is a bit crazy about Sanskrit, and fascination for anything except God is dangerous.

Pai: Mother, for one who leaves his body after reaching the Supreme State, is there another birth?

Mother: Only if he wishes. Even after giving up the body, he can maintain a subtle, separate existence according to his own *sankalpa*. He will not completely dissolve in *Brahman*. By his own self-will he can again accept a body. This coming back is for the benefit of the world.

SARVATRA SAMADARSHINAHA
Seeing All as One

Venu: What kind of actions are you expecting from me, Mother?

Mother: Son, selfless service, even-mindedness, seeing good even in the mistakes of others, these are things which Mother likes. If you children love Mother, you should love and serve all living beings. Only then can it be said that you children love Mother. Do not think only about your own comfort. Do not think even for a moment that "This is my body." See everything as your own *Atman*. Whatever others tell you, listen carefully and with *sama chittata* (even-mindedness). Speak to them only after they have finished speaking to you. Aversion should not be felt towards anyone. Like a river flowing without hindrance, let your mind flow with the sound "Hrim." Like the links of a chain, there should be an unbroken remembrance of God. The cool air resulting from

this will give freshness to everyone. Whomever you see, remember God's Form. Then everything will rise up from
within.

Son, there is only one Self. It is omnipresent and omnipotent. When our mind becomes expansive we can merge
with the Infinite. Then there will be neither selfishness nor
ego, for Infinity means vastness. There everything is equal.
Serve others without wasting even a moment. Help the suffering. Do not expect anything from anyone mentally or
physically. For a *sannyasin* there is no particular God dwelling in the sky. Both heaven and hell are on earth alone.
There is only one thing he has to do, that is to see God in
everything. For a true seeker, the Guru is everything. In fact,
the Guru and God are one and the same; the Guru's will is
God's Will.

Usually the Guru will give ochre cloth to the disciple
only when he has reached an advanced spiritual state, that
is, when the disciple no longer prays for any selfish things.
God has no form nor taste. He is infinite. When our ignorance is removed, we can see everything equally in any circumstance.

Ganga was sitting nearby listening to all that the Mother
was saying. He was looking down, hanging his head. Turning to him, she said,

Mother: Son, you had a desire to wear the ochre cloth. You
believed that it would help you to overcome worldly desires.
Mother has caught hold of you because during the time
when you came here, goodness was already obscure. You always talked about *Brahman*. As far as you were concerned,
there was no God. You thought that only Ramana Maharshi

was great, that no one else had any greatness. Even then, you did not try to understand who Ramana really was. You had seen that "person" alone. You did not try to study him. You did not think about his equal vision, selfless service and devotion. You were only convinced "I am the greatest." Darling son, at least now, correct that ignorance.

GURU MAHIMA
The Guru's Glory

5 September 1982

A woman named Mahatti from Tamil Nadu who was doing her doctoral research came to see the Holy Mother. From a very young age Mahatti had been interested in spiritual matters. *Brahmacharin* Madhu from Reunion Island had told her about the Mother. She needed an interpreter, so the Mother sent for one of the *brahmacharins*.

However, that *brahmacharin* had been scolded that morning by the Mother for not milking the cow at the usual time. Because he was upset from the scolding, he replied, "I can't" in a tone as if he were talking to his biological mother. The Mother calmly replied, "Son, you can say anything to Mother. Mother will forgive. But Nature has recorded your words and you will not get forgiveness from that. Such words should never come from one who meditates." The Mother called another of the *brahmacharins* and the talk began.

Mahatti told the Mother about certain spiritual experiences which she had, and sought instructions regarding her path for further spiritual attainment.

Mother: Daughter, do you have a personal deity?

Mahatti: No, I don't. I have no inclination at all towards any form of God or Goddess. But I have an intense thirst to realize the formless Self.

Mother: Daughter, name and form are ladders to reach the Formless. We who are limited cannot conceive of the Unlimited. And so, form is needed to reach the Formless. A second thorn is needed to remove the thorn which has pierced our foot. Once the thorn is removed, both can be discarded. Likewise, after reaching the Ultimate Goal you can abandon all names and forms if you want. Child, even when you meditate on the Formless Self you need a pure conception which itself is nothing but a thought. Thus it is also a concept, is it not? And when you meditate on a form of God or the Goddess, you are not really meditating on an external object, but only on your own Self.

Mahatti: That is a convincing point, but can't Mother suggest another method which suits my mind?

Mother: Mother can understand your difficulty in following meditation on a form. So, you can do one thing. Whenever you feel like it and have the time, sit in solitude and try to visualize everything as pure light. Look at the vast sky and try to merge in that expansiveness. Look within and observe the thoughts, tracing them back to their source. Instruct the mind in this way, "O mind, why do you long for unnecessary things? You think that this will give you happiness and satisfy you. But it is not so. Know that this will only drain your energy and give you nothing but restlessness and unending tension. O mind, stop this wandering. Return to your source and rest there in peace." Try this, daughter. It will enable you to gain peace and tranquillity.

Upon hearing the Mother's words, Mahatti's face became bright, her smile revealing her inner contentment. "Mother, I am so happy to hear an instruction befitting my mental constitution. I am very grateful to you for this valuable piece of advice. It will help a lot in my search to realize the Supreme." The Mother affectionately patted her back as Mahatti prostrated before her.

The Mother came out of the hut to meet the other devotees who were waiting to see her. She sat on the verandah in front of the temple as the devotees one by one prostrated to her and sat nearby. A few of the *brahmacharins* were also present and one of them seemed to be dejected. The Mother enquired about his gloomy mood. Even though she is aware of everything, she also knows the soothing affect of a motherly enquiry on the hearts of her children.

Brahmacharin: Mother, before seeing you I was a devotee of Lord Krishna, but now there is nothing like that. Everything is Mother alone.

Mother: Son, one who has a real Guru will have devotion to no particular God. One can say that God and I are one, but a disciple will always have a higher place in his mind for the Guru than for God. Son, don't think that the Guru and one's Beloved Deity are two. In reality, they are one and the same.

Brahmacharin: Mother, what books are suitable for us to read?

Mother: The *Srimad Bhagavatam* is good. All the inner principles are explained in it. A good storyteller will not start telling the story from the very beginning. At first, he will amuse the people by relating certain non-essential incidents. Only once the listeners start paying attention will the real story begin. So it is in the *Bhagavatam*. Many interesting stories are told. After these introductory stories have been told, it gradually enters into a discussion of the Real Principle. It is enough to read the eleventh chapter only. All principles are contained in that one part.

In the beginning stages aspirants should only read books like the *Bhagavad Gita*, the *Bhagavatam* and the life stories and teachings of great saints and sages. Devotion must be developed first and then *jñana*. Otherwise, egotism will develop.

After reading the *Advaitic* book,"I am That," Venu is imitating certain things without understanding their real principles. What Nisargadatta Maharaj says in that book is that he faithfully served his Guru for three years. He had perfect devotion to his Guru. It was only after completing his *sadhana* that he said, "I am *Brahman.*, I am That."

Brahmacharin: Is meditation on a form necessary, Mother?

Mother: Son, when we meditate on a form, it is not the form but we who get peace and concentration. In *rupa dhyana, laya* (dissolution of the mind) will take place. In reality, even then we are meditating on our own Self. Form is a ladder. After some time it will be felt that form is a mere shadow. All experiences will be gained from this.

8 September 1982

Today the Mother and the *brahmacharins* visited Srimati Mohanan's house in Quilon. She was an ardent devotee of the Holy Mother. In her excitement, Mohanan was running here and there not knowing how to welcome or to serve Mother.

It was ten o'clock in the morning. The Mother sat on the front verandah conversing with Mohanan. "Mother, while in the state of *Krishna Bhava*, will you return to your normal state now and then?" Mohanan asked.

Mother: No, at that time I am Krishna alone. There are many who are still not aware that Mother assumes *Krishna* and *Devi Bhavas* by self-will, nor are they aware that Mother and Krishna are one. Even so, they have a special love and reverence for Mother. Mother will only strengthen the faith of those who believe her to be two. Mother would say that their belief is helpful for the progress of their devotion. It would shake their devotion to feel that both are one. *Bhaya bhakti* (reverential devotion) would go. Sometimes Mother will play with them and make jokes, won't she? That is why they will think, "This innocent child cannot be Krishna or Devi." How many things each one tells Mother during the *Bhava Darshan* which they would not tell her at other times. These people believe that after Devi and Krishna have heard them, they can go away and nobody will know what they have said.

The *brahmacharins* felt a little sad at heart to hear the Mother's reply. When Mohanan went to the kitchen, the Mother turned to them and said,

Mother: You believe that everything is Mother,.ut do not try to make others, who see Mother and Devi or Krishna as separate, understand this thing. They get great benefit from their belief.

It was afternoon and the Mother was lying on a cot in the inner apartment of the house. Mohanan was fanning her, while her two children sat near the Mother, holding her head and feet on their laps. A few of the *brahmacharins* were sitting on the floor. The Mother told them,

Mother: If one practices celibacy for twelve years, a new nerve will be created in the body. The power of the seed which ordinary man throws away for the sake of trivial enjoyment is what is changed into nectar in a *yogi*. As concentration deepens, the length of the tongue will increase and then, bending back, it will rise towards the top of the head through a hole in the uvula palate. During a particular state of meditation, some will drink this nectar by slightly severing the tendon that joins the tongue to the throat. If even a single drop is imbibed, they become immortal. This is the inner meaning of the saying that the gods used to quaff nectar. Remember that it is this potential power which is deterred each time a drop of semen is lost. Such discharges will take place in both men and women after they reach the age of fifteen. This loss may occur while awake, or while dreaming also. It will not happen if we are alert during sleep. Do not use much oil in your food. Wherever you go, try to overcome any attraction to women by seeing everyone as your Mother. If a lustful woman passes by, that is enough to make a chaste man lustful. We can experience the intoxication of real liquor and *ganja* if the power of celibacy is acquired. Just like a drunkard, we will experience an intoxicated state at certain stages of meditation. But that experience is lasting; whereas, the happiness gained from liquor and *ganja* will flee.

Brahmacharin: Even though I have done intense *sadhana* for so many years, my mind does not become still. It is due to the lack of Mother's Grace. Therefore, I am going to commence a vow of silence and fasting from tomorrow onwards.

Mother: Son, how will you get Grace if you continue to think "I am doing?" You do not have the proper attitude of surrender, which is characterized by the feeling that you have offered everything to Mother, and that Mother will save you. This is not *sannyasa*. Mother will not let you walk along whatever path you like. Your thoughts should be, "I am doing *sadhana* not for my own selfish purposes, but for the good of the world." Son, do your *sadhana* sincerely and with utmost care. Don't waste your energy thinking of the fruit. It must come if your effort is intense and sincere.One must forget the fruit of the action if one really wants to get its full benefit. Patience and self-surrender are very necessary for an aspirant.

10 September 1982

It was the occasion of Sri Krishna's birthday, and the Ashram and surroundings were being prepared for the auspicious celebration. The reading of the *Srimad Bhagavatam* was going on. The Holy Mother participated in the recitation by reading and listening.

Uriyadi began in the evening. *Uriyadi* is a folk custom typically celebrated on Lord Krishna's birthday. It is a game which depicts the childhood sportings of Lord Krishna ~ in particular, His escapades of stealing butter, milk and curd from the houses of the *gopis*. First, Mother herself would dress the young village children like Krishna and the *gopas* (cowherd boys) and each would carry a staff in his hand. A clay pot containing butter, milk and curd would dangle from a rope slung over a bamboo pole some thirty feet high. As the boys came dancing up to the pot aiming to break it with their staffs, it would be pulled up and down and swung like a pendulum. At the same time, two of the *brahmacharins* who stood on either side would splash water in the children's faces as they ran by. This game went on until seven o'clock in the evening. The Holy Mother, like a small child, was laughing and clapping her hands as the play went on. The bliss enjoyed by everyone present was altogether in-expressible.

Later in the evening there was an old-style Kerala folk dance called 'Thiruvathira Kali'. It was performed by women and young girls and was accompanied by the sung praises of Sri Krishna. Next there was a long *bhajan* after which the Mother sat in the front yard of the Ashram with some of the *brahmacharins* and householder devotees.

Venu: Mother, what is experienced in *samadhi*?

Mother: Bliss. There is neither happiness nor sorrow. There is no "I"or"you." This state can be compared to deep sleep, but there is a difference. In *samadhi* there is full awareness; but not so in sleep. When we wake up from sleep, no *jñana* has been gained. Instead "I," "you" and the world re-emerge. Because of our ignorance, we feel that all this is real. To remove this ignorance, constant practice should be done fixing the mind on one object.

Ganga: The *Puranas*[51] say that Vishwamitra was a Realised Soul, but he was sometimes seen as hot-tempered. Why is this?

Mother: Son, whatever a Perfect Being does is for the good of others. In reality, Vishwamitra was testing the devotion of Harischandra. All the quarrels instigated by the sage Narada were also for the benefit of others.[52]

Ganga: That reveals a lot. If Mother's grace is present, I can do many good things in this world.

---

[51]Ancient scriptures written in story form by the sage Vedavyasa.

[52]Vishvamitra was a sage who deprived King Harischandra and his wife of their kingdom and put them through other intense and prolonged trials. The sage Narada has also been depicted as doing similar things.

Mother: Son, you should have your own power. Mother is telling you that she and you are One. Due to ignorance, the all-pervading Truth cannot be seen. But you must try to see everything as Mother's form.

Do not become angry with anyone. If somebody gets angry with you, immediately think, "The thing which is called 'I' is the same in me and in him. That is the *Atman*. *Atman* is only one. So with whom shall I get angry?"

ONE-POINTEDNESS

Brahmacharin: Mother, how can concentration be gained?
Mother: Son, if there is the intense desire to reach the goal, *ekagrata* (one-pointedness) will arise. There was a boy who had never done any work in his life. His father was a coconut tree climber by profession. One day the boy's father died. After his death, all the people would still come and call the son to pluck the coconuts from their trees. But, what could the boy do? He did not know coconut tree climbing. This boy could find no other way to earn a living, so he decided to try to learn to climb coconut trees. This had to be learned with great care. If he would happen to fall, his arms and legs would be broken and it would not be possible for him to climb any coconut trees. His life would be wasted. Therefore, with great care, he tried to climb a coconut tree. Placing each foot with utmost care and embracing the tree tightly, he would climb a little way and then come down. The next day he would climb a little higher. After several days' effort, he learned coconut tree climbing. Through practice, he was able to ascend and descend the tree very quickly.

A *sadhak* should be like that. God alone is Truth. Only if this is realized will life be fulfilled. God-Realization must be life's only goal. That alone is the food for all eternity. But there are obstacles in the way of reaching this goal. If immense care is not taken, we will slip and fall. One's life will be wasted if one falls down. One should have this kind of attitude in the beginning stages of *sadhana*. Only then will concentration be gained. Try for that, children.

While singing *bhajans* the Holy Mother rejoiced and danced blissfully, like a small and innocent child. This made all the devotees feel that Lord Krishna had once again taken birth on this earth. Everyone was very happy and content.

Around ten o'clock the *Srimad Bhagavatam* was again read. The readings were taken from the chapter describing the birth of Krishna. At midnight, *bhajans* were sung and *arati* performed in celebration of the auspicious occasion of Sri Krishna's birth.

GUDAKESA
Conqueror of sleep

15 September 1982

At quarter past five in the morning, the *Bhava Darshan* was just ending. Even after sitting for thirteen continuous hours without moving from the seat, the Holy Mother was very energetic. She did not go to her hut but remained with the devotees and began talking to them.

Ramesh Rao was a young man from Haripad who wanted to stay in the Holy Mother's presence. He had been forcibly taken by his family and friends to a mental hospital in Trivandrum to undergo a series of treatments for mental abnormality. Pai, a close friend of Rao's and a spiritual son of the Mother, told her what had happened. The Mother sat quietly for a long time deep in thought.

Brahmacharini Gayatri had been recently admitted to a hospital in Quilon after symptoms of cancer had been detected, and on this day she was to undergo surgery. It was, in fact, the Mother who had first pointed out that Gayatri was suffering from cancer and had instructed her to immediately get medical care. The diagnosis proved Mother's words to be perfectly true. This was not a wonder to anyone, as they were well aware that Mother knows everything. Yet the news of Gayatri's operation had created a feeling of sadness in everyone's mind.

Now and then devotees would invite the Mother and the *brahmacharins* to their homes, and the day would be spent blissfully singing, reading the *Bhagavatam*, conducting the *archana*, and other spiritual disciplines. The previous night a woman had come to the Ashram to invite the Mother to her house the next day. However, it was not the right time to leave the Ashram since the Mother had many things to do in connection with Gayatri's operation, Rao's abduction and other things of concern. The Mother explained to the devotee that she was unable to visit her house on that day and the woman left with a dejected and disappointed mind.

As mentioned before, some devotees saw the Mother as different from Devi, and would approach the Mother during the *Bhava Darshan* with silly matters. For the past two days the Mother had neither slept nor rested even for a moment. It was at about six o'clock in the morning and the Mother was getting ready to visit Gayatri in the hospital. One *brahmacharin* requested, "Mother, please sleep a little." To this she replied, "It is not for sleeping that Mother has come here. All of you can sleep. Mother has to take care of so many people's problems."

MOTHER OF THE HOUSE

18 September 1982

Today all of the Ashram work, from sweeping the grounds, to cooking meals and cleaning all the vessels and utensils, was done by the Mother herself, since most of the *brahmacharins* were bed-ridden with severe fever. As if she were their natural mother, she made hot gruel and went to each one making them drink it. Even in the midst of all this work, she noticed the dirty clothes of one*brahmacharin* who was about to go outside for some purpose. She lovingly scolded him for wearing them and asked him to change. It should be pointed out that even at this time the Mother found the time to give spiritual instructions.

Talking to a *brahmacharin* about how an aspirant should control his diet, she said,

Mother: Food intake should be controlled. A *sadhak* should not eat much tasty food. Due to the attraction towards taste, it will become difficult to overcome many other obstacles. However tasty a thing is, it is not possible to know the taste once it goes down the throat. Tasty food will increase in the quantity of semen, and because of that, lust will increase. Both tasty and tasteless food should become the same. Practice eating bitter things. Not only the tongue but all the sense organs should be overcome. Going to places that stink, try to overcome your aversion to unpleasant smells by sitting there for some time.

In the evening the Mother cooked tapioca root for every-one. On certain days the Mother would do all the Ashram work, including cooking, while the *brahmacharins* sat for meditation and *japa*. She would bring rice gruel and ba-nanas to the place where they were sitting.

At about four-thirty p.m. a man from Bangalore named Srinivasan came to see the Holy Mother. Although he had been working as a doctor in the United States for the last ten years, his deep-rooted devotion to Lord Krishna which had begun during his childhood in India still remained with the same intensity. He had arrived from the States only on the previous day and had come to see the Holy Mother, in-spired by a dream which he had had. Balu, the first person who he met in the Ashram, was curious to know more about Srinivasen's dream, but did not ask anything, thinking that it would not be proper to do so before the man had seen the Mother.

At five o'clock the doctor was called to the Mother's hut. Balu noticed how his face blossomed and shone when he beheld the Mother's form. His whole body was trembling and his eyes were filled with tears. Mother tenderly wel-comed him and made him sit near her. After some formal enquiries Mother said to him, "Son, tell Mother what you want to say." Controlling his emotions, Srinivasan spoke.

Srinivasan: It was a vision rather than a dream. I had not even met or heard about the Mother then. The most striking aspect of the vision was the place where I was when it oc-curred. It took place in the airplane, yes, the same flight on which I was traveling to India this time. I had a window seat. For a long time I gazed at the sky and chanted my man-tra. As I was chanting the *mantra*, I slowly glided into a

semi-sleepy mood. Then, in the sky appeared a strong efful-
gence which slowly assumed a form. To my wonder I found
that it was the beautiful form of Krishna, my Beloved Deity.
I was really thrilled and felt that each and every cell of my
body was dancing in bliss.

As I was drinking in the beauty of my Lord, there appeared just beside Him another equally radiant and splendid
glow. That also assumed a form. It was that of a lady
wrapped in pure white clothes with a beaming smile on her
face. Her nose ring sent forth rays which blinded my eyes. It
seemed as if two suns had appeared in the sky. My mind
soared, and I could not contain the tremendous amount of
bliss which was generated then. Both of these figures, dark
blue in hue, smiled at me. A few moments passed thus
when Krishna turned to the woman, who was still smiling at
me, and pointed His index finger towards her. As He remained in that position, both of them vanished from my
sight. I suddenly woke up.

I was still enjoying the bliss and was quite sure this
hadn't been a dream but a vision. Even the semi-sleepy
mood I'd felt was as circumstance created in order for this
divine drama to take place. I knew that this was a hint for
me to do something. But who is this woman, I thought? My
eagerness to know the significance of this dream became so
intense that I could not eat or sleep during the remaining
part of the trip. My thoughts were focused only on the vision; nothing else entered my mind. It was to be a sixteen
hour flight, and this divine drama had taken place just four
hours after the departure from the New York. Twelve hours
were left. I became very restless.

The next morning at eleven o'clock I reached home. My
parents and my older brother welcomed me with open arms.

But in spite of all their love and affection, my mind was not at rest. The vision grew more and more clear in my mind, especially the smiling face of the woman. I thought, "What is this?" I'm a devotee of Krishna, but instead of being attracted to His divine form, this lady's face was overpowering me. My parents and elder brother noticed my strange mood. I was very confused and therefore could not give them a satisfactory answer. I was doing everything more or less mechanically. When I eventually entered the room which had been arranged for me, the first thing which caught my attention made me almost dumb with wonder. Pasted on the wall was a picture of the same woman who had appeared in the dream. Overwhelmed with joy I turned to my parents and asked, "Who is this lady?" "People say that She is God," my elder brother answered. He continued, "I found this picture in one of the newspapers and felt a strange attraction to it. This room was occupied by me until yesterday evening. For your convenience I moved to another one." Rejoicing at heart, I requested him to tell me more about her.

Thus I am here, Mother. Please tell me, what am I to do? I am yours, please guide me. Bless me by giving me implicit devotion and faith.

Mother: Mother is very happy to see your innocence. This is something extremely difficult to get. Even though you have been living in the midst of worldly pleasures, you are able to maintain strong devotion and faith. It is this innocent devotion and faith which has caused all this. Keep up this attitude, that is enough for your spiritual progress. Child, Mother is always with you.

He cried like a small child, keeping his head on the Mother's lap. With great affection and love, the Mother caressed him. He left the Ashram at seven o'clock having paid his homage to the Holy Mother and requesting her to be in his heart always.

22 September 1982

Today the Mother and all the others left in a boat to go for *bhajan* in a nearby place. It was twilight time. The expansive blue sky, the coconut trees growing on both sides of the backwaters, and the gentle breeze which caressed the water's surface, all made for a truly inspiring scene.

The Holy Mother rose from her seat and started dancing. Unable to control her bliss, she cried out, "Hoi, Ho, Hoi, Ho..." and, raising her hands upwards she sang:

> The Sea of Compassion art Thou.
> If Thou art not compassionate to me,
> Who else is there to give me refuge?
>
> My heart keeps on waiting for Thee.
> Will this day also be lost in vain, O Mother?
> Will this day also be lost in vain?

Everyone sang along with the Mother's song. Taking water from the river with her cupped hands, she threw it in the air calling, "Devi, Devi..." All of a sudden she went into *samadhi* and stood still in the boat, her hands uplifted still. After a few minutes she slowly opened her eyes and asked Venu to sing a song. He sang:

> O ever youthful Mother,
> Because Thou art not showering

Mercy on Thy children,
Grief is intensifying in their hearts.

O ever youthful Mother,
Allow me not to fall and sink down
Due to delusion, like the sun
That gets covered by clouds.

When the song was over, he asked, "Mother, this time is good for meditation, isn't it?"

Mother: Yes son, at this time Nature is calm. Dusk is a suitable time for *sadhaks* to do *sadhana*. More concentration will be had by those who meditate now. But in worldly people, more worldly thoughts will occur at this hour because their minds are immersed in that. Twilight is the confluence of day and night, is it not? Two different natures are present here. While the *sadhak* can get more one-pointedness if he tries, the undisciplined mind won't stay in anything at this time. All living beings will want to sleep. Everybody will be thinking of their day to day lives. This is a time when there are lot of worldly vibrations. If all of that is breathed in, worldly waves will be created in us as well. It is because of this that people chant the Divine Names loudly at dusk. Leaving off bad thoughts, the mind will become concentrated on God, and the atmosphere will become pure. Don't eat or sleep at twilight. Because the atmosphere is impure it will affect us through food. Just as changes are taking place externally in Nature at that time, changes will occur within us also. There is a special relationship between the body and Nature. Just as there are planets in the external universe, there are subtle planets within us also. They are rotating as well. Solar eclipses, lunar eclipses and everything else is within us also.

In the olden days Mother used to cut grass for the cows from the shore of these backwaters. With friends, Mother used to bathe here and, standing in the water, Mother would meditate.

Brahmacharin: Mother says that *sraddha* is needed. What is *sraddha?*

Mother: Son, suppose somebody is talking to you angrily. Listen to him with patience. Don't feel angry at him. Anger comes when we think that we are the body. No anger or hatred will be felt if you think that "I am not the body, but the Supreme Self." With whom can you be angry then? There is only one all-pervading Self. It is in everyone. We must understand perfectly that we are not the body but the *Atman.* All this together forms *sraddha.* Using discrimination is *sraddha.* Faith and detachment are signs of *sraddha.*

Brahmacharin: Mother, why am I not getting any experience even after doing so much meditation?

Mother: Son, due to lack of *sraddha* there is no concentration. Experience will come only if *sadhana* is done for at least four years with proper *sraddha.* Meditation should be done always. Don't waste even a moment. To one who has a Guru, complete faith in the Guru is enough.

Brahmacharin: Mother, after experiencing *brahmananda* (absolute bliss), do you feel that the time you spend talking with us is wasted or that this is insignificant compared to that?

Mother: In the olden days when Mother talked with someone, she used to feel that the time was being wasted. But today Mother sees all the children as *Iswara amsa* (part of God). Just as a weaver goes on spinning thread even while talking to those sitting nearby, Mother's mind is fully immersed in *brahmananda*   even while she talks to her children. Mother sees nothing but God. Therefore, there is no question of wasting time. Mother's dwelling place is in her childrens' hearts.

Brahmacharin: Sometimes it seems that Mother is worried while thinking of her children. In reality, does Mother have any attachment to anyone?

Mother: No, Mother is not attached to anything. She feels neither sadness or sorrow. But the vibrations that emanate from her children when they are sad will reflect in her. It is for their peace of mind that Mother also will grieve.

If there are no desires then there will be no sorrow. We must be able to love without expecting anything from anyone. Always think that we are the servants of all.

THE GURU AND DISCIPLINE

23 September 1982

One *brahmacharin* was not well. He expressed a wish to go home and take a rest for a few days.

Mother: Today is a *Darshan* day and Nealu will have to do all the work alone if you go. Not only that; this is an ashram and since you have settled down here, Mother does not like for you to wander out. If your body is trying to make you its slave, you should not easily give in to it. Overcome the body through strength of mind. There is nothing that cannot be accomplished through courage and faith.

The *brahmacharin* gave up his idea of going home. Because it was a *Bhava Darshan* day, devotees started coming from noon onwards.

Mother: (To one *brahmacharin*) The *prema* (loving devotion) of these householders is very deep. They are very innocent. A few days ago Mother became oblivious to the world while singing *bhajans*. Crawling on all fours, she went to the other side of the yard and sat under a coconut tree. There was no external awareness at all. It was not until she regained consciousness that Mother knew where she was sitting. Do you know why Mother did that? One daughter who lived in a nearby house had an intense desire to see Mother. Because she could not come here, that daughter was crying and crying, and looking over to this side. It was then that Mother unknowingly moved to that side of the compound. So intense is the love and devotion of some householder devotees.

Brahmacharin: Why is Mother always creating sorrow in our minds?

Mother: Son, it will be like this until complete surrender and refuge are sought. Complete surrender and discipline under the Guru's guidance are both needed. Is this not a life of renunciation? It is not possible to get closer to God if there is no sorrow of some kind. Therefore, through Mother, God will create some kind of difficulties. Having heated the iron in the fire, the ironsmith beats it. It is not possible to beat the metal into a shape without heating it up properly. The iron cannot be re-shaped if it thinks, "I will not allow myself to be heated in the fire." The Guru will create obstacles and sorrows which the disciple should overcome through intense *sadhana*. Spirituality is not for idle people. The difficulties of the subtle level are difficult when compared to the sorrows of the external world. There is nothing to fear for one who dedicates everything to a *Satguru*.

Brahmacharin: Mother, why is it that sorrow comes to me now and then?

Mother clearly knew that the *brahmacharin* thought that Mother had less love for him and that his was the cause of his sorrow.

Mother: It is due to the lack of complete faith. If there is faith, you won't be sad thinking, "Mother has more love for them does for me."

Brahmacharin: Mother, what do you mean by 'faith'?

Mother: Complete obedience to the *Guru's* words. In the presence of a Guru, a disciple should be like a servant in front of his master. The servant has no opinions of his own, only complete obedience to whatever the master says, no opinions at all. When obedience awakens in the disciple, the *Guru's* grace will automatically flow to the disciple. Grace will be there when the servant-like attitude, "I am nothing," is held. The *Guru's* heart will be filled when he sees the disciple's innocence. One's goal will be realized by worshipping God and serving the devotees of God with a servant-like attitude.

30 September 1982

It was the time of *Navaratri*.[53] All over India the *Durga puja* was being celebrated. From early morning onwards the neighbourhood children came to the Ashram to place their books in front of Saraswati, the Goddess of Knowledge, in order to get Her blessings for success in their studies. Also present were many devotees with their sons and daughters.

---

[53]Nine days festival and worship of the Divine Mother.

The Mother was joking and playing with the children. She was cutting sugar cane and making them eat it. The Mother herself seemed exactly like a small child. It was amazing to watch her. Some people recalled the Holy Mother's words, "God has the nature of a small child. God won't even look at those who do *tapas* with ego, but He will shower His grace on the innocent-hearted ones who do not do anything. This may be due to His childlike nature."

The Holy Mother continued playing with the children. The devotees' hearts and eyes took delight in watching the her innocent sports. Knowingly or unknowingly, they also partook in her bliss.

COMPLETE FAITH & LIBERATION

1 October 1982

Today the *brahmacharins* went with the Mother to visit Sreekumar's house. They waited a long time for a bus in Vallickavu, but it did not come. The Holy Mother would not permit a taxi to be taken, explaining that "spiritual people should not spend money unnecessarily." Finally, a bus came and they reached their destination. As the Mother was walking from the bus stop towards Sreekumar's house, she said to one *brahmacharin,*

Mother: The enthusiasm you once had is not seen in your meditation nowadays. Do one hour of physical work, and meditate the rest of the time. Don't spend time looking after Mother's needs. You children will become weak-minded if you think Mother is sick or weak. If you think Mother has power, you children will also get power. Unshakable faith is needed. None of you children have full faith in Mother. Complete faith means Liberation. What is necessary for you children now is a regular routine.

About eating food prepared the previous day, the Mother said, "The food which we eat will influence our character. Don't eat the food cooked on the previous day. It is *tamasic* (conducive to dullness or inertia)."

Next, the discussion turned to *kirtana*. Somebody said something about *Brahmacharin* Unni's songs. Mother said that some of Unni's *kirtanas* had come from his meditation. When the mind becomes pure enough through meditation, it is possible to cry to God. At that time, songs can be composed without effort.

Brahmacharin: Mother, will the mind subside by itself?
Mother: The mind can be controlled only by constant practice.

All of a sudden the Mother stopped. An elderly lady sitting by the side of the road was looking at her. The Holy Mother approached the old woman who, with great difficulty, tried to prostrate to her.

With great affection, the Holy Mother lifted the old lady up and gave a kiss to her hand. The Mother then continued walking. The previous day the woman had found out from Sreekumar's father that the Mother was coming, and so she had waited by the side of the road to see her.

Continuing to answer the brahmacharin's question, the Holy Mother said,

Mother: Until yesterday we were living thinking, "I am the body." In the beginning there will be some waves in the mind. Through practice they will go. It is to control these waves that *sadhana* should be done sitting steadfastly in one place. The waves will not subside if you simply read some books. Instead, they will only increase. In the deep sea there are no waves. It is on the shore that the waves break because there is little depth there. Peace can be experienced when through *sadhana*, the mind becomes expansive and deep.

Many people had come to Sreekumar's house to see the Mother and listen to her *bhajans*. After supper all the children gathered around the Mother. The Holy Mother said, "The passing of time is not known when I am with these children." Catching hold of her hands, the children walked with the Mother, following her wherever she went. Because they were fighting with each other to be able to sleep near her that night, the Mother made each one of them lay down beside her for five minutes. Whenever they see the Holy Mother, the children do not want their own mothers. On their own, they would come and gather around the Mother. When she sat somewhere they would all sit around her. If the Mother happened to sit quietly, these children would sit near her gazing at her face. Many times when the Mother sat in deep meditation, they would also sit with their eyes closed. This natural attraction of the children towards the Mother is proof enough of her unconditional love. This pure love, which is always radiating from the Holy Mother, has remolded and transformed many lives which were about to be ruined. If Pure Love is God's nature, then why can't we call such a phenomenon God?

4 October 1982

Following her operation, Gayatri was recuperating at

brahmacharini Vimala's house. She had been staying there for a few days when Mother decided to visit her. Accompanied by some women householder devotees, the Holy Mother started from the Ashram. Even though she was going only a short distance away, the *brahmacharins* felt very sad to see the Mother leave. With great emotion they stood watching her as she walked away. Some among them sought Mother's permission to follow, but she left saying she would return soon. The *brahmacharins* would feel pain in their hearts even if the Mother left the Ashram for only a half an hour or an hour. This experience is beyond words. In those days, to be away from the Mother even for a moment would cause the residents unbearable agony. Those who were happy and smiling would become like living corpses when separated from the Mother.

Sometimes when the Holy Mother left the Ashram, she would take only a few *brahmacharins* with her. But before reaching the bus stop she would suddenly stop, saying that a particular son or daughter was crying. She would then send someone to fetch him or her. When the person who was sent back reached the Ashram, he would find that what the Mother had said was correct. The one he was sent to fetch would be there crying, his heart broken. The Mother would proceed only after that boy or girl had reached her. Only those who are very close to the Holy Mother can understand the intensity of that pain. The heart will feel pain as if being wrung like a wet cloth. At that time they could neither eat nor sleep. They would sit in a corner crying like a small child who had been separated from its mother. The mental pain of the residents was like the excruciating pain of the *gopis* of Brindavan when they were separated from their beloved Krishna.

5 October 1982

At two o'clock the Holy Mother returned from *brahma-charini* Vimala's house. Everyone prostrated to the Mother and she then summoned all the residents and distributed sweets to everybody. It seemed as if the Ashram regained its lustre and glory with the Mother's return. Bhargavan, an ardent devotee from Mother's village, came before the evening *bhajan* started. He believed that the Mother was only divine during the *Bhava*. He had much love for Sri Krishna and owing to this, he would take a little freedom during *Krishna Bhava* by playing with Mother. Mother would really glorify his innocence. When she saw him, the Mother said, "Krishna has come." She then told the others,

Mother: Father Bhargavan's innocence is very deep. During *Krishna Bhava* he will say, "Krishna, this man behaved in such and such a way, that man behaved in such and such a way. I went there, I went here." His attitude is that Krishna is his own. Having told him all these things, he will simply look at Krishna and laugh. He could easily go up if the real path were known.

Because the Holy Mother's birthday was the following day. Many devotees started arriving. Some were decorating the Ashram and its surroundings. The *Bhava Darshan* went on until five-thirty a.m. The Mother sat for twelve hours on the *peetham*, receiving the devotees without moving from that spot. On certain days she will sit for fifteen or sixteen hours and will still be cheerful and full of energy. Tirelessly working for the well-being of the world, she puts new light and life into meaningless lives, instilling faith and restoring peace.

BIRTHDAY

6 October 1982

Today is *Trikartika*, the Holy Mother's birth star. Having gotten up early and taken their baths, all the devotees waited outside the hut to receive the Holy Mother and to offer their salutations. The *brahmacharins* chanted the *suprabhatam*.[54] After many requests and prayers, the Holy Mother sat on the seat which had been especially prepared for her. One by one the devotees offered their salutations. Some put garlands on her while others offered flower petals. The *brahmacharins* worshipped the Mother's feet and Pai did the *arati*. The whole time the Mother was absorbed in deep *samadhi*. When she finally became somewhat normal, the Mother arose from the seat and distributed *prasad* to everyone. With her own hands she gave sweet pudding, rice gruel and clothes to the village children. The reading of the *Srimad Bhagavatam* and the singing of *bhajans* took place at the same time. As part of the celebration, in the evening a folk dance known as *Kôladi* was performed by some girls. They stood in a circle, rhythmically beating two small wooden sticks which they held in their hands as they danced to the music sung by others. The song glorified the Holy Mother, highlighting her great and beneficent qualities and asking how to repay her for the transformation which she had brought into the lives of so many.

> Today is the Kartika star
> Which is my Mother's birthday,
> A day shining forth with beauty
> Causing us to overflow with joy.

[54]A song sung in the morning to God or the Goddess requesting Them to awake and bless the devotees.

You have made us blessed
And liberating us from worldliness,
You have made us devotees
And given us peace.

You have showered immense love on us
And we drank it forgetting everything.
O Mother, we have nothing, nothing
To repay You with for this divine love
Which You have showered on us.

How many births have I done tapas
To gain this, Your Divine Presence?
I bow at Thy Holy Feet millions of times
For making this life fulfilled.

One child was watching the *Kôladi* with great attention.
Seeing that, the Mother said,

Mother: Look, have you seen the concentration of that
child? This kind of concentration and desire should be there
for God. Not even a moment will be wasted if we have love
for God. All-encompassing bliss is there for him who dwells
close to God.

After the evening *bhajan*, the chanting of the Thousand
Names of the Divine Mother took place. The residents and
brahmacharins decided to offer the worship to the Holy
Mother. When everyone requested, the Mother finally
agreed to sit. The worship started. All the *brahmacharins* sat
around Mother forming a circle. *Brahmacharin* Unni led the
chanting of the *mantras* while the others responded. One by
one, lotus flower petals were offered at the Mother's feet.

The Mother entered into *samadhi*. At a particular stage of the worship the Mother started offering flowers to her own body and then to other's bodies also. She sees the same Consciousness pervading everywhere. The Ashram was saturated with concentration and devotion. Everyone was at the peak of bliss. When the *archana* was over, there was a big heap of lotus flower petals around Mother. The Holy Mother looked like Mother Durga sitting on a large lotus. The sight was a feast for the eyes and devotional ecstacy to the heart. At the end, all the devotees again saluted the Holy Mother.

WHAT IS THERE AFTER DEATH?

An ardent devotee of the Holy Mother died in the beginning of October 1982. This incident inspired *brahmacharin* Venu to ask the Mother about life after death.

Mother: There is a very subtle sheath covering our gross body. All our thoughts are imprinted on this layer. Like a tape recorder, this covering will record all acts which we do mentally, verbally and physically while we are alive. This forms a covering of thoughts. After death, when we leave the body, the thoughts and covering will rise up with the individual self. According to the actions done, each *jiva* will go to a particular plane. In that state the *jiva* has no gross body. Even then, the *jiva* will feel hunger and thirst. Due to the actions done in its previous birth, it will feel as if it is in mid-ocean. It will have a lot of unfulfilled desires but it cannot fulfill them. Some *jivas* will attack other living beings in order to fulfill their desires. Entering into them through their breath, they will destroy the other beings' consciousness. After that, they will make them eat according to their will. But they cannot give life to a dead body. It is possible to attack only those who have no mental power. The next birth will be according to the thoughts one has at death. The *jiva* will go on accepting bodies until all desires are eliminated. Usually it is through the breath or food that a *jiva* enters into other bodies. According to their *karma*, some *jivas* accept other bodies without much delay after death, Some others will wander around. It is for those that wander that the rituals are done by the relatives who are still living. By chanting certain *mantras* with concentration, it is possible for the wandering *jivas* to get a higher birth and stop their wandering.

But the case is different as far as a Liberated Soul is concerned. He will merge with the Absolute just as the air in a soda bottle rises up and dissolves in the atmosphere on bursting open.

7 October 1982

The Holy Mother was sitting by the side of the backwaters looking at the water. A few minutes passed and she said to those sitting nearby,

Mother: Our mind is like this canal. Due to the stagnant water, how many people are smelling the foul odour produced from it. Make this water flow and unite with the ocean and there will be no more odour. Likewise, at present the mind is dirty owing to accumulated tendencies. It should be cleaned by making all the thoughts flow towards God. Then the mind will become expansive.

Brahmacharin: Mother, why do you behave differently and sometimes in an incomprehensible way to different people?

Mother: For some time Mother will deliberately slacken the hook and let you nibble. Then when you are fully hooked, Mother will catch hold of you. You children have been living in the illusory world since birth. One day you come to Mother, calling, "Amma," but she cannot suddenly discipline you in the very beginning. The disciplining should be slow and steady, with proper understanding of the mental constitution and assimilating power of the student. The Guru must have patience and forbearance to train the disciple. Above all, selfless love must be the basis of everything. A *Satguru* will have all these qualities. You children will throw everything away and leave if Mother manifests the Guru *bhava* (attitude of a Guru) at the very beginning.

The Mother got up and went to the hut. At that time Saraswathi Amma, a householder devotee of the Mother, arrived. Whenever she came she would bring food for the *brahmacharins* as well as for the Mother. Saraswathi Amma was waiting outside Mother's hut with a packet in her hands. Seeing her, the Holy Mother smilingly said, "Ah, you have come. Today Mother thought of you. Everything is straightened out, is it not?"

Hearing this, Saraswathi Amma started weeping, falling on Mother's lap. Her eldest son was in great difficulty due to not having a job. With Mother's permission and blessings he went to Bombay and was appointed to a good post. She received a letter from him on that day informing her about his appointment. Before she could utter a word about it, the Holy Mother smilingly revealed that she already knew as if to tell Saraswathi Amma that nothing happens without her knowledge. That is what made the devotee cry.

The *brahmacharins* also waited for a chance to sit in the presence of the Holy Mother and to listen to her nectarous words. Taking this as an opportunity, some of the *brahma-charins* entered the hut. At this time, Venu tried to stealthily take some of the edibles which Saraswathi Amma had brought. Watching the Mother's face, he slowly pulled the packet towards himself pretending as if nothing was happening. Just at that moment, the Mother glanced at him and catching hold of his hand said, "You little thief! Are you trying to steal from the Greatest Thief? Aren't you Mother's son? She knows your nature fully well." Everyone laughed and Venu blushed from embarrassment on being caught.

Shortly after, a *brahmacharin* asked, "Mother, is scriptural knowledge necessary?"

Mother: Didn't Sankaracharya and other great souls study the scriptures? Knowledge of the scriptures is a must. Study is a *sadhana*. It should not be to inflate your ego but to get rid of it. The scriptural statements and dictums will act as weapons to fight against mental conflicts and weaknesses which might arise during the course of *sadhana*. While studying the scriptures, one should feel that "I am studying divine *mantras*."

Venu: Mother, why is *Bhagavan* (Sri Krishna) not coming in front of me?

Mother: Definitely He will come if you have such a wish. Some more alertness should be there externally. Patience should be instilled into the mind. *Asana siddhi* (being able to sit three hours in one posture without moving) should be there. Today, if you sit two hours in one *asana*, tomorrow you must try to sit five more minutes. Afterwards it should be made ten more minutes. Like this you should be able to sit three or four hours in one *asana*. Thus, when patience is there, everything else will come of its own accord. We should imagine that the form of our Beloved Deity is walking beside us and smiling at us while we walk, bathe, sit, etc. Cry to your Deity, imagining that your Beloved is standing in the atmosphere. More time should be utilized in the night for meditation.

In the days long before there was an ashram, Mother would do *sadhana* in the night without even sleeping. She would not waste any time at all. When innocent devotion arises, whatever we see, we will feel it to be our *dhyana rupa* (form of meditation). When she was very small, while plucking grass or sweeping the ground, Mother would imagine that Krishna was playing and dancing with her.

One *brahmacharin* had an intense desire to meditate sitting on the seashore during the night, but sometimes he would feel fearful. Hearing this, one among the *brahmacharins* asked, "Mother, do ghosts and evil spirits really exist?"

Mother: Son, Mother won't say that there are no subtle beings. But they cannot do anything to spiritual people. A meditator's proximity will give them much happiness. They can easily attack us if we don't have mental power. At a certain stage, it is possible to see subtle beings if one is meditating in a graveyard.

Brahmacharin: Is there any harm in showing *siddhis?*

Mother: If the laws of Nature are transgressed, it is harmful. Also, others will be too fascinated by such displays. As far as possible, a Perfect Man will avoid showing *siddhis.* But, by manifesting such psychic powers, he has nothing to lose because he is already full. If the energy which is used in showing *siddhis* were to be used to instill renunciation into one, that would be more beneficial to the world. One will only get diverted from the goal if one is deluded by *siddhis.*

Brahmacharin: Mother, I have committed many mistakes. What is the redress?

Mother: Nothing particular is needed. It is enough if you meditate well. Mother has sought forgiveness from God for your faults.

Just like Sri Ramakrishna's devotion to Devi, you children have devotion to Mother. You realize this when you stay away from Mother for some time. Many children have come and told me, "Mother, when we are away, whatever women we see we will only feel that they are Mother, especially those who wear white clothes." When Mother is near, the children will think, "Mother is near, so why should we meditate?" That is why in the very beginning Mother told you not to meditate on her form. Once you believe that Mother is one with God, then your mind should not falter even for a moment. Such firm faith is needed. Don't think, "Mother has more love for him and she has less love for me." All this shows lack of faith.

8 October 1982

This morning, soon after dawn, the Ashram premises had still not been swept. The Holy Mother came to the scene with a broom in hand to do the sweeping herself. Seeing the Mother, the *brahmacharins* also started cleaning the compound. Within a few minutes the *Ashram* and its surroundings were clean. Rather than take the easy way and tell others what to do, the Mother sets an example herself although it means exertion on her part. In her eyes, no work is low; all is sacred and a means to reac2h God.

CONTROL OF FOOD

Almost all the *brahmacharins* were from wealthy families and had led comfortable lives. Sometimes, due to their old habits they would eat something at odd times. The Mother, if she saw them doing so, would scold and correct them, accepting no excuses. She would always remind them, "Children, without giving up taste, you cannot progress spiritually."

One day the Mother noticed one *brahmacharin* eating some titbits taken from the cabinet.

Mother: This son is only thinking of food. That is very bad. In the beginning food should be definitely controlled. Everything is excreta once it goes inside the body. If you sit thinking of food, then where is the time to remember God? Just experiment and see what happens after taking plenty of tasty food one day. You children will lose your semen at least in the dream state. It won't happen if you eat only *sattvic* food. When your seed is lost you will be angry with Mother. The complaint is that this happened because of the lack of Mother's Grace. What does it matter if you get angry with Mother without controlling your food? Those who are intent to reach the goal will control themselves.

The *brahmacharin* felt ashamed and became a little offended. He said, like a son to his mother, "Am I the only one who eats everything?" He then left the room. After a few minutes, this *brahmacharin* approached the Mother with great remorse and confessed his mistake. He sought forgiveness for his indiscriminate act.

The usual evening *bhajan* was over at eight. One *brahmacharin* had been meditating and did not attend.

Mother: This is an ashram. A general routine should be followed. Everyone must come during the *bhajan*. One person meditates, another one does *pranayama* and some others do *bhajan*. This is not right.

Though she gives such general instructions, there also are exceptions. The Mother will exempt those who can meditate well from all other works and from the general routine. The Holy Mother will allow them to spend as much time as they can in meditation. They don't have to come even to the *Vedanta* classes or the *bhajan*. The Holy Mother says, "I am ready to serve them and look after their needs myself." But, Mother is very particular that the others who cannot do meditation for long hours should actively participate in the daily routine of the Ashram, which also includes a total of six hours of meditation done at different times of the day.

MAKE ME INTOXICATED WITH YOUR LOVE

9 October 1982

Today at three o'clock in the afternoon the Holy Mother was sitting on the front verandah of the temple. Calling "Sreekumar!" the Mother started singing a song. Sreekumar came with the harmonium and sat near the Mother. The Mother gave certain instructions regarding the song and its music. She herself set the music to it and began singing each line. In between, she told Sreekumar certain things about the beat of the song. She clapped her hands according to the rhythm. Balu, Pai and Ganga came and sat near the Mother and Venu came and played the drums. Such occasions,

when the Mother and her spiritual children compose and
sing music, are certainly blissful moments. Unforgettable
and unique are these times.

Eventually the Holy Mother sang the song which created
an overflow of devotion, bliss and love which engulfed everyone there.

> O Mother, make me mad with Thy Love!
> What need have I of knowledge or reason?
> Make me drunk with Thy Love's wine.
>
> O Thou who stealest Thy devotees' hearts,
> Drown me deep in the Sea of Thy Love!

Intoxicated by the song, the Mother stood up and
started moving around and around. She was in an abstracted mood. The speed of her circling increased and in
that state of total absorption, the Holy Mother now and
then burst into blissful laughter. No sign of an end was to
be seen. Sugunanandan, who was watching the whole scene,
became very anxious about his daughter and in great con-
sternation caught hold of her calling, "My child!" and made
her lay down on his lap. He didn't stop there. Before anybody could prevent him, he poured water on the Mother's
head. Totally transported to a world unknown to those of
gross intellect, the Mother burst into an uproarious laugh. It
became louder and continued unabated. Half an hour
passed as the laugh of uncontrollable and overflowing supreme bliss continued.

All the family members gathered around the Holy
Mother. The Mother's sisters started crying and Mother
Damayanti also cried calling the Divine Mother. Owing to
their spiritual ignorance they thought that the Holy Mother

was going to lose her mental balance. It took a long time for
the Mother to come down to the normal state. Afterwards, it
seemed as though she was struggling to keep her mind
down. Her eyes went up and got fixed at the point between
the eyebrows. About three and a half hours later the Mother
regained her external awareness. She got up from her father
Sugunanandan's lap and told him, "Father Sugunanandan,
hereafter don't touch my body on such occasions." The
brahmacharins as well as some learned people several times
had told Sugunanandan and the other family members not
to disturb the Mother during such times. But they could neither control their emotions nor could they understand the
situation. Later, the brahmacharins, as instructed by the
Mother herself, would sing bhajans during that time. In
those days the Mother would lose her external awareness almost every day. It would take a long while, some times even
hours, for her to come down. As the number of brahmacharins increased, the Holy Mother controlled herself
from getting totally absorbed. About this, she said one day,
"If Mother always lets herself get into that mood of supreme
bliss, then the very purpose of taking this body will be de-
feated. Mother has a lot to do including the raising of the
brahmacharins which is very important."

11 October 1982

Today the Mother was going to a devotee's house in
Quilon. At seven o'clock in the morning everyone was preparing to go. Having noticed the dirty dhoti worn by a brahmacharin, the Mother said,

Mother: Son, go and come back wearing a good dhôti.
Cleanliness is what is necessary. Even if there is only one set

of clothes, wash it daily and wear it. Bathe, at least scrub-
bing with sand. External cleanliness is what is needed first.
Wherever you go, take your own seat for meditation. You
children should not use things which are used by others.
Things which are urgently needed should be taken along.
Henceforth, a vessel for eating will be purchased for each
one of you.

SADHANA AND VASANA

When the Holy Mother reached the devotee's house, she
became like a small child. Everyone took delight seeing the
Mother's childlike innocence and sportings. The Mother
danced as she was eating peanuts given by a devotee. Like a
child she said, "No, I won't give this to you." It was an unforgettable day for the members of the devotee's family. They
watched the Holy Mother as if they were looking at something very attractive and precious. The next moment, the
Holy Mother walked towards the family shrine room and entered it, leaving behind the peanut packet which she had just
said she wouldn't give to anyone, . This act of the Holy
Mother's reminded the *brahmacharins* of the Mother's own
statement that God's nature is like that of a child. He is not
attached to anything. After entering the shrine room and
looking at the portrait of the Divine Mother, the Mother
said in a childlike way, "Hey Grandma, look after the needs
of these children." Afterwards, she went to the terrace and
lay down on a mat which was spread there. All the family
members were sitting around her. The Mother was eating
ice cream fed to her by the youngest girl of the house. It was
quite obvious that she was eating it only for their happiness.
When she had three spoonfuls she said, "Enough. It was
only for daughter's satisfaction that Mother ate it."

The head of the family who was a spiritual aspirant asked, "Ammachi, why do more *vasanas* rise up as we do *sadhana?*"

Mother: When we clean a room all the superficial dirt will go first. The room will seem as if clean but when wiped harder we can see all the mud coming out. The *vasanas* lying subdued within come up when we do *sadhana*. They come up only to get exhausted. Those are all illusions (*mithya*) and ever-changing.

The next day when the Holy Mother was about to return to the Ashram, the little daughter of the house expressed a wish to go with the Mother in the car. But saying that her classes will suffer, the parents did not take her. As the car started and moved away, the little girl cried aloud looking at the Mother, "Ammachi...Ammachi!" Because the parents were very much interested in her studies, the Mother thought that it would not be fair to say anything. The car moved forward but suddenly stopped after going five kilometers. There was more than enough fuel. The driver checked the car but couldn't find any trouble. No matter how much the driver tried, the car would not start. After some time, the Mother, who was keeping quiet until then said, "The car will start if you try to go back to the house." They obeyed the Mother's words and the car immediately started. There was no trouble at all. They were amazed when they reached the house and saw the little girl who wanted to go with the Mother crying out loud, lying in the shrine room. When the girl saw the Mother, she came running to her calling aloud, "Ammachi!" and embraced her tightly, crying and crying. Returning to the Ashram with the girl at her side, the Holy

Mother said, "It is this daughter's *sankalpa* that caused the car to stop. There is nothing which cannot happen with a pure and innocent *sankalpa*. Small children can get it easily."

13 October 1982

Mother was talking with four year old Shakti Prasad, a child born out of the Mother's blessings.

Mother: Son, you must become the *sannyasin* teacher of this entire world. You should teach everyone.
Shakti: I will become a teacher by studying in the school.
Mother: Son, sing a song. Let Ammachi hear it.

Shakti Prasad sang with great concentration folding his hands on his chest,

> Through my mind, speech and actions
> I am remembering You incessantly.
> Why then are You delaying to show
> Your mercy to me, beloved Mother?
>
> I am a miserable destitute.
> I have none but You, Mother.
> Please stop Your tests and
> Extending Your hand, pull me up...

Someone walked near by and Shakti Prasad looked in that direction. Mother said, "Don't look at whoever comes. You must sing with concentration." Shakti again sang. When the song was over, Mother made him repeat the English alphabet.

Mother: Mother's son should learn Sanskrit. Son, show how you meditate.

Shakti sat in a perfect posture and meditated. Seeing this, the Mother and the others all rejoiced at his innocence.

THE MOTHER WITHIN

It was three o'clock in the afternoon. Gayatri, Nealu, Venu and Ganga were sitting near the Mother.

Question: Mother says not to look at the external Mother. No spiritual progress will be gained if we sit looking at Mother's external form. What is the meaning of this?

Mother: Son, Mother said that so that you children will look inside. If you don't have strong faith in Mother, doubts will crop up in your mind regarding Mother's actions. You may feel, "Why is Mother talking to that person for such a long time and not even looking at me." Such doubts will create many obstacles in your spiritual path, due to your seeing only the external Mother. This will not happen if you enshrine Mother within. You must also have the strong conviction that Mother is not the body but the all-pervading Consciousness. Staying with Mother for some years, you will have to fight. Only then can you win wherever you go. Children, the ignorance of ego should be pulled out and thrown away with its roots. Sincerity towards the Guru will come only if the disciple stays with the Guru for some years.

Question: Mother, what should be done to control lustful thoughts (*kama vikara*)?

Mother: Through constant association with the *Satguru* all those thoughts will automatically be removed. Desireless love will also help to attenuate lust.

Just before the *bhajan* the Mother was talking about the Ashram affairs.

A new brahmacharin: Mother, how are the Ashram needs being met?

Mother: Children, whenever there is a lack of something, then and there God will have it sent. Mother has given everything to Him. He will look after things. Mother doesn't need anything. For Mother, her children are everything. Mother's heart will become full when she sees each child growing spiritually. Now what is necessary is for you children to do spiritual practice. You don't have to pay attention to anything else. Somehow the things will come. Mother doesn't like anybody serving her. You should meditate. It should go on very well. That is what is necessary.

TAKING ON DISEASE

14 October 1982

It was a *Bhava Darshan* day. The *Devi Bhava* was over by four in the morning. At the end of *Devi Bhava* the Holy Mother sucked blood and pus from the head of a leper. On certain days, due to accepting the illnesses of many people, the Holy Mother would become sick but would recover within a few minutes. The Mother says,

Mother: A perfect person is filled with compassion when he sees a leper or such other persons; he will not feel disgust or aversion. Through concentration and divine power he can absorb the disease into himself. The sick people who are coming here might have been carrying around their disease for the last ten or fifteen years, undergoing different kinds of treatments and still not finding any cure. If Mother accepts that, she will have to suffer only ten or fifteen minutes and those poor people will be saved from any more suffering.

The time was three in the afternoon. The Holy Mother was lying on the cot in her hut. Some of the residents were sitting down on the floor.

Question: Mother, no improvement is seen in my *sadhana*. What should be done for that?
Mother: Children, don't worry. That will come. It is enough if you try. While sitting in an airplane as it is flying across the sky, we will not feel that it is moving, but once having reached the destination, we understand that we had been travelling all along. Likewise, we are progressing but it is too subtle for us to understand. After reaching the goal, everything will become clear. Concentration, that is what is needed. A person who has concentration can conquer this entire world. Just by hearing his voice, people will feel an attraction. One look at him is enough to bring someone to the spiritual path, no matter how wicked a person might be. Concentration should be increased somehow. It is possible through practice.
Question: Mother, can meditation be done imagining oneself as the form?
Mother: No, that is not necessary. The ego will come if meditation is done on oneself. Not only that, it is always better to choose a Perfect Being as your form of meditation. Whichever form you meditate on, eventually we will come to the understanding that we and That are one. During the period which Mother meditated she saw herself as Devi.

FAITH IN THE GURU

15 October 1982

Mother was in Quilon at a devotee's house. In the evening there was *bhajan*, *satsang* and chanting of the Thousand Names of Devi. Many people were there to see the Mother and to participate in the *bhajan*. A great soul, Nisargadatta Maharaj, had left his body recently. One devotee brought it to the Mother's attention.

Devotee: Mother, it has been said in the book "I Am That" that Nisargadatta Maharaj met his Guru at the age of thirty-four and that by the age of thirty-seven, he had realized the Self. He had reached the goal within only three years. Is that possible?

Mother: Son, you must keep in mind one thing. Was it not said that he had complete faith in his Guru? If such faith is there, then there is no difficulty at all. It is not enough to consider only the time it takes to attain the goal. Faith, disposition inherited from the past birth, and practice must all be considered.

20 October 1982

In the afternoon at three o'clock, the Holy Mother was sitting in front of the *Vedanta Vidyalaya* (*Vedanta* School) surrounded by the residents. There were some visiting devotees as well.

One devotee: Mother, is there any harm if there happens to be a break in the *puja* performed to a particular form of God or Goddess?

Mother: Son, when we do worship to a form, it gets power. It is we who transmit life to it. In fact, when you children salute someone with concentration, power will flow from you to him and from him to you. However, if the worship is discontinued, the same power can do harm to you.

Question: Mother, it is said that there is godliness in human beings. If that is true, can a human become totally identified with God or can he become God?

Mother: He is God. There is nothing to become. But at present, he is not aware of this great Truth because of his accumulated tendencies. Son, even if it is said that God is in man, there is a Power that transcends everything. That is the Supreme Reality. That power is unique. That exists even beyond a Liberated Soul. The waves and the ocean are not essentially different, but the wave does not contain the ocean. The ocean stands as the substratum of the wave. There is no tree that touches the heavens and no root that reaches to the netherworld. This means that all names and forms are limited.

THE CAUSE OF THE MANGO TREE AND THE SEED

Brahmacharin: Will the atheists agree that there is a God?

Mother: You should ask the atheists, "Which came into being first, the mango tree or the seed?" If it is the mango tree, then a seed should be there. And if it is the seed, then a tree should be there. Because there are no answers to these questions, we can say that beyond both, there is a Power which is the cause of everything. That power is God. As we progress in *sadhana* we will understand everything. There is no use in unnecessary dispute.

The topic suddenly changed to the narration of the Mother's experience during the period of her*sadhana* . The Mother continued,

Mother: In the old days Mother was not even able to say "Krishna." If she did, body-consciousness would be lost immediately. If concentration was not gained in meditation, I would angrily jump towards Devi's portrait shouting at Her. I used to beat my head on the wall. But what is there to say about other times! I would embrace Devi's picture with overflowing love and crumble it into pieces. In those days, Mother would see only Devi in whoever came. If I happened to see any good-looking girls nicely dressed up, I would leap and jump out of bliss. I felt all of them to be Devi.

About her spiritual children, the Mother said,

Mother: All the children have that kind of devotion. Children, if you see someone who looks like Mother, don't you stand gazing at them? When you are away from Mother, won't you cry if you see someone who has a face which closely resembles Mother's? That devotion will help a lot. If you stay away from Mother, you will be able to cry and call to Mother. No matter how elevated a state a disciple may have attained, he will have a kind of selfishness when he comes in front of the Guru. Children, don't you have the feeling that Mother should have more love towards you than towards others?

Now one *brahmacharin* who had gone out of the Ashram for some purpose suddenly returned. He had waited

a long time at the bus stop without being able to catch a
bus. Having prostrated to the Mother, he sat near her.

Mother: Son, haven't you gone?

Brahmacharin: I couldn't catch a bus. I waited almost one
hour.

Mother: Is this a *brahmacharin* who is saying this? Hasn't
God given you good health? Don't you have hands and legs?
Can't you walk? If you had walked instead of waiting for the
bus, you could have gone and returned, having accomplished the thing for which you went, couldn't you?
Will the time be wasted if you chant your mantra while
walking? On the way, if the bus comes you can still get in ,
can't you? Hereafter, you children should not waste time
waiting in the bus stop. While you are standing there,
people of different characters will come and you will talk
with them. All that will help to create new *vasanas*.

INACTION IN ACTION

25 October 1982

In the morning the Mother suddenly came to the
kitchen and began doing all the work. She sent all the *brahmacharins* from the kitchen saying, "Go and do meditation."
Yet some stood there, hoping to help.

One brahmacharin: Shall I simply stand here looking on
while Mother is working?

Mother: Children, Mother does not feel that she is doing
anything. It would have been enough for you to have stayed
at home if it was simply for doing work that you came here..

Otherwise, think over whether you can do work with an attitude of dedication to God. Mother doesn't think that you can, and therefore you children should meditate without breaking the daily routine. That is enough for Mother.

Venu: Mother, how many days are still needed to attain Truth?

Mother: Children, you work. Don't be sad thinking of time. God will give everything.

Brahmacharin: No matter much work I do, if Mother's Grace is not there, there is nothing. If Mother's *sankalpa* is there I will be liberated this very moment.

Mother: Son, don't talk like that. That is weakness. If you work you will get the wages. God will not simply give anything to anyone without their working for it. Self-effort and grace are interdependent. If *tapas* (spiritual discipline) is performed sincerely, you can then see God's Grace flowing into you. Sitting behind the closed doors of a room, saying, "The sun is not giving me any light," is foolish. Open the door and light will enter. Likewise, open the doors of your heart by removing the obstacles of egoistic thoughts and by developing such qualities as love and humility. That requires effort. Prepare your mind to become a befitting instrument of God's Grace which flows in a never-ending stream.

You should pray to God to always be given work. You should not feel that "Having done this much, I still did not get anything." God is to be loved without desiring anything. Wishing for a vision is also a desire. This is what God said when He was approached, "To overcome the mind is more difficult than finding Me. See everything with an attitude of equanimity. Overcome the mind."

Don't argue with others unnecessarily. Tell them, "I don't have time to waste talking unnecessarily. My Mother has told me 'Truth is God. It is in you also. It is everywhere. When you find That, you will know your Self.' Mother hasn't said even to have faith in her." Also tell them, "I am trying to know myself, to love and serve all with a brotherly attitude. My aim is not to attain Liberation."

Brahmacharin: Mother, what is the nature of *Atman*?[55]

Mother: No attributes at all. Changeless like the sky. It cannot be said what It is. There is no motion at all. There is no "you" and "I." It can be known only through experience.

MAHABALI[56]

Venu: Mother, why did Vamana push Mahabali down to the netherworld? Why was he not sent to the heavens?

Mother: Son, even heaven is not permanent. When the merit which was responsible for sending one to heaven is exhausted, one will come down again. In fact, Vishnu was testing Mahabali's devotion. He asked for three feet of land. After Vishnu measured two, when there was no other place, Mahabali offered his own head. Mahabali's devotion was revealed then. It was Eternal Liberation that Vishnu gave to him. Whether in heaven or hell, there is no change for *Atman* at all. The *Atman* has no trouble even if pushed down to hell.

Marriage celebrations were going on the house of a family related to the Idammanel family.

---

[55]The Self Absolute.

[56]Mahabali was a king of ancient times who was approached by Vamana, the dwarf Incarnation of Lord Vishnu, who asked for three steps of land. Vamana showed his Universal Form and covered the entire cosmos with the first two steps. In order to remain truthful to his promise of giving three steps of land, Mahabali offered his head as the third step.

One brahmacharin: Mother, do we have to go to the marriage at the other house?
Mother: Don't ask such questions. What does it matter for us? *Sadhaks* should never participate in such functions. Help them, but only if they ask for help.

UNSTEADINESS

28 October 1982

One *brahmacharin* had a wish to go somewhere to practice meditation in solitude.

Mother: Mother will not allow you to do that. You want to escape without confronting and defeating the obstacles rising within. After two days you will come back. If you go somewhere, *sadhana* should be performed staying there at least for a month, without moving around. But you won't do that. You would say that staying with the Mother is the best. Go and meditate after changing your clothes.

The Holy Mother was sitting in the Ashram library after lunch.

Balu: Can a *Jñani* (Knower of the Self) bestow Liberation on one by mere *sankalpa*?
Mother: Certainly, but the disciple should have alertness and faith. One who has faith will not ask any questions of the Guru. He will obey the Guru's words implicitly. That is service to the Guru. There is no benefit if one who does service has no "*visala buddhi*" (expansive vision). Obedience and proper discipline are necessary. The Prime Minister entrusts each section to the other ministers. What if they walk

around to serve the Prime Minister without doing their job?
Is that correct? Will he be happy? The same is the case with
the spiritual Guru. God doesn't need anything, neither service nor flattery. Devotion, faith and obedience are all
needed.

SRADDHA
Alertness

The Holy Mother was working in the kitchen. It is interesting and at the same time amazing to watch the Mother's
kitchen work. She works very quickly but she is very careful
and alert. She can cook rice and the necessary side dishes
with less spices and still they are tasty. Within an hour and
a half, she can have the meal prepared for all the residents.
As the cooking was going on, the Mother told the *brahmacharini* who was assisting her,

Mother: You have burnt the mung beans by not pouring in
enough water. While doing one thing your full attention
should be in it. Only then will *sraddha* come. Do not distract yourself by chewing things or talking to anyone while
doing work. Your *mantra* should always be chanted within.
We should always be centered within. A person may be rowing the boat for some time, and then he sits and rests on his
oars without rowing for awhile. Even then he is alert as to
whether the boat is going straight or not. In the same way,
we must have inner alertness whether we are doing external
work or taking a rest. Even if the Guru scolds, beats or kicks
you, offer everything completely at the *Guru's* feet thinking
that everything is for our own good.

The Holy Mother noticed that one brahmacharin had not removed a banana peel which had been lying on the floor for a long time.

Mother: (to the brahmacharin) Son, you still haven't removed that banana peel even though you have seen it lying there for a while. If it lies there, unknowingly somebody may step on it and fall down. Are we not the one at fault for not removing it even after seeing it?

Understanding his mistake the brahmacharin picked up the banana peel.

Mother: Likewise, you should be alert while walking along the road. If there are any stones or pieces of glass, they should be removed. Egoistic people won't think about this. But we should so that no one will slip and fall.

Brahmacharin: Why is it said that one should stay with the Guru?

Mother: Son, the Guru alone can remove the *vasanas*. Otherwise, if one doesn't have a Guru one should at least have a very strong spiritual disposition. Sitting in one corner of the jungle the fox may decide, "I won't howl at the dog henceforth." But it will be the same old case when he sees one. It is the same with *vasanas*. When we are alone we may feel that all the *vasanas* have subsided, but when a difficult cirsituation arises, we can see all of them rising up. If there is faith in the Guru, *sadhana* can be done sitting somewhere. Wherever he is, the disciple will get the *Guru's* grace. Faith is what matters. When they think of Mother with concentration, those children who stay at a distant place will have intense longing. They will get what they need even without Mother's knowledge.

Brahmacharin: Mother, sleep comes during meditation. What should be done to remove this?

Mother: Son, it is due to the lack of *sraddha*. You should be alert. When sleep comes, you should know that sleep is coming. Then you won't sleep. At that time you can either repeat the *mantra* with eyes open or get up from your seat and repeat the *mantra* walking to and fro. The mind is very tricky, don't let it enslave you. In the beginning stages, all the dullness will come up. But if you have alertness and enthusiasm you can overcome this in due course.

7 November 1982

At seven in the morning, the Holy Mother was sitting in the front yard of the temple where the coconut trees were growing. She was in an abstracted mood. After half an hour she got up and walked around as if intoxicated. Sometimes she turned around with eyes closed and showed a particular *mudra* with her right hand. And at other times, she uttered certain words as if she was speaking to an unseen person.

For some time Mother roamed around fully absorbed; then all of a sudden she broke into a rapturous song,

> O Mother, for the satisfaction of my life, give
> a drop of Thy love to my dry burning heart.
> Why O why dost Thou put burning fire as
> fertilizer to this scorched creeper?
>
> O Devi, chanting the Name 'Durga, Durga'
> my mind has forgotten all other paths. O my
> Durga, I want neither heaven nor Liberation.
> I want only pure devotion to Thee..

Hearing the song, the *brahmacharins* who were watching from a distance, slowly gathered around the Mother. As she sang, tears of bliss and devotion rolled down her cheeks. When the song was over, in a semi-conscious mood, the Mother slowly sat down and remained still for a while. Then turning to the *brahmacharins*, she softly said,

Mother: Children, the sweetness of devotion is incomparable. Once you've tasted it, you will never again like to taste the objects of the world. Children, don't speak about *Brahman* to worldly people. Tell them only about pure love and devotion. To those who are a little educated and rational say, "I am searching for my Self."

THE MEDITATION OF A JNANI

Brahmacharin: Mother, does a *Jñani* who has attained Perfection need to meditate?
Mother: No, son. It is not necessary for them to meditate. Once perfection is attained they will not perceive anything as separate from themselves. Even so, in order to set an example for others, they will meditate. If Mother sits idle without meditating, you children will imitate her. That is why Mother meditates. Even after attaining Perfection, many *Mahatmas* did *sadhana*, did they not? It was not for their own sake, but for setting an example for others. In the *Srimad Bhagavatam*, it is said that even Sri Krishna practiced meditation.
Brahmacharin: While living as a householder, can one attain salvation?
Mother: Certainly, but one must be a real householder. All one's actions must be performed with full dedication. One

must always discriminate thinking, "Everything is God's, nothing is mine. He alone is my true Father, Mother, friend and relative." A *grahastashrami* should always be careful not to get too attached to his wife, children, parents and other relatives. Attachment will cause sorrow. In the past everyone had faith. At the time of birth itself, a *mantra* would be chanted in the ear of the child. The child would grow up leading a chaste and austere life. After finishing his studies in the hermitage of his Guru, he would enter into the life of a householder by marrying. His wife would also have been brought up in the same spiritual way. While she was pregnant, she would have taken a vow of silence and performed rituals in rememberance of God for the first six or seven months of pregnancy. The husband would also have done the same. Therefore, the child born to them would be preeminent, it's nature having evolved according to the character of the woman's thoughts during the time of pregnancy.

Brahmacharin: Mother, I am not getting concentration during meditation.

Mother: Son, in the beginning for at least three years, you should keep looking at the form of meditation. Only then will the form be properly fixed within. Looking at the middle of your forehead or the tip of your nose, you must try to achieve concentration. You must control food; otherwise food will control the mind. You must be careful about that. Good food and bad food, these are all just delusions of the mind. It is possible to live eating only grass. As we attain concentration in meditation, we get all the essence of food from within. There should be the desire to meditate. It is because of the lack of detachment that one doesn't feel like meditating.

THE TASTE OF WORK

12 November 1982

The *brahmacharins* were building their own huts to live in. The Holy Mother was helping them. No one wanted to let the Mother do the work, but whatever was said, it was of no use as the Mother was definitely going to work.

Mother: The difficulties of life will be understood when we do hard work. When we do this much work we feel tired. So what must be the weariness of those who work like this day in and day out? Only if we work like this will we develop compassion. Actually this is nothing. Mother has to make you children carry still more of a burden.

Food is to be taken after having worked. Only then will the taste of work be known. What happens in most of the Ashrams? Some books will be read, and the knowledge to speak will be gained. My children, Mother won't allow that. She will make you work hard.

One *brahmacharin* asked permission to go home.

Mother: Until yesterday Mother gave you children that freedom. But from now on it will not be possible. This is an *Ashram*. There is a discipline here. You should live here observing it. Be careful while associating with worldly people. When you get home, your mother, grandmother and all the others will come and tell you many worldly things. You will also get immersed in that and new *vasanas* will be created as a result. If you go to any worldly house, sit silently. If you are asked anything, answer with a few words. What you children need is to remove ignorance.

18 November 1982

The building of the *brahmacharins'* huts was continuing. There was no water to mix the cement for the floors.
Mother herself was bringing water in a big pitcher. As she
was carrying the pitcher on her hip, one of the *brahmacharins* who had just finished washing clothes was about to
throw away the remaining detergent water from the bucket
after taking his clothes out. This had been used for washing
just one *dhoti*. The Holy Mother noticed this and said to the
brahmacharin,

Mother: You children have no *sraddha* at all. You have not
been through any difficulties. You are wasting things like
this because you have not known what suffering is. You
must have alertness in each and every thing. Don't waste
this much detergent for only one dhoti. This can be used to
wash other clothes as well. *Sannyasins* should not waste anything. Then the value of work will be known."

One *brahmacharin* was about to go out wearing a big
black *rudraksha* rosary over white clothes.

Mother: Son, remove that rosary or people will stare at you.
We don't require any external show. Devotion is not in all
that. In this *Kali yuga* we must wear good clothes and comb
our hair. It should be without any external show that we
teach spirituality to others.

Another *brahmacharin* came near the Mother and said,
"Mother, I am not seeing the full form of the Deity during
meditation."

Mother: In the beginning it is difficult to get the full form. Therefore try to visualise the feet of the Deity and focus your mind on them. Once the form gets absolutely clear, we become That. For this, continuous practice is needed. All that is seen should be imagined as the form of your Beloved Deity. Everyone is to be seen with a vision of equality. Imagine "I am the servant of everyone." If everything is the Self, then who is there to hate? A real devotee's heart must pant for God just like a fish taken out of water. He won't waste even a moment. Some cannot meditate for even two hours. Therefore, they should learn Sanskrit or study scriptures. Knowledge of the scriptures is also necessary. Others can then be taught, can't they?

Brahmacharin: Mother, why have you come down? Do you know what your real nature is?

Mother: Son, it is the body that is coming and going, the Self remains unchanged. It is all-pervading. From birth itself Mother knew that God alone is the Truth and that all that is seen is not true. She could see her own reflection in each and every object as if in a mirror. Mother would constantly remember God and would cry, singing God's name. In the night time she would sing loudly. I always had the strong feeling that without realising and becoming one with Him I could not live. Worldly pleasures and all other objects were meaningless and equal to poison to me. How many said that Mother was mad! Even the family members would always say, "She is giving a bad reputation to the family." But Mother did not care. Mother has not come just to do something and go. Mother has a clear goal and will not go leaving in the middle without fulfilling it.

A NEWCOMER

9 September 1983

Just after the Mother's birthday, a college professor visited the *Ashram* for the first time. The big decorated shed which had been used during the celebration still remained. He had seen the Mother's picture and an article about her birthday in the newspaper. When he saw her photo he felt strongly attracted to her and was inspired to go see her immediately. He sat waiting for the Mother on the front verandah of the temple. It was around noon and one *brahmacharin* told him that the Mother was in her hut reading the day's mail and would come soon.

The professor, who later compiled the Conversations of the Holy Mother in Malayalam, experienced inexpressible peace and divinity in the atmosphere. He later related, "I was certain even at that time that there must be a highly evolved spiritual personality as the heart and soul of this divine centre."

In a few minutes the Holy Mother arrived. Without blinking his eyes, the professor gazed at her. Full of cheer and vigour, she came and sat on the verandah as the professor prostrated to her. She looked at him with a smile that registered deeply in his heart. Whoever has met the Mother will never forget her smile. A few moments passed silently, then the Mother asked:

Mother: Have you eaten anything, son?
Professor: Yes.

The Mother again smiled. This was followed by another silence. The Holy Mother seemed totally absorbed. Showing a *mudra*, she whirled around her right hand and uttered "*Shiva, Shiva.*" The professor watched in amazement. "Where am I sitting?" he thought. "She is not just an *Avadhuta* or *Paramahamsa*,[62] but something transcending both. What a tremendous peace there is in her presence." As such thoughts passed through his mind the Holy Mother addressed him. "Say something, son," she said.

Professor: Mother, you please speak. I will listen.

Mother: No, son, you say something. Let Mother hear.

Professor: I came to hear Mother's words. That is the tradition, is it not?

Mother: Son has read a lot. Enough. Now you should perform some *sadhana*.

The professor could not help but wonder. From an ordinary standpoint he was a total stranger to the Mother; but this was not at all reflected in the conversation. He was quite convinced by the Mother's statement that she knew everything about him, because it was indeed a fact that he had studied much but had practiced little.

Mother: Son, everyday you must meditate for some time.

Professor: While seeing you, on whom else could I meditate with eyes closed?

Mother: That is all right, but even then, the Vision of God is also needed within so that no trouble will occur. If you only see the external form, sorrow may come.

One *brahmacharin* came and sat down on the sand near the Mother.

Brahmacharin: Mother, some devotees have an idea to

publish a souvenir brochure about you. Would you agree to this, Mother?

Mother: Darling son, this Mother of yours does not need any publicity. Son, don't be hasty. All the wealth of this world is Mother's. Don't hurry for anything. Everything will take place at the correct time and when it is needed. Children, you go and meditate without thinking about all this.

The professor then cherished a desire to know about the *Ashram*. The Holy Mother, as if understanding his thoughts said,

Mother: Son, it has been only two years since the *Ashram* was registered. There were so many obstacles! Especially since Mother's form is that of a woman, there was no freedom. Different people had different doubts. Father Sugunanandan of this house had no faith in me at all in me.

Professor: (Hesitantly) About the needs and necessities of the *Ashram*...

Mother: Look son, here in this *Ashram* there is nothing. Some times there will not even be a penny. Forty or fifty people need to have their livelihood met with also. The children would come and ask in the beginning, "Mother, what should we do for tomorrow?" Mother would sit quietly. Whatever was necessary would come here just the day before it was needed. When things went on like that, the children stopped complaining to Mother.

Some devotees had just arrived and prostrated to the Holy Mother. They offered apples, mangos and other fruits at the Holy Mother's feet. She distributed it as *prasad* to all the devotees present.

One devotee: Not having seen Mother for some days, my mind became restless. Therefore, I came today.

Mother: Son, Mother is there within you. She is always with you. Sorrow will result if you think Mother is only this body. Mother is everywhere and within everyone. Therefore, don't worry.

Hearing the Mother's words, the devotee's eyes were filled with tears. The Holy Mother is always simple and humble in her statements but there are occasions when unequivocally and precisely, she declares her total identity with the Supreme. Such declarations spring forth spontaneously and unexpectedly when a suitable situation arises.

Devotee: What should we do, Mother?

Mother: Chant God's name. Repeat the *mantra* while making each step. That is enough.

Devotee: *Pranayama...?*

Mother: Breath control is not necessary. *Kumbhaka* (retention of breath) will come by chanting the Divine Name itself.

Devotee: Mother, even the so-called believers in God abuse us for coming here. How can they give an opinion without having come here and seen for themselves?

Mother: Don't blame them, children. It is most difficult to remove egoism and jealousy. These are seen even in advanced *sadhaks*. We should not give importance to what those ignorant children say. Don't get angry with them. We will only lose our power by doing so, that's all.

Another householder devotee: What should I do, Mother? My desire is to join the *Ashram* as soon as possible.

Mother: Son, for the time being you stay in your home.

The egg will hatch when the time is correct. Don't break it open before that. The bondages of the family will fall off in due time when your desire to realise God becomes stronger.

Professor: What are Mother's plans for the future activities?

Mother: Mother's aim is to raise these *brahmachari* children, making them do spiritual practices and disciplining them. In this way, they can become good *sannyasins* who propagate *Dharma* in the future. Mother has given them a regular routine. As there are no hired workers here, all *Ashram* work is done by the *brahmacharins*. A *brahmacharin* should not cling to anything or anyone. He should be free. The habit of self-dependence is needed.

The Holy Mother was sitting in the front yard of the *Ashram* where there was a small coconut grove. A song exemplifying the oneness of Lord Shiva and Lord Vishnu filtered through the small speakers in front of the temple,

> Hare Keshava Gôvinda
> Vasudeva Jaganmaya
> Shiva Sankara Rudresa
> Nilakantha Trilôchana...

A householder devotee came and sat silently near Mother. She opened her eyes after some time saying "Shiva, Shiva." Moving her head sideways with the rhythm of the music, the Mother was enjoying the singing. At the same time, she looked at the devotee and smiled at him most naturally. After some time, the devotee asked the following,

Devotee: Please tell me what is needed by me spiritually, Mother.

Mother: What does Mother know, son? She knows nothing. Mother is just telling some crazy things, that's all.
Devotee: Mother is playing tricks with me.
Mother: (In a low tone as if to tell a secret) Now, now, son, Mother will tell you something. One day when the three gods Brahma, Vishnu and Shiva came to see Saraswathi, the Goddess of learning, they found her sitting, holding a book. When they asked, "What are You doing?" Devi replied, "I am studying." Son, that is how infinite knowledge is. Won't humility come when we remember that? Even Saraswathi is studying. Then, what about Mother? Never let go of humility.

Understanding that the Mother was asking him to always be humble, the devotee said,

Devotee: Mother has understood me correctly. Humility, that is what I lack. I have never been able to yield to anyone.

BHAVA DARSHAN

Outside the *Ashram* compound, on the other side of the canal, fisherwomen were beating coconut husks to make rope. Looking at them, one devotee said, "It is amazing that the Mother felt to take birth in this place where coconut husks are beaten."

Mother: Son, look at that rotten coconut husk. How black and dirty it is. Have you seen them refining it by beating it again and again? Likewise, the mind should be made pure through intense *sadhana.*
Devotee: Mother, isn't this ordinary mood enough for you? What is the purpose of the *Devi* and *Krishna Bhavas?*

Mother: Maybe it is *Iswara's sankalpa* (God's Will). If Mother sits at that time as she ordinarily does, many people will not speak what's in their hearts. But they have no hesitation to tell everything to Mother during the *Bhava*. At that time they are talking to *Bhagavan* (Lord) and *Bhagavati* (Goddess), aren't they? The people think that afterwards Mother cannot remember anything. Thus, so many people are consoled by unloading their burdened hearts before God. Therefore, is not the *Bhava* beneficial for others? Everything is His Will. Infinite and multi-faceted is God's play.

One *brahmacharin* who went home for some purpose had just arrived and prostrated before the Mother.

Mother: Son, why are you late?
Brahmacharin: It was late when I got the bus, Mother.
Mother: It is not good for *brahmacharins* to go home during the period of their *sadhana.* Don't stand at bus stops and other such places where people are of different characters. Instead, walk keeping your destination in mind and if the bus comes, you can get in. You will reach the place where we have to go even if you cannot catch a bus. Something can be purchased and given to beggars with the money that you save on the fare. That is real and selfless service. By renouncing our own comfort, we serve others. What happens when we wait for the bus? Sometimes we may have to wait four or five hours. If the bus does not come, we will have to go back and will feel disappointed. This is not proper for one who wants to lead a spiritual life. Therefore, you must walk without waiting for the bus.

The Mother looked at the householder devotee. Even though the Mother had been speaking to the *brahmacharin,* what she had said seemed applicable to householder devotees who do *sadhana*.

Mother: Also, a *brahmacharin* should not eat food from a shop. Shop keepers are business minded. Taking each and every ingredient, the shopkeeper's only thought will be how to make more profit. While making tea he will think, "Is this much sugar necessary? This much milk is not needed. Oh, the tea powder is a little too much." In this way he does everything in a miserly fashion, calculating just to gain profit. His mind is not concentrated, but filled with vacillating thoughts. This will affect those who eat the food as well.

Although he was not in the habit of reading them, a *sannyasin* dreamt about newspapers . The newspaper and news appeared clearly in front of him during his sleep. He wondered why he had dreamt such a thing, and an enquiry was made. It was then discovered that the person who had prepared his food had been reading the newspaper while cooking. Due to carelessness, the fire in the oven would get extinguished while he read the newspaper. So he would re-light the fire and again read the paper. This was the way the servant cooked the food. The vibration created by his habit was reflected in the *sannyasin*.

Different types of people come to shops. We will hear different things there. The thought vibrations in the atmosphere will affect us. If control is not maintained, it will become a habit to eat from shops as soon as hunger comes. Without *tyaga* (renunciation), it is not possible to study ourselves . Plantain fruits and lemon juice can be taken while traveling. If necessary, milk and water can also be had. In the beginning stages an aspirant should be very careful. Until their roots are firmly fixed, plants should be raised with great care. The same is the case with a *sadhak*. When his roots are firmly fixed, then he won't go astray.

Hearing the reading of the *Srimad Bhagavatam* from a distant place through the loud speakers, one devotee asked, "Mother, is it right to read the *Srimad Bhagavatam* and accept money for it?"

Mother: Son, it is not wrong to receive a *dakshina* (offering) if a householder does not have any other means to earn his livelihood. But reading the *Bhagavatam* desiring money is not correct.

The devotee: Mother, what is the meaning of the saying that God is of the nature of Love *(prema svarupa)?*

Mother: It simply means that He can give nothing but love. In fact, He is the only One who truly loves us without expecting anything. Children, even if all the creatures in the whole world love us, that cannot equal an infinitesimal fraction of the love we experience from God in one second. There is no other love which can compare to God's love.

A child stricken by illness was lying in a hospital. The doctors and nurses treated the child with great care. Seeing their expression of affection, the child was also very interested in them. When the illness was cured the parents made ready to take the child home. The child said to the father, "How loving these people are." Before he could give an answer the nurse handed over the hospital bill to the father. The child wanted to know what that was. The father said, "This is the bill for which they have loved and served you. A separate amount is shown for each and every thing they have done. Their love was selfishly motivated." In this world, whoever loves you will have some selfish interest. We will

get real love only from God. Real love is selfless. Unconditional love will be seen only in God. What else can such a
God be except the embodiment of Love? But how many
know the glory of that selfless love? Those who have known
at least a little taste of that love won't run after worldly happiness.

7 October 1983

The beginning of *Navaratri* celebrations were taking
place in the *Ashram*. A big oil lamp was lit in front of the
portrait of *Vidya Devi* (the Goddess of learning) for the first
day of worship. The reading of the *Srimad Devi Bhagavatam*
had already begun. Worship with the Thousand Names of
the Divine Mother was going to be performed. The Holy
Mother and the *brahmacharins* were preparing margosa
(bilva) leaves for the worship and Gayatri was sitting near
the Mother , helping prepare the leaves.

One brahmacharin: Mother, all these leaves are damaged
by worms. They are not good for the worship.
Mother: Oh, that doesn't matter, son. It is enough if we
give importance to our devotion. We can do the worship
with these leaves. It is not really the leaf, but the innocent
mind and heart that we are offering at the Feet of the Lord.
It is enough if we take care of our mind so as to not to let
that be destroyed by worms.

A newcomer who had not had the opportunity to learn
anything about the Mother asked, "Mother, do you have a
Guru?"

Mother: (While preparing the leaves) Mother has neither Guru nor *sishyas* (disciples). Mother bows down to everything in the world. All are Mother's Guru. Mother has learned everything from Nature. At a particular state of meditation we will get knowledge about the essential principles from any object in Nature.

The western horizon was very cloudy and showed signs of a heavy downpour. The roaring sound of the ocean could be heard.

Mother: There, do you hear the roaring of the ocean? The sound will be louder in places where there is no depth, but where it is deep it will be calm. Evil-minded people will walk around making a commotion. Personalities with profound ideas will be calm in any circumstance. They won't be disturbed by anything.

Devotee: Mother, which is better, the philosophy of non-duality or the path of devotion?

Mother: Son, the path of devotion suits the majority of people. Can the majority be discarded for a few non-dualists? Sri Sankara, the greatest exponent of *Advaita Vedanta,* propagated *bhakti,* did he not? Didn't he compose many poems glorifying gods and goddesses and install statues of them? He knew that the path of devotion is what is needed by ordinary people.

Ganga told me that Ramana Maharshi was a *jñana margi*[57] and that he did not accept *bhakti.* Mother did not agree with Ganga, but he argued saying that *bhakti* shows weakness. Without having read any books, Mother said that

---

[57]One who follows the path of knowledge and does not accept devotion as a valid path to Realisation.

Ramana Maharshi approved of *bhakti*. How could Ganga agree with my point of view? Soon after this conversation, Ganga went to Tiruvannamalai. The first book which he took from the Ramanashram library gave Ganga a surprise. It was a text written by Ramana Maharshi glorifying *bhakti*. That finished son Ganga's doubt. Ganga believed that Mother was speaking through Ramana Maharshi in that book.

GOD'S GRACE

8 October 1983

At eight o'clock in the morning, the chanting of the Thousand Names of the Divine Mother was about to be completed. The Holy Mother entered the temple and sat near the holy seat. One *brahmacharin* began to get up immediately after the worship.

Mother: Don't get up immediately after the worship is over. Sit still for a while; the taste should be enjoyed at least for some time. The effect of taking a medecine may not be felt immediately. It must be given some time to pervade the system. Likewise, the energy gained by doing japa and meditation must be given some time to take effect by sitting silently for a while.

The Holy Mother sang,

> O Divine Mother, Mother of the world,
> O most courageous Mother,
> Giver of Truth and Divine Love,
> Thou art the Universe Itself...

All joined in. The singing reached the peak of devotional heights. It seemed as if the Holy Mother was carrying
all the others with her and soaring high in the vast expansiveness of infinite bliss. Now and then the Mother burst
into an ecstatic laughter, followed by her calling *"Amma,
Amma!"* which penetrated into the hearts of the *brah-
machaains* and other devotees, surcharging their minds as
well as the whole atmosphere with spiritual energy.

The singing went on for about forty-five minutes and
ended with the *arati*. After a while the Mother came and sat
in the front verandah of the meditation hall. A few householder devotees and some *brahmacharins* were also present.

Brahmacharin: What should be done to get God's Grace?
Mother: Son, if there is the load of ego and desires, the
wind of God's Grace won't lift us. The load must be less-
ened. In her youth Mother never thought about anything
other than God. When the wind blew, having touched her
body, she would call out loud, crying, "O Mother, are you
running away having touched my body? Mother, why are
you not taking me with you?" One will certainly get God's
Grace if that kind of devotion is there. But it is not possible
without reducing the weight of worldliness in the mind.
Devotee: Is there a particular position one should sit in for
doing *sadhana?*
Mother: It does not matter if you cannot sit in one position
for a long time without moving. Assuming any sitting posture, you can repeat the *mantra* or meditate. *Japa* can also be
done while walking. But you must sit and practice *japa*. That
will teach you patience. Sitting comfortably in one position
without moving is called *asana siddhi*. This is good for
meditation.

ASTROLOGY AND ITS RESULTS

Devotee: It is said that one's horoscope cannot be changed. Is that true Mother?

Mother: What is seen through astrology are the results of the actions done in the past. The fruits of action can be deflected through other actions ~ such as actions dedicated to God. A stone which is thrown upwards can be caught before it falls down. Likewise, the course of our actions (karma phala) can be changed before they bear fruit. A horoscope will give way before God's Will (sankalpa). It may show in a man's horoscope that he will marry. But the horoscope will change if he does spiritual practices and happens to get satsang (the company of sages) at a young age. Thus he might be able to become a sannyasin. His horoscope will certainly change, provided there is good spiritual disposition and satsang. Self-effort also is indispensable, as are spiritual practices like worship, japa and meditation.

OBLATIONS TO THE DEPARTED

Devotee: Are oblations to the deceased ancestors necessary?

Mother: Mother will narrate an incident. The son of a person who lives near here was a vagabond and one who did wicked deeds. Seeing his son's bad ways, the father would scold him. Even then, the son did not care and continued in his ways. Therefore, one day the father said, "After I die, don't let him perform my death ceremonies. If he does, his sin will also come to me. I won't accept the offerings even if he does do the ceremonies after my death." When the father died, the son performed the ritual saying, "I must see for myself whether or not he will accept the offerings." Even

though he performed the ritual several times, at the conclusion when the balls of rice which he offered for his deceased
father were offered to crows to eat, they would not even
touch them although they would peck at everyone else's.

Just as the correctly addressed letter will be received un-
failingly by the addressee, the benefit of the rituals performed by chanting *mantras* with concentration will reach
the soul of the intended person, wherever he is. But as far
as a real*sadhak* is concerned, he does not have to do any of
these *karmas*.

SRADDHA AND NISHTHA
Alertness and Discipline

9 October 1983

Because it was the time of *Navaratri,* more devotees
than usual were present. Some of them were newcomers. At
eight o'clock in the morning the Holy Mother came out of
her hut smiling benignly at the devotees. All prostrated to
her, and she in turn touched each one, greeting them with
all humility. Calling everyone, the Mother went to the front
yard of the temple where the coconut trees were growing.
Some devotees spread a mat under one tree where she sat
and started meditating, asking everyone to join her. About
thirty people were present. All of them sat together and began to meditate. Seeing this unusual sight, the passersby
could not help themselves from stopping and gazing for at
least a moment. Shortly after the Mother closed her eyes, the
devotees opened theirs and remained gazing at her. After
some time when the Mother opened her eyes, she found
that everyone was sitting there looking at her. An elderly

man who was a retired doctor softly whispered to his friend sitting nearby, "On whom to meditate when the personification of love is sitting right in front of us? But the Mother is simply playing games with us. What do we know about this divine play?"

Raising her voice, the Holy Mother asked, "What are you saying, doctor-son? (Turning to the other devotees) Doctor-son is of the opinion that doing meditation when this crazy Kali is sitting here is not correct."

The doctor was struck with wonder when he heard Mother repeating the sentence that he said a few moments before. He was sitting in the rear which was too far away for the Mother to have been able to hear their conversation. He exclaimed, "How did Mother hear it?" Saying this, he got up from his seat, and having approached the Mother, he prostrated at full length before her.

The Holy Mother caressed him with great affection but did not say anything but "Shiva, Shiva." The doctor shed tears of joy which the Mother wiped with her own hands as they rolled down his cheeks. Greatly moved by this show of love, he cried loudly, calling out "Amma Saranam Saranam..!" (Mother is my Refuge). Everyone silently shed tears. After a few moments he returned to his seat. An unusual peace pervaded everywhere. The atmosphere was extraordinarily calm and serene. A few more moments passed in silence. Everyone seemed as if they were in a contemplative mood. All of a sudden, a young man broke the silence by raising a question.

Young man: Mother, why has God given happiness to some and sorrow to others?
Mother: God is not making anyone sorrowful. It is the demon which makes us sorrowful.

Young man: Is not God in the demons also?

Mother: Son, it is a person's character that is said to be like a demon *(asura)*. It is the *asura svabhava* (the demoniac nature) which makes us sorrowful.

Young man: How is that?

Mother: Suppose there is a blazing fire. Someone tells you not to jump in it. Without listening you jump and burn yourself. If fire is *Brahman*, the person who told you not to jump is also *Brahman*. In the beginning, using your discrimination, only do things which are needed. But usually when certain circumstances arise, we will lose our discriminative power and do as our ego tells us. The ego and its products have *asuric* qualities. They will spoil our life and personality. In the olden days, both men and women would be trained at a young age to control the demonic forces. They would become masters of their minds through scriptural studies and their practical application.

A child will study out of fear of his father. But later when he becomes aware of his place in the world and in society, he studies for himself. In the beginning, guidance and discipline are needed. Having loaded yourself with sorrows by acting as you please, don't blame God for your lack of obedience. Alertness *(sraddha)* is needed. Nothing is possible without that.

Sraddha and *nishta* (alertness or faith and strict observance) are necessary. Once two fishermen went fishing in a river. Standing near a canal with thick vegetation, the first man said, "See, I am going to catch fish here by making a bund around this vegetation. Would you like to join me?" The second man said, "No, if I join you I may have to work until evening and if I don't get any fish my children will starve today. I shall go somewhere else and try." Having said this, he left. Now the first fisherman started to build a bund with the mud and grass which was at hand. He had no tools with him and so he started to bail out the water with his hands. With patience and faith, without even a slight change in his attitude, he continued his work. Not being made strong enough, the bund broke in many places and water started to gush out. But with a steady mind and firm faith the man went on repairing and continued his work. At last in the evening he succeeded in his task and obtained plenty of fish. At that time the other fisherman, after wandering here and there, returned to this place empty-handed. The first fisherman supplied him with fish and made him happy. Because of his unshakable faith and perseverance, he could save himself and the other man as well. The one who had no faith did not achieve anything at all. Furthermore, his whole time was wasted and he unnecessarily dissipated his energies for nothing. Dear children! Wherever one may be, if one has strong faith in God, he will succeed in everything. This is what we have to understand.

GURU

Young man: Mother, is a Guru necessary?

Mother: Son, a Guru's presence is unique. Even though wind is everywhere, nowhere but under a tree will we find coolness. Doesn't the breeze that filters through the leaves of a tree give soothing coolness to those who are living in hot climates? Likewise, for us who live in the scorching heat of worldly existence, a Guru is necessary. A Guru's presence will give us peace and tranquillity. One whose goal is Self-realization must have a Guru. Without a Satguru, Realization is hard to attain. The dormant subtle vasanas can only be removed by a Perfect Master. Even for gaining worldly knowledge a teacher is necessary. What can be said then about spiritual science, the subtlest of all branches of learning?

Devotee: It is said that satsang is good for one's spiritual upliftment. What is your opinion about this, Mother?

Mother: Yes, that is true. If there is *satsang* it is not necessary to do *sadhana* in the beginning stages. But it must be real *satsang*. Real *satsang* is the yoking of *jivatman* and *Paramatman*. God or the Guru represents the *Paramatman*, disciple or devotee is the *jivatman*. Yoking happens when the disciple or devotee applies the *Guru's* teachings. Scriptural discussion is also a kind of *satsang* because it remind us of the Truth with which we are trying to have a companionship.

CUSTOMS AND DISCIPLINE

Young man: Mother, is a discipline necessary for *sadhana?*

Mother: A road is required for the buses, cars and cycles. Traffic rules are also necessary; otherwise, accidents will happen. Similarly, ordinary people should have a discipline. There are no traffic rules for the wind and the bird. In a like manner, a Knower of *Brahman* does not need any discipline.

One devotee: In the Bhagavad Gita, Lord Krishna says, "Abandoning all *dharmas*, take refuge in Me alone; I will liberate thee from all sins; grieve not."

Mother: What does that mean? Is it saying that everyone should abandon their *dharma?* The Lord won't say so. *Dharmas* are not needed for those who have the attitude of complete surrender. But this does not mean that *dharma* is unnecessary. Beginners must perform their duties but in a direction that leads them towards God.

The questioner was surprised upon hearing the Mother's interpretation of the Sanskrit verse. He might have wondered how Mother, who has no knowledge of Sanskrit and has not read any books at all, could give an explanation about a particular verse taken from the Holy Gita.

Young man: Mother, I have no peace of mind. What is the way to get it?

Mother: Son, this attitude of yours to want to know the way will itself open the door to the path. Now what you need is to do sadhana.

Devotee: Mother, some people say that the knowledge of *Brahman* is enough and that image worship is not necessary.

Mother: Son, ordinary people need images and temples and other such aids. When we are about to go to the temple we remember God and after reaching the temple we remember God. Thus the temple awakens the remembrance of God in us. There is yet another thing. The *atmachaitanya* (consciousness) of the devotees will be reflected by the image. There is a special power in the temple where the devotion and concentration of the people remains saturated. By going to temples we will get concentration and devotion.

Young man: Mother, there are those who say that temples are not wanted because of the crimes committed by people who believe in religion.

Mother: If it is so, medical treatment and hospitals should also be done away with because of the mistakes committed by a few doctors. Instead of trying to correct the mistakes, should one be obstinate, saying that to correct the mistakes is unnecessary?

Young man: Is not applying sacred ash to the forehead simply a custom?

Mother: It is very good if you apply ash baked out of cowdung. First, grass is transformed into cowdung. Then, after drying out in the sun, it is slowly burnt in a fire made from paddy husk. Having removed all the dirt (sand) through purification, ash is obtained. Then after going through several changes, this ash becomes an infallible medicine. It will destroy the bad germs in the hair pores. When we see ash, we should remember the end of our life (death). Ash reminds us that at some time, this body will turn into ash. Ash from a burnt corpse is the best.

It was lunch time. The Holy Mother took everyone to the dining hall. She asked the *brahmacharins* to serve food quickly. The Mother said, "All the children may be feeling hungry." The devotees said, "Mother should also eat." "Mother doesn't need to now. Children, you eat. Mother will sit here." Saying so, the Holy Mother sat in the dining hall. Everyone ate but the Mother didn't, even though everybody requested that she eat. The *brahmacharins* begged, "Mother, you haven't eaten anything at all. Please eat at least a little rice." Mother kept quiet. She laid down in the dining hall. It was three o'clock. At that time a devotee of the Mother named Karunakaran came running to the Mother. He was carrying a bag. He saluted the Holy Mother but soon marks of sadness appeared on his face. Seeing the devotee, the Holy Mother, like a small child, snatched the bag from the devotee's hand, saying, "What were you doing until now? My head is spinning due to hunger." The bag contained rice and other dishes especially cooked by his wife to offer to Mother. The devotee's joy knew no bounds when he came to know that Mother had not eaten anything until then. With tears in his eyes he said, "I know that you would not eat because my wife was constantly uttering your name while preparing it."

Having finished cooking early in the morning, the devotee, cherishing the desire to feed the Holy Mother, set out from his house intending to reach the Ashram before noon. But unfortunately, he missed the bus and reached there only at three o'clock. It was quite obvious that the Holy Mother was waiting to fulfill the devotee's pure and innocent wish.

After lunch the Mother laid down on the sand under some trees. Some *brahmacharins* and householders insisted that she lie on a mat, but the Mother would not agree. A devotee who had not visited the Mother for many months came to see her at that time. Pointing to him one *brahmacharin* said, "Mother, an old son has come."

Mother: Are there old and new sons?

Those devotees who were sitting at a distance came closer and sat near Mother when she began talking. The Holy Mother got up and sat down next to one devotee. He said, "I have visited several times but never brought my wife and children. Mother has never asked anything about them. Sometimes I feel sad about this."

Mother: They are Mother's children even from before, aren't they? Doesn't your wife cook Bengal gram and keep it in the shrine room in front of Mother's picture every day before the usual evening *bhajan?* Whenever you scold your children, don't they say, "We will tell Vallickavu Amma that you have scolded us and she will scold you!"

The devotee, hearing these words from the Mother's own lips, was overwhelmed with joy and wonder. He said,

"Yes, I am a fool to think that the all-knowing Mother does not know or care about my family." He bowed down at the Mother's feet and chanted the following verse with tears in his eyes.

> O Annapurna Devi, the Ever-Perfect,
> The Beloved and Wife of Lord Shiva,
> In order to get Wisdom and Dispassion
> I am begging of Thee, O Mother Parvati.

> My Mother is Goddess Parvati,
> And the Great Lord is my Father.
> The devotees of Lord Shiva are my relatives
> And the three worlds are my home.

Devotee: I heard Mother saying that in the *Kali Yuga* (the present age of materialism) concentration is gained more by singing devotional songs than through meditation. Therefore, can meditation be wholly given up?

Mother: Children, what Mother said was that nowadays the atmosphere is filled with a lot of bustle and sound and therefore to attain concentration, *kirtana* (devotional singing) is better than meditation. A silent and peaceful atmosphere is needed for meditation. Other sounds can be overcome by singing devotional songs loudly, can't they? Even beyond concentration is *dhyana* (meditation). *Kirtan* , concentration, *dhyana* - this is the progression.

Devotee: It seems that in Kerala there are more devotees of Krishna and Devi. Why is that, Mother?

Mother: In each place the custom is different. It depends on the mental disposition inherited from the previous birth. (Humourously, with a smile) Whoever they might be, they will be in trouble if they have not pleased Devi. In the olden days, the Guru, after initiating the disciple, would give him a *Lalitasahasranam* book (Thousand Names of the Divine Mother). Only then would he be sent to do *tapas*. The disciple would be asked to chant it everyday.

Only one endowed with the spirit of renunciation can realize Sri Krishna. This is because in order to please Krishna, who is the Embodiment of *Suddha Sattva*,[58] one must become like Him. Feelings of self-important and other such egocentric qualities should not exist. Whoever one may be, without renunciation one cannot realize God. During his course of spiritual practice, a devotee may have to undergo different kinds of trials and tribulations. Destroying your sense of "I" and "mine," God may deprive you of all your wealth and even then, only if you catch hold of His Feet will He give His Darshan. Sri Ramakrishna said that he had undergone great difficulties to realize Krishna. But the bliss that you experience will be infinite and inexpressible, compared to which the sufferings are nothing.

In olden days, a *Lalitasahasranam* book would be given not only to those who worshipped Devi, but also to the person getting initiated into Krishna's *mantra*. Do you know why? So that the initiate should not be in want of food and clothing. Devi will look after that. Motherhood is predominant in God in the form of the Divine Mother. Children will have a natural attraction towards their mother and a mother will be naturally loving and compassionate towards her children and will look after their needs. So also is the case with the Divine Mother. To get your bread, Devi should be satisfied. That is why She is known as "*Bhukti-Mukti-Pradayani*" or the One who bestows both material happiness and Liberation.

[58]Absolute purity or pure sattva.

Devotee: Mother, what is the meaning of the verse "Without doing anything, She does everything?"

Mother: Devi doesn't do anything. That She does everything is only an illusion. The sun does nothing, but without him, nothing can continue. He stands as a witness, yet he does everything. In this way, Mother is only a witness. Although She is doing everything, She is not bound or attached to it. Therefore, She does nothing though doing everything.

One householder devotee: What is to be done for gaining mental peace?

Mother: Son, daily you should give some solitude to the mind. God's Name should be chanted. Have faith in a Perfect Guru. A ladder is needed to climb a coconut tree. The Guru is the ladder. When children are young, they study mainly out of fear of their father, mother and teacher. Therefore, it is clear that in the beginning stages, *bhaya bhakti* (devotion endowed with reverence and fear) is necessary. Thus, mental peace can be gained if one moves forward adhering to the *Guru's* words.

Devotee: In order to gain mental peace, I have gone to several *sannyasins* but I got nothing from them. All were fakes.

Mother: Son, *shanti* (peace) will not be had if you search outside. It should be sought within. God dwells within. He will be known through introspection.

Son, you have abused *sannyasins*, haven't you? You should not do that. Look at Sri Sankara, Swami Vivekananda and others. You can see that it has been *sannyasins* who have done lasting good in the world. Siddhartha, who was an emperor, became the *sannyasin* Buddha and did so much good to the world. But there are also fake sannyasins, aren't there? But are fakes found only among *sannyasins*? Do those who are virtuous ones become worthless because of the impostors? When going to the market, if you find that one of the shops is illegally selling goods does it mean that all the shops are doing the same?

A young man: I feel that there is no meaning in temples.

Mother: Son, that is not the case. When we see an artificial apple we are reminded of the real one. When we see temples and divine images, we will be reminded of God, is it not so?

Young man: That is right.

DISCRIMINATION

Mother: It is not enough if you simply agree with everything. You must do *sadhana*. Sweetness will not be had if you write on a paper "sugar" and lick it. You must eat sugar. Studying books alone is not enough. *Sadhana* has to be performed. If you need to get inspiration to do *sadhana*, observe life closely and gain understanding of life. After all, what is marriage nowadays but another bondage? It is a relationship of two bodies. It has nothing to do with the relationship of the souls. Without the relationship of the souls, there is no essence in the marriage. In the olden days marriage and married life were considered as divine and were means to attain Self-Realization. A man and woman's spirits were united, rather than their bodies. This unity led to peace, tranquillity, and eventually culminated in God-Realization. Nowadays it is nothing but another means to satisfy lust. There is no real love in the union, only selfishness. Who will listen and contemplate deeply if one is told that the body is a bag of stools and urine! Children, don't think that Mother is telling you to completely discard

worldly life. What Mother is trying to say is that you should
use this life in a more intelligent way so that this world and
your life will become more joyful and beautiful. Discriminate
and see. Is the love that we get from our relatives, wife, husband or children real? Is it not for fulfilling their selfish
ends that men love women and women love men? What will
happen if she or he runs away with another man or woman?
Then the attitude becomes just the opposite. You will be
ready even to kill her or him. Is this love?

Mothers will say that they love their children. In fact, do
they? If they do love them, why do they not love the children
of the neighbouring houses? What they really love is
"mine." Mother would say that even the birth of a child is
accidental. It occurs during the course of the parents' effort
to satisfy their lust and because of other selfish motives. If
parents really loved their children, they would make them
understand and assimilate the spiritual truths which would
give them mental strength and control needed to confront
the challenges of life. But instead, they throw them into the
world without giving them proper spiritual education, and
force them to lead the same kind of life that they themselves
do.

We say that we love our children. But would any of
those who love their children be willing to die for them? It
is not seen or heard of that someone is ready to save their
child's life by sacrificing their own at the time of the child's
death. Do you know how many have told Mother this? A
woman was watching when her child fell into a well seven-
teen rings deep. That woman was not ready to jump into the
well to save her child from death. She cried and shouted
aloud. The child was already dead by the time he was taken
out by the diver who was brought by a neighbor. Rare are

such people who are ready to save another life by sacrificing their own.

To be frank, worldly pleasure is equal to a dog's excreta. From one drop of semen we are losing energy equal to a hundred drops of blood. For a spiritual aspirant, *brahmacharya* (celibacy) is his wealth. As far as he is concerned, worldly life is indeed equal to a dog's excreta. For a dog, human excreta is like nectar, but for human beings it is an object of detestation. For a spiritual person, worldly life is something to be loathed. Only if he has this attitude can he attain the goal. Otherwise, his energy will be dissipated by the objects of the world.

Real *vairagya* (detachment) will develop if one discriminates like this. Then it will become possible to perform intense *sadhana*. A *sannyasin* should acquire inner wealth by doing *sadhana*. *Sannyasa* is not child's play. It requires tremendous courage, courage born of sense control. It is enough for a married person to look after his wife and two children, but a *sannyasin* has to carry the burden of the whole world.

In the middle of the conversation a lawyer, a devotee of the Holy Mother, arrived and sat with the Mother, having offered his salutations to her. Hearing Mother's words, he raised a question concerning his own mind and life.

Lawyer: What is our fate, Mother? We are walking around getting involved in court cases, quarrels, lies, etc.
Mother: That is alright, son; it is the *dharma* (duty) of a lawyer to argue for his party in court. That is not wrong. A lawyer is only performing his duty when he argues for a murderer. But accept only truthful cases as far as possible.

The sin does not go to the lawyer if the criminal is saved by
the arguments put forth by him. The criminal is only saved
from the court of law. He cannot escape from God's court.
One must bear the fruit of one's actions.

Like others, abandoning worldly life when real *vairagya*
has dawned in him, a lawyer can come to spirituality. Until
then, *svadharma* (one's own *dharma*) should be performed,
dedicating everything to God.

The Mother took the fruit offered to her by the devotees
and having made them into small slices, fed the devotees
with her own hand. Everyone was happy with their hearts
overflowing.

11 October 1983

The Holy Mother was sitting in the front yard of the
Ashram in the coconut grove at eleven o'clock in the morning. A group of householder devotees from Trivandrum arrived. They saluted the Mother and sat near her. Some *brahmacharins* who had just finished their meditation also came.
They prostrated and sat with the other devotees. Mother expressed a wish to hear devotional songs. Sreekumar brought
the harmonium and the Mother sang with full devotional
fervor,

> O Devi, O Ambika, Beauty Personified,
> Thou who art affectionate towards devotees,
> May Thou dwell here in order to end
> The sufferings of the devotees.
>
> For how many days have I been desiring
> To see Thee? I am praising Thee

Without losing even a moment.
Did some mistake happen on my part or is it
That Thou hast no mind to end my sorrow?

The *brahmacharins* sang along with the Holy Mother. Tears of bliss rolled down the Mother's cheeks as she called out, "*Amma ente Amma* " (O Mother, O my mother). All the devotees were immersed in the Mother's songs. Some shed tears of devotion and others sat with closed eyes. The atmosphere was calm and quiet, except for the chanting of the fishermen which could be heard as they pulled the fishing nets from the ocean nearby.

Half an hour passed before the Holy Mother opened her eyes. A young man asked, "Mother, what are the signs of a person who has conquered his mind?" Another devotee interrupted, "It is enough to look at Mother!"

Mother: This crazy one? Very good! Children, one who has conquered the mind is like a child. He has no attachment to anything. If a child sees gold, he will take it. Then throwing the gold away, he will grab a charcoal if he happens to see it lying nearby. This is a child's nature. He does not have attachment to anything, no bondages. There will not be any ego at all.

One devotee: (Humorously) Mother is a very egotistic person. Mother is the All-Witness and therefore everyone's ego is Mother's. The ego in me is also not mine, it is hers.

Mother: That is the attitude that is needed, son. This is the perfect way of thinking. But you should apply it in your life also.

Devotee: But in Mother not even a speck of ego is found.

The Holy Mother laughed like a child.

NAME AND LOVE

A woman householder devotee came. She saluted and kissed the Mother's feet.

Mother: It is a long time since this daughter has been seen!
Devotee: It is one year, Mother. There has been no time available to come here.
Mother: There is time to go to the hospital if the child is sick. No matter how long it might be, there is enough time to stand waiting in bus stops. There is also time to stand in the long queue in front of the movie theatre, even in the scorching heat. But there is no time to go to temples or to come here. You will go running to the place which you like and to gain objects that you love.
Woman Devotee: What should be done to develop love, Mother?
Mother: Daughter, when the Divine Name is chanted constantly, spiritual hunger will come. Consequently, a taste for the Name will arise followed by love for God (*Isvara prema*). We are saved if love is obtained.
Devotee: How can one repeat the Divine Name while working?
Mother: You can chant during leisure times, can't you? Then, through chanting and chanting during those times, the constant chanting will become a habit. At that time, even when we are doing worldly things, our breath will go on repeating the Divine Name. Thus, a state will come when we can do japa as well as worldly activities simultaneously.

After seeking the Mother's permission to go, one devo-tee came and prostrated to her. Touching his back, Mother acknowledged his gesture. This is Mother's usual way; she bows down to the indwelling Truth in all.

THERE IS NO MATTER, EVERYTHING IS CONSCIOUSNESS

One man who heard about the Mother came to see her in person. He went on babbling about his own glories and achievements. Later when he left, the Holy Mother jokingly said about him,

Mother: Son, once the tape starts playing, shouldn't the song finish? Is it possible to easily wash away the tough stains that have accumulated over many years?

A science student who was interested in spiritual matters as well asked, "The *rishis* (seers) declare that everything is *Brahman*. Modern science also says that everything is energy. Is there any connection between these two?"

Mother: Son, when we enter into the higher states of *sadhana*, we can hear all the stones and pieces of wood talk-ing to us. They are not inert but conscious. Then it will become clear that they are also talking. What is known as matter is only matter at the empirical level. In reality, there is no matter. Everything is one and the same Consciousness.
An aspirant: Mother, why is it that the circulation of the blood through the veins is not felt?
Mother: At a particular stage of meditation when the mind becomes one-pointed, we can hear the sound of the harmo-

nious flow of the blood through the veins. It can be experienced. It will be felt as if water is rushing through thousands of small pipes. Such experiences are not born out of any physical disorder. There is nothing to worry about. Several experiences of this kind will occur when we progress in meditation. (Hugging a small girl) See, look at this daughter. She is only seven but meditates like a great *yogi*. This daughter asked Mother, "Mother, where does the body go while meditating?" When I lie down, she would fan me as she sits in the lotus posture repeating the *mantra* with her eyes closed. If Mother has her eyes closed, thinking Mother is asleep, she would embrace Mother's feet and start crying and shedding tears. What kind of girl is this, O God?

Mother laughed loudly like a small child. Everyone joyfully laughed with her. The little girl also expressed her joy, smiling and embracing the Holy Mother.

12 October 1983

Mother with some other devotees was preparing *bilva* leaves for the *archana* at eight o'clock in the morning.

One devotee: Mother, what happens if all these ants die getting entrapped in the *bilva* leaves?
Mother: Children, you don't have to worry about that. All those will return to where they came from. Prepare the leaves chanting the Divine Name (*mantra*) endowed with *sraddha* (faith).
Devotee: Do the *brahmacharins* practice *pranayama?*
Mother: A little bit. It shouldn't be practiced too much. *Kumbhakam* (retention of the breath) will automatically come

when concentration is attained through chanting of the Divine Name. On its own, the *kumbhakam* (serpent power) will awaken. For that, no particular breath control is needed. How is it possible to practice *pranayama* during this age when even pure air is not available? *Pranayama* should be practiced with discipline under the guidance of an experienced Guru. It is a dangerous path if not done correctly. *Japa* is more than enough.

One *brahmacharin* came and made some complaint about another one.

Mother: Son, *brahmacharins* should not even think anything which is not conducive to *sadhana.* All the power that is acquired through *sadhana* will be lost. There should be no anger at all. It is more difficult to remove jealousy. The mind should always be vacant. Son, go and meditate.

The *brahmacharin* retired after having offered his salutation.

One householder devotee: Mother, can a *grahastha* take *sannyasa?*

Mother: (Laughingly) Oh, have you attained that state? (All laugh) A *grahastha* should look after his family. Don't abandon them. But you can give them up, if there is complete detachment. Then you can leave the house. After relenquishing that, not even a thought about the house should enter into the mind.

It was time for lunch. The Holy Mother went to the hut after instructing the *brahmacharins* to feed the devotees.

STORY OF SANDEEPAKA

After lunch the Mother narrated the following story to the *brahmacharins*:

Angiras was a great sage endowed with immense spiritual power. He had many disciples. One day, summoning all of them, he addressed them as follows:

"Due to the fruits of past *karmas* my body will soon be afflicted by blindness and the terrible disease of leprosy. I would like to spend those days in Kasi (Benaras). Now, I want to know which one among you is willing to follow me to Kasi and serve me during those days of suffering?"

Looking at each other, the disciples all stood silently. At that time, Sandeepaka, the youngest among Angiras' disciples stood up. In all humility he said, "Respected Guru, I am ready to come with you."

The Guru replied, "You are too young. Also, you don't know what service is."

Sandeepaka said, "Revered Master, I am ready and will certainly come with you."

Angiras explained, "It is easy to undergo suffering oneself but to serve the one who suffers is much more difficult."

But Sandeepaka was determined. Such was the intensity of his desire to serve his Guru. Thus, the Guru and his young disciple went to Kasi.

Soon after reaching there, Angiras was afflicted by the fell disease and lost his eye sight. Sandeepaka sincerely and devotedly served his Guru day in and day out. He would never go out leaving his Guru alone except in order to beg for their food or to wash his *Guru's* clothes. He was constantly engaged in looking after his Guru and took the utmost care to meet even his *Guru's* slightest needs. He would say, "My Gurudev is Kasi Vishvanath himself (Lord Shiva presiding over the city of Kasi)."

In spite of little Sandeepaka's unshakable devotion and utter dedication, the Guru would severely chastise him and accuse him of having made mistakes which he had not done. Sometimes he would scold Sandeepaka saying that the clothes were not properly washed or that the begged food was sour and so on. At other times he would show great affection and love to him and would even say that he was putting Sandeepaka to so much trouble.

One day, Lord Shiva appeared in front of Sandeepaka and said, "I am very pleased with your devotion and dedication to your Guru. Please ask for a boon." But Sandeepaka was not willing to ask for a boon without first having the consent of his Guru. He therefore ran back to him and after prostrating to Angiras, asked him, "O Revered Guru, may I ask a boon of Lord Shiva to remove your disease?"

Angiras angrily replied, "You are not my disciple but my enemy. Is it your wish to make me suffer more by having to take another birth? Don't you wish that I become liberated in this birth itself?"

Sandeepaka sadly returned to the presence of Lord Shiva and said, "O Lord, forgive me! My Guru doesn't like that I ask for the thing which I would like. As for me, I do not want anything for myself."

Years rolled by and Sandeepaka, the embodiment of devotion to the Guru, still continued to serve his Guru with the same amount of love and surrender. One day, while he was going to the town to beg food, Lord Vishnu appeared before him and said, "My child, I am very pleased with your devotion and dedication to your Guru. I am ready to give whatever boon you ask. You did not ask anything of Lord Shiva but this time you should not disappoint Me as well."

Struck with wonder, Sandeepaka enquired of the Lord, "Even though I haven't served You or even remembered You once a day, how could it be that You are pleased with my service?"

Vishnu smilingly replied, "The Guru and God are not different but are one. It is your service to your Guru which has pleased me."

This time Sandeepaka also went to seek his Guru's permission to ask for a boon. The Guru said, "Sandeepaka, if you want some boon for yourself, go ahead and ask. Don't ask anything for me."

Sandeepaka returned to Lord Vishnu and said, "O Lord, give me more wisdom and knowledge so that I can understand how to serve my Guru according to his wishes. Most of the time, due to my ignorance, I am not able to understand what he likes. Therefore, O Lord, grant me the knowledge to serve my Guru properly." Lord Vishnu was very pleased and saying, "So be it," He disappeared.

When Sandeepaka returned from the presence of Lord Vishnu, Angiras asked him what was the boon that he sought from the Lord. Sandeepaka told him everything that had happened. Immediately, all the symptoms of leprosy disappeared from the Guru's body and his sight was restored. He stood smiling at his disciple and hugged him. The leprosy and blindness had been self-imposed by the Great Master Angiras in order to test the devotion and dedication of his youngest disciple. Being established in the Supreme Truth, he had no karma to work out. Graciously blessing Sandeepaka, the sage said, "I am very pleased with your devotion. No harm or danger will come to those disciples who serve their Guru with as much devotion and dedication as you have served me with. May all of the disciples and their disciples for coming ages be blessed because of you."

Children, this is real *bhakti*. If there is such devotion, then nothing else is needed.

MITHYA MEANS CHANGING

13 October 1983

A person belonging to the neighbouring house had epilepsy. The relatives of the patient came to see the Holy Mother. The Mother was sitting on the front verandah of the old temple facing east.

The Great *Mantra (Mahamantra),* "Hare Rama, Hare Rama, Rama Rama, Hare Hare, Hare Krishna, Hare Krishna, Krishna Krishna, Hare Hare" was echoing through the *Ashram* .

Mother told the relatives of the sick man, "For diseases like epilepsy and hysteria, practicing meditation is better than medicines. Those who have practiced meditation according to Mother's instructions have received a cure for such diseases."

A young man sitting near Mother asked, "How to meditate, Mother?"

Mother: Children, it is not the same path for everyone. Son, you should meditate on the form of your Beloved Deity and chant the *mantra* of that particular Deity. While meditating, you can fix the eyes either in between the eyebrows or on the tip of the nose. If you find it difficult to concentrate on one of these, then visualise your Beloved Deity's form within the heart lotus. As far as householders are concerned, it is better for them to meditate in the heart. The *mantra* can be chanted always, irrespective of time and place. Chanting the *mantra* using a rosary will help to attain more concentration and to maintain alertness.

Young man: Mother, how is it possible to remove sorrow?

Mother: We have been thinking that the body is eternal. That created sorrow. Now we should think in the opposite way ~ that *Atman* (the Self) is eternal. It should be realized as well. In order to convince ourselves that the body is non-eternal, we must train the mind, using the weapons of discrimination and detachment. Look here, son, if you put your finger in the nostrils, mucous will come out; from the eyes dirt will come out, and from the ears the same. Now, if you do not brush your teeth for a day, your breath will smell terrible. If a wound gets infected with pus, a putrid smell will emanate. In a similar manner, take every part and every organ of the body. What is it, after all, except a bag of stools, flesh and blood? This is the thing that you dress with beautiful clothes and golden ornaments? Try to pierce through and see the Real Thing which makes it beautiful and shining. That is the Supreme Consciousness. This is how you have to discriminate and detach yourselves from the body and the world of objects. Once you are convinced of the ephemeral nature of the so-called pleasure-giving objects, then you won't desire them. There ends sorrow.

Young man: This is really useful for any practice. Mother, some say that there is no God.

Mother: Children, it is like saying with the tongue that I have no tongue. It is with the power given by God alone that one denies God. Not only that. When one denies the existence of something, he is actually affirming its existence. In order to reject something, one must first have a general idea of that particular thing. For example, when somebody says, "There is no book," it is quite certain that in the past, he has had or has at least seen a book. It is the same with God. The existence of God or the Self is purely a matter of experience. It is not a subject for argumentation.

Young man: Is there any difference between the mind and the *Atman?*

Mother: Pure mind alone is *Atman.*

Young man: It is said that the world is *mithya* (an illusion).

Mother: Son, *mithya* only means changing. To say that the world is *mithya* doesn't mean that it is non-existent. It means simply that it is not permanent. If rice is ground, first it becomes powder, then it transforms into edibles and finally into excreta. There is only transformation. The object is still there. There is no change for *Brahman* (the Absolute), but there is change for the world. *Brahman* alone is the Truth; the world is illusory. To understand *Maya* (illusion) or *Brahman* (the Absolute) is very difficult.

Young man: Mother, is not Kurukshetra[59] only found within us, or is it outside also?

Mother: The battlefield of Kurukshetra is there both outside and inside. Symbolically, it is the constant war which is fought within each one of us between righteousness and unrighteousness, vice and virtue, untruth and truth, evil and good, the demons and God. We cannot deny the fact that this Kurukshetra battle was also an historical truth. If you simply interpret everything symbolically, all these happenings which occured long ago will lose their splendour and significance. People will become egoistic and arrogant thinking "O everything is inside, then why and whom should I fear?" It must not be interpreted in that way. Rama, Krishna, Buddha and Christ were all historical personalities who each led a life that was perfect in every way, setting an example for the entire human race. You cannot simply say that Dvaraka (a city where Sri Krishna was living) is the *Sahasradala Padma* (the thousand-petalled lotus chakra in

[59]The battlefield where the Pandava and the Kaurava armies arrayed and fought the Mahabharata War.

the head) and that Krishna is the Supreme Power who dwells within. These and similar esoteric interpretations are foolishness. Suppose that after a hundred year a grandfather tells his grandchild, "Child, you know what Mahatma Gandhi did? He fought against the British without any weapons. His weapons were truth and non-violence. He stood smilingly in front of the machine guns of the British without thought of revenge or enmity. Indians arrayed behind him and obeyed his words with utter submission. Even when he was shot dead, he didn't cry but uttered the name of Lord Rama. Above all, physically he wasn't a striking personality. He always dressed like a peasant." The boy would tease his grandfather saying, "Grandpa, that was a beautiful story even though it is a fabricated one." Later, somebody else may say that Gandhiji is an inner state. Children, it is foolish to interpret things like this.

Young man: Mother, is there life after death?

Mother: Yes, there is. During our life time, all our thoughts and actions will be recorded by a subtle sheath which functions like a tape recorder. According to the impressions gathered during one's life time, the *jiva* (individual soul) will take another body during which the recorded impressions will be replayed. Children, we can see some people very talented in music, mathematics or in science since birth, even though they haven't undergone any special training in those particular fields. Neither their parents nor any of their family members or ancestors will have been a musician or a mathematician or scientist, but this particular boy or girl will manifest these qualities even from a very young age. This is where we have to agree with certain mysteries connected with our past birth. Anyhow, it is difficult to convince everyone about these things, but even so, it still remains a fact.

DETERMINATION TO REACH THE GOAL

Young man: Mother, what is to be done to attain the goal?
Mother: Be intent on the goal. To be first in the class is the aim of a student who studies for a degree in engineering. He won't go to movies. He won't waste time making friends or spend too much time with them. Even while traveling, he will study while sitting in the bus. Circumstances will not obstruct one who is intent on reaching his goal. If the intense desire to reach the goal should arise in a person, he must have discrimination of what is proper and what is improper. He should have the awareness, "How meaningless are the things of the world." Bliss is not in all those things. If we want to have peace, Truth should be enquired into. Mother doesn't tell her children to worship God or to worship Mother, but she says to know "who you are."

Worldly relationships are like the relationships at the bus stop. All will get down at some stop. You alone will remain. Therefore, what Mother says is to search for the Truth without getting engrossed in dreams.

15 October 1983

It was the day of *"Pujayeduppu,"* part of the *Navaratri* festival. At six-thirty a.m. many children were already present. Many parents brought their children for initiating them into learning the first letters of the alphabet. As a concluding ceremony to the worship, all ~ irrespective of age ~ are asked to sit before the Goddess Saraswati. Considering themselves as beginners, they pray to Her to shower Her grace upon themas they trace the first letters of the alphabet in a tray of rice or sand. The Holy Mother made all present write each

of the syllables in the sand and asked them to respond as
she herself repeated each one s in a loud voice. It was truly a
blissful time, and everyone was overwhelmed with joy.
Women, men, elderly people and children all gathered together, and all were initiated into learning by the Holy
Mother.

All of a sudden, a young man ~ a medical student from
the northern part of Kerala, who was only twenty-five or so ~
started crying, laughing, dancing and rolling on the ground.
It was the first time he had come to visit the Mother. He
called out, "O Goddess, O Saraswati, O Amma Saraswati,
here is your child, teach me, teach me, O Saraswati!" The
Holy Mother smilingly went near him, caressed his forehead
and chest, and said, "Calm down, child, calm down,
Mother is here." In a few seconds he became normal. He
stood up and seeing Mother standing in front of him, prostrated at her feet with tears of joy in his eyes.

Later, when asked, in a voice choked with emotion the
youth related, "I was gazing at Mother's face as I wrote the
syllables as instructed by her. All of a sudden, even while
my eyes were wide open, the Holy Mother's form transformed into that of Goddess Saraswati seated on a beautiful
white lotus holding a *vina*, the*Vedas* and a rosary in Her
four hands. She was dressed in pure white. But I could easily recognise Her face because it was the Holy Mother's enchanting countenance. Tremendous light was emanating
from all over Her body as if a thousand suns had risen up
together. I could not control the bliss which I experienced. I
became totally oblivious of the surroundings." Before he
could finish the sentence he again burst into tears.

By this time the *bhajan* started with all accompaniments.
The Holy Mother sang:

O Kali, the Holy Consort of Lord Shiva,
Parvati, Sankari, my only refuge is
Thy beautiful Lotus Feet.

Hail, hail to the Goddess of Knowledge,
Hail to the Mother of the Universe,
Hail to the Mother who bestows
Auspiciousness on Her devotees.

Victory, victory to the Goddess of Sound
Who holds the vina in Her hands,
Victory, victory to the Goddess of Speech
Who is the Ruler of the Universe.

O Lalita, the Power contained
In the seed letters,
The Embodiment of Knowledge and
The Liberator of the Universe, I humbly
Bow down to Thee praying for Thy Grace...

The singing lasted for two hours but the time passed like
five or ten minutes; such was the bliss radiated by the Holy
Mother.

17 October 1983

The Holy Mother was sitting in the front verandah of
the meditation hall facing east. Many devotees were sitting
on the steps as well as on the ground. Now and then a few
of the residents came to seek the Mother's opinion on certain matters concerning the administration of the *Ashram.*
Some others came with questions so as to find a way to
come near the Mother and hear a word or two from her.

One devotee: Mother, how could you attract these children when they were still very young?

Mother: I haven't attracted anyone. On the contrary, they were attracted by something in this crazy girl. It is their *samskara* (latent tendencies) which brought them here. Anyhow, it is better to turn to spirituality when you are young. The more you live in this world, the more will be the worldly experience and *vasanas* (resultant habits). Each experience is an addition to the already existing one. It will become more and more dense. A tender stick can be easily bent but a dry one will break if you try to bend it. Training young people is easy because they have comparatively fewer conceptions and ideas about life in their mind; whereas, others have many ideas about life and most of them are misconceptions. Still they cling to their ideas strongly, believing that they are right. However, the case is different if they have self-surrender and devotion.

Son, attraction is the nature of a magnet. In reality it doesn't attract anything, but iron filings get attracted to it by its mere presence. The magnet simply is.

Devotee: Mother, how is it possible for you to behave equally towards all?

Mother: Children, a spiritual person is not seeing the external appearance but only the Essence or God. When he sees a rock, the sculptor beholds not the rock, but the beautiful statue which he can carve from it. A *sadhak* should see only God, which is the Essence in everything. Only then will equanimity *(samatva bhavana)* come. The electricity which comes through a fan, bulb or refrigerator is one and the same. The difference is only in the medium. It is the same Consciousness which dwells in all living beings. We will not feel hatred or anger towards anyone when we think that the

Consciousness which dwells in him is the same as that which dwells in us.

SCRIPTURES ARE BILLBOARDS

Devotee: Mother, can one attain the goal through scriptural studies?

Mother: Son, suppose there is a billboard on the roadside saying that there is a jewelry shop in a certain place. You won't get gold if you ask the billboard for it, will you? If you want gold you must go to the jewelry shop. Scriptures are like billboards. They are pointers. They point out the goal. That is the only use for them.

We cannot get coconuts from the picture of a coconut tree. Scriptures are like the picture. Having drawn the blueprint of a house, we cannot possibly live in it. We have to build a house according to the plan, only then can we live in it. Scriptures are like the blueprint. We ourselves have to work and attain the goal.

One *brahmacharin* was making scrawlings in the sand with his fingers. The Holy Mother noticed it.

Mother: Children, don't move your legs and hands unnecessarily. Movement shows the vacillation of your mind. Wherever you sit, sit with concentration, without moving your hands and legs unnecessarily.

A devotee just arrived to offer *dakshina*[60] to the Holy Mother. The Mother declined to accept it. When the devotee insisted, Mother said, "Mother has not given *dakshina* to

---

[60] A gift to a revered person like a preceptor in connection with an auspicious occasion.

anyone. Then how could Mother accept it? Mother has neither a Guru nor disciples."

GURU BHAKTI

A householder: Mother, some people say that a Guru is
not necessary. Is that correct?

Mother: Consecration is not needed for a *svayambhu linga*
(a self-manifest object of worship). Discipline under a Guru
is not necessary for those who are perfect from birth. Even
such people might accept a Guru in order to set an example.
Sri Krishna studied in a *gurukula* (a *Guru's* residence), didn't
he? Whereas, those who haven't attained perfection need a
Guru. Is it proper to say that only for *Atma Vidya* (Self-
Knowledge) one doesn't need a Guru when a Guru is
needed for all other arts? He who says that a Guru is not
necessary is an egoistic person who is not ready to bow his
head down in front of another. He will not make any
progress unless he serves a *satguru* who will help him remove his ego.

Suppose someone wants to learn carpentry. First he
must find a master carpenter. Then he must listen with patience and attention to the carpenter. After that, he must reflect on all that has been learned and try to assimilate it.
Then follows the practical application of that by making a
door, table or window. The same is the case with spirituality. The *Guru's* words must be listened to with great attention and devotion. Next comes discriminative reflection, followed by application of the teachings in one's own life.
Without a Perfect Master and His Grace, Realization is most
difficult.

The Guru will test the disciple in different ways. Only
one who is endowed with strong determination can with-

stand all those tests and proceed on the spiritual path. But once those tests are passed, then the infinite Grace of the Guru will flow towards the disciple unimpeded.

There was once a Self-Realized Guru who had a single disciple. One day, the Guru summoned the disciple and told him to sculpt an image of the disciple's Beloved Deity, Sri Krishna. Seeing that it was his *Guru's* wish, he made the statue applying all of his skill and talent. On seeing it, the Guru smashed it to pieces and said, "What is this? How ugly! Make another one." The disciple patiently and silently obeyed his *Guru's* words and made another statue with even more care.

This time the Guru severely scolded him saying, "You are not sincere and do not obey my words. This image is even worse than the first one. Make another one." He smashed the beautiful idol of Krishna which the disciple had made for the second time.

The disciple made nine statues, all of which met with the same fate. Yet, he accepted the *Guru's* words and actions submissively without getting impatient or angry. Only he felt sad that he could not please his Guru. Finally, when he brought the tenth statue, his Guru hugged him with over-flowing love and said, "Now you are fit enough." Upon say-ing this, he touched the disciple on the forehead. Immedi-ately, the disciple experienced the ecstasy of *samadhi*. By his *Guru's* Grace he was able to sustain that high experience.

Children, there is nothing that the Guru cannot give. The Guru is Supreme Consciousness Itself. Selfless service and utter dedication are the two things which make one fit to receive the *Guru's* Grace.

After staying in the *Ashram* during the *Navaratri puja* and performing his spiritual practices in the presence of the

Holy Mother, a devotee from Kottayam[61] came to take his leave. He saluted the Mother. While patting him on the back the Mother said,

Mother: Son, go happily and return. Mother is always near you. You have stayed here for many days. Even after going home, reflect on the memory of this experience. Remember the Divine Mother while walking, sitting or working.

Devotee: Mother, please give me some instructions.

Mother: You should get up early in the morning. Having washed your face, hands and legs, do *japa* for some time. Then, after finishing your nature calls and bath, chant the *Lalitasahasranam*. Don't chant it for namesake. Do it sincerely and with devotion. Visualise the enchanting form of the Divine Mother standing in front of you and offer flowers at Her Feet. It is enough to offer mental flowers if actual flowers are not available. Son, if you find it difficult to visualise the full form of the Divine Mother, try at least to see Her Feet. Meditate for a few minutes when the chanting of the *Sahasranama* is over. Try to repeat your *mantra* even while at work. You should sing *bhajans* at dusk. Control your food and sleep. Meditate for some time every day.

The Holy Mother took the rosary which the devotee was wearing on his neck. The Mother meditated for some time keeping the rosary in her hands. Putting it back on the devotee's neck the Mother said,

Mother: Chant your Beloved Deity's *mantra* on this rosary. Avoid mingling with people too much. Speak softly and behave sweetly towards your wife and children. If they are not

---

[61]A town which is about 65 kilometres away from Vallickavu.

interested in spiritual practice, slowly try to make them understand the importance of it and try to make them
participate in the practices that you are following. When you
return home after work, talk moderately only about absolutely necessary things. Entering the puja room, do japa
sitting there.

22 October 1983

A beautiful morning dawned, the rising sun's soft rays
filtering through the coconut trees and the leaves of the
mailanchi plant which grew in front of the temple. This dif-
fused light along with the gentle breeze produced a wonderful soothing effect. The chirping of the birds and above all
the reverberating sound of the ocean waves made the whole
Ashram atmosphere more lovely and graceful.

The Holy Mother was sitting on the front verandah of
the old temple with a group of educated young men. Cheerful as ever, the Mother's countenance was lit up with a
bright smile.

One young man: Mother, we simply wanted to see you and
therefore we came. But when I saw you I was inspired to ask
something. May I ask?
Mother: A question? To this crazy one? (Mother laughs and
after a pause) Yes, yes, you can, son.
Young man: Mother, some say that this world is total chaos
and confusion. Some others say there is a harmony beyond
all these seeming diversities. What is your opinion about
this?
Mother: Son, these are two different points of view derived
from two different levels. Those who run after the external

world will always experience nothing but chaos and confusion. Whereas those who go deeper and enquire into its real
nature, will certainly find that there is only harmony and
oneness and no diversity at all. Children, everything depends on the mind. If the mind is well balanced, you can
experience peace and tranquillity everywhere in the world,
but if it is agitated, the world will seem agitated. When we
are on the earth we can see many things ~ houses, trees,
huge buildings, forests, animals, different kinds of people...
But when we are traveling in an airplane, flying very high,
there is nothing; everything is one, a whole. Son, now there
are many thoughts in the mind accumulated from different
experiences of life. When there are so many thoughts, we
will not get any peace of mind, wherever we are or whatever
we have. When there are fewer thoughts, we can find peace,
even if we are not provided with any comforts or proper fa-
cilities. Those who lessen the thoughts through practice can
find peace, irrespective of place and time. For them, the so-
called world of chaos and confusion becomes an abode of
peace and harmony. For others it remains as a hell forever.
All spiritual practices are methods to decrease the thoughts
and to increase peace. By doing *sadhana* , slowly man can
become God. When one has reached this state, not only
does one enjoy peace oneself, but one can give peace to others as well.

The Mother suddenly stopped and turning to one of the
boys who was carelessly looking here and there said, "Son,
stop fighting with your parents." One could easily see the
visible shock that the boy had as soon as the Holy Mother
uttered these words. His face turned pale. Hanging his head,
the boy sat silently for a few moments. The Holy Mother,

who was smilingly watching the boy, now burst into laughter and asked, "Did Mother scare you, son?"

The young man, who still had an amazed look on his face, asked Mother in a soft voice, "No, but how did Mother come to know that? Even my close friends do not know this. Did anyone tell this to you?" The Mother patted his back and said, "No, Mother was simply joking, don't worry." The young man in a firm voice said, "No, Mother it wasn't a joke. What you said is true. I always fight with my parents. I am not at all hesitant to admit this right in front of my friends and Mother. Almost all the time it is my ego which makes me quarrel with them. I argue with them because they will not give me money for my lavish way of living."

The Mother lovingly asked, "Is that proper, son?" Now he could not control his emotions. His eyes were filled with tears. In a broken voice he said: "No, Mother, I know it's not. I was never aware of the fact that an unseen person is always watching me. Now this is clear, Mother. I won't repeat it. I promise in front of you." The other young men were silently watching the whole scene with wonder. Tears rolled down the young man's cheeks. The Mother consoled him saying,

Mother: Son, don't be sad. This remorse is itself the best redress for the mistakes that you have committed. The errors committed when we were ignorant will be forgiven by God. But once you become aware that they are mistakes, from then and there onwards try your best to refrain from doing them. Stop brooding. Forget about the bad actions that you have committed in the past. Once you take refuge in God and refrain from bad actions, they become like a cancelled cheques.

The young man gazed at the Holy Mother's face and again asked surprisingly, "Still, I am wondering about how Mother came to know all these things." The Mother just smiled, looked at him and upturned the palm of her hands (a gesture which means "who knows?").

At this time a householder devotee came with his family and prostrated to the Holy Mother. This was their first visit to the Ashram. Mother asked them to sit on the verandah.

Mother: Children, have you eaten anything?
Devotee: Yes, we had breakfast.
Mother: Children, you know *bhajans,* don't you? Please sing some songs.

The devotee, his wife and children looked at each other in amazement. They were wondering how Mother came to know that they sang *bhajans.*

Mother: (Loudly) Oh, my son Sree, bring the harmonium.

Sreekumar came with the harmonium. The devotee and his family sang togetherin praise of Krishna:

> Nandalala navanita chora natavaralala gopala
> Devaki vasudeva kumara deva deva gopala
> Mohana murali gana vilola
> Mohana venu gopala

Mother: (In great joy) Sing, sing!

They again sang:

He nandala gopal
Shyama gopal venu gopala
He nandalal...
Giridhara gopala radhe gopala
Shyama gopal venu gopala

Mother: (In a begging tone) One more, please!

The devotee and his family sang:

Nanda ananda krishna sundara gopala
Ananda govinda gopi gopala
He madhava He keshava
Manamohana krishna jagadiswara

The Holy Mother was very happy. She enquired about the devotee's children's education and their general welfare. The Mother drew very close, as if she had known them long ago, saying, "Children, come on, let us go to the seashore."

The Mother took them to the seashore. There was a stump set deep on the seaside. Only about one foot of the stump was visible from the ground level. Pointing to the stump, the Holy Mother said: "Formerly it was sitting here that Mother used to meditate."

The Holy Mother with the devotees went very close to the ocean waves. A giant wave suddenly rose up and broke on the shore. Like a small child, the Holy Mother laughed and called out "*Shivo, Shivo!*" Looking at the sea, the Mother said: "Where it is not deep there are waves and agitations. The deep sea is calm."

The Mother with her index finger wrote in the sand, "Mother Sea". When the waves rolled up and washed it away, the Mother, like an innocent child laughed aloud.

It was lunch time when they returned to the *Ashram*. The Mother herself served food to the devotees and fed each one with a ball of rice with her own hand like a real Mother and her children.

After lunch the Holy Mother went to her hut. Some of the devotees conversed with the residents and others began reading spiritual books. Some of them sat in the coconut grove and sang *bhajans*.

It was dusk when the Holy Mother came out for the usual evening *bhajan* at six-thirty. The Mother sang:

> O Mother, even though Thou art near
> I am wandering unable to know Thee.
> Even though I have eyes,
> I am searching unable to see Thee.
>
> Art Thou the beautiful moon
> That blooms forth in the blue winter night?
> I am a wave that, unable to reach the sky,
> Beats its head against the shore...

Such is the despair of the limited individual selves who wish to attain the Unlimited. Knowingly or unknowingly, they search for that Supreme Goal, but like the waves, they fall down again and again, unable to reach the heights of Self-Realization. This search which began aeons ago, continues until death, only to begin once again.

23 October 1983

When the Mother came out of her hut at ten o'clock in the morning, she was dressed in pure white, wearing ash on the forehead and ornaments made of *rudraksha* on her ears,

hands and neck. The Mother smilingly received her devotees.

Her nose ring shone in the sun's rays, making her be-
nign smile even more beautiful. The Mother walked towards
the coconut grove and sat in a shady place. All the devotees,
having offered their prostrations, sat in front of the Mother.

The Holy Mother became absorbed in deep meditation.
Some of the devotees also sat in contemplation while others
gazed at the Holy Mother's form. Now and then the Mother
showed different *mudras* (divine gestures) with her hands
and blissfully smiled as if she was beholding something
beautiful. When the Mother came out of meditation, a
woman from a nearby house approached her and began
explaining her woeful story. She talked to the Mother as if
to a friend or neighbor. It was quite obvious that her understanding about the Mother was poor. As there were many
people sitting around, the woman quit the place without
spending much time near the Mother. When she had gone,
the Holy Mother said,

Mother: People go to see doctors when they are afflicted by
some disease. One should go to spiritual centres when the
mind gets sick. There one will get mental peace. But, usually
they won't feel like going. They simply suffer. God is waiting
to help. But there is nobody to receive the help.

Look, haven't you seen that woman? During *Krishna*
and *Devi Bhavas* she will come and tell everything to *Bhagavan* and *Devi*. She thinks that Mother doesn't remember any
of those things afterwards. Then again she will come like
this and tell many other things but only things concerning
herself and her small family. What a pity! All are living in a
little world made of their own dreams. (Mother laughs) No

matter how much sorrow comes, these people won't properly turn towards God.
Devotee: Why is that so, Mother?
Mother: What Mother would say is that it is due to *karma
phala* (fruits of past actions). That is how *vasanas* control
people. They lack *sraddha* (care or heedfulness) and will not
do what is necessary even if somebody tells them to. It is all
a result of their previous birth.

The Mother noticed one *brahmacharin* going to do
something else during the hour of meditation. When
Mother questioned him, he gave certain lame excuses.

Mother: (To the *brahmacharin*) Children, when we set a
disciplined routine, we must follow it regularly and without
fail. Punctuality in following one's discipline is most necessary. A person who has picked up the habit of drinking tea
every day at a fixed time will get a headache if he doesn't
drink it for one day at that particular time. This is the nature
of habit. You children should feel that kind of longing if you
fail to perform your practice one day. That will show your
intensity and *sraddha* to reach the goal.

The *brahmacharin* returned to the meditation hall. The
Mother says that one should not get up even for nature calls
during meditation.

Mother: A *sadhak* should have forbearance and endurance.
Nothing should move him. Before meditation, you should
tell your mind, "Whatever may happen, I will get up from
here only after the pre-determined hour of meditation is
over."

The crows made a big noise cawing while perching on the trees and flying haphazardly in the sky. It seemed that they had seen some food somewhere and were fighting for it. On the other side of the backwaters the fisherwomen were beating coconut husks. That sound mixed with the cawing of the crows echoed in the atmosphere.

Woman devotee: Mother, what is our path?

Mother: You children are householders. You should look after your children, husband and home. But all the time chant the Divine Name. Chant your *mantra* while doing any work. Both spirituality and worldly life should be carried on simultaneously. Let your world be firmly fixed on spiritual foundations.

Daughter, haven't you seen a person feeding ducks while guiding them through the backwaters? He will be standing in a small canoe. There will not be even enough space in the boat for him to stand properly. If the ducks happen to stray, he will guide them in the correct direction, making noise by splashing the oar in the water. All the time he will be rowing the boat as well as smoking a cigarette. If water happens to enter into the boat through any hole he will bail it out. He will also talk to someone who is standing on the shore. But even while doing all these things, his mind will be fully concentrated on the balance of the boat. If his attention is distracted even for a moment, he will lose his balance and fall into the water. This is how you have to live in this world. Whatever you are doing, your mind should be fixed on God. This is possible through practice.

Whatever they are,it is better to tell your sorrows to God rather than to your husband. You should pray like this, "O God, please give peace of mind to my husband. Please bless my children." In this way, do everything thinking of God. Usually women think only about their family. They should be a little more broad-minded. Remember that all are God's children. If thorns are lying in front of our house, we will remove them. Why do we do so? To avoid pricking the foot. To avoid falling down we remove a banana peel from the house or yard. In the same way, we should remove it if it is lying on the public path or road. Think of all as our children or as God's children. Our attitude should be that no one should fall, even a person who, out of his ignorance, angrily jumps forward thinking egoistically, "I am everything." Don't think, "Are they not somebody else's children? Let them fall, why should I care about them?" Our mental attitude should be, "O God, let even the ego centered person be able to pass by without falling down."

First of all, our neighbors should be good. Is it possible for us to sit quietly in our house if a quarrel takes place in the next house? Can concentration be gained for meditation if some thorns are lying around? You will go on thinking restlessly, "Oh, it will pierce someone's foot. That will hurt." Or if there are bad thoughts in the surroundings, they will adversely affect us. Concentration will be lost. Therefore we should pray like this, "O God, make everyone virtuous. It is because of their *samskaras* (mental tendencies) that they are saying and acting like this. O God, give your light to all, pardoning everyone." Always chant your *mantra*. Whomever you meet, don't forget to chant your *mantra*.

Daughter, don't waste time talking about worldly things. Life will be wasted if you cling to worldly things forever. Suppose you live eighty or so years in this world. Why should you spend your entire lifetime only desiring, enjoying and thinking about worldly pleasures? Can't you think

about and turn to a higher way of living once you understand the momentary nature of these worldly objects? Otherwise, it is foolishness and one leads nothing more than a
pig's life. The family man's mind stays in the world, with
worldly thoughts gnawing away at his vitals. Even then, ways
to save himself are not wanting.

Woman devotee: Why do you say like that, Mother?

Mother: Remembrance of God is like a*vettuchembu.*[62] Do
you know what is unique about the *vettuchembu?* In most
plants once the seedling decays in the root it won't sprout
again; whereas, this is not the case with the *vettuchembu.* No
matter how much it decays, if there is even a little bit of
green somewhere, the shoot will come from there. Similar is
the case with the remembrance of God. Suppose that the remembrance of God has entered into our mind at some time
or other. It doesn't matter how much the mind is spoiled or
how long it has remained under evil influences. When spiritual awareness dawns, that former thought of God will
spring up and sprout. This is the special feature of Godly
thoughts. So, we don't have to be afraid now, do we?

Nothing will happen if you simply sit feeling happy
about life. If you want spiritual progress, intense *vairagya*
(detachment) and *sadhana* are needed. It is laziness to think
that everything will turn out well without any effort. This
tamas (inertia) is a great obstacle.

From the very beginning you should move with care.
Suppose we are sowing some seeds. After they sprout, we
spread thorns around that particular area. Why? To protect
the seeds from getting destroyed by hens and human beings.
In the beginning it is dangerous because the thorns might
pierce people's feet, but will the seeds sprout if you think in

---

[62]The root of a kind of tuber plant.

this way and do not spread the thorns? In the beginning thorns should be strewn in order to protect and help the seeds to sprout and grow. In the beginning stages the *sadhak* should protect himself from evil influences to help his spiritual progress. For that, *yama* and *niyama* (the do's and don'ts of yogic discipline) are necessary. Whoever comes your way, don't mingle too much with them. The seed of devotion will not sprout if you gossip and cling to your worldly manners in order to please everyone. All that will be trampled and destroyed by relatives and friends. Don't pay heed to their hatred. They cannot save us. They can only harm us. *Bhagavan* (the Lord) alone is the Savior. Therefore, whatever happens, hold on tightly to God.

We will lose the certificate from God if we act wanting or expecting a good certificate from the relatives. Those who remember God alone are our real relatives. Only those who help us towards that goal become our near and dear ones. Others are destroyers. When such people come, tell them, "You have your own path. My path is another one. Please don't feel angry. I take this as the correct path. I must be like this now."

When milk is set for curdling it should be kept still. Only in that way will it become curd. In the beginning *sadhana* in solitude is necessary. After the seed is sown, care should be taken to prevent the hens from pecking or scratching it. Once it germinates and grows up, there is no problem. In the beginning, don't mingle too much with everyone. Women householder devotees should particularly be careful about this. Sitting alone you should do *japa, dhyana* and sing *kirtans* without wasting time talking unnecessarily with the neighbors.

Woman devotee: Mother, what if they come to quarrel with us saying that we are having enmity with them?

Mother: Daughter, try to make them understand the matter. They will listen if they care. Otherwise, don't bother with them. We shouldn't have hatred towards anyone. Tell those who are about to develop ill feelings, "Look, it is not be-cause of any bad feelings that I am saying this. It is after how many births that we get this human birth? The aim of human birth is God-Realization. Forgetting the goal, we have passed our time thinking that this body is eternal. Now that awareness has dawned, why should we commit mistakes again? Why should we talk ill of others and find fault with them? What is the use of it? We can chant the Divine Name instead, can't we?"

Children, we spoil our lives thinking of our near and dear ones like husband, children and relatives. Are the so-called children our children? Where were they before birth? Whose children were they then? Whose children are they when they die? We say that the children are ours. If that is so, can we stop them from going when death comes? It is certain that they are not our children. All are His children, the Lord's children. It is He who gives life and takes it. He alone is the real owner of the *jiva* (individual soul). Chil-dren, what foolishness it is to think of them as ours! We say that husband is ours. Is he our husband? If so, we must be able to seize and detain him when death comes, mustn't we? If that is not possible, how can we say that he is "our" hus-band? How can a thing which is not under our control be ours? Therefore, the husband is not ours. Everything is owned by Him. See and behold only the Essence in others. It is not the cashew fruit but the nut that we need. The fruit will get rotten after two days, but the nut won't decay. It is not the husband's body but the soul that we should see. Not only the bodies but the spirits should be united as well.

Thinking and contemplating thus, let us move forward surrendering everything to Him. You should give good advice
to your friends and relatives. Even then, if they become envi-
ous, don't pay any attention.

We should direct all our attention to God discarding everything else. When our child is sick, we will run to the hospital to see the doctor and obtain medicine. On the way
while you are running, one after another people will ask
you, "Where are you going? Where are you going?" You will
say, "No time now." There is no time to stop on the road
and give the answer because you will miss the bus and won't
be able to see the doctor. Thus, ignoring everything else, we
should go towards God. When you sit somewhere doing
nothing, try to tell stories of the Lord instead of indulging in
gossip and finding fault with others.

The woman devotee was very happy and seemed quite
convinced. It was a moment filled with grace. All the devotees bathed in the Holy Mother's nectar-like words. It
seemed as if none had even taken time to breathe. Everyone
sat motionless like statues, as they listened to the great
truths which the Holy Mother expounded in such simple
and lucid terms. She made these truths alive and under-
standable through examples taken from daily life. Her words
went directly into the hearts of the devotees. Only if the
Mother finds that the listeners are inquisitive does she give
such long talks. Such occasions are rare. Sometimes when
people are not interested in spiritual matters but ask questions just for the sake of asking, and the Mother will not
even open her mouth. To put it in the Mother's own words,

Mother: No matter how much I try I cannot even utter a
single word to them. I will just get up and leave. Mother

cannot talk or show love artificially. For this, a feeling must spring forth from within. Everything depends on the children's character. Mother doesn't have any particular feeling towards anyone. But unknowingly, Mother will feel a closeness to innocent-hearted people. Even if they are atheists or rationalists, Mother will answer the questions of those who are truly eager to know.

But the case is different when people who are eager to know ask questions even if they are atheists or rationalists.

Woman Devotee: We heard that Mother couldn't sleep last night due to some reason.
Mother: (Joyfully laughing) Yes, yes, that son's call. Oh, what an innocent call it was! Eventually that son slept thinking and thinking of Mother. From wherever children call, Mother will hear it.

The devotees did not understand anything about the son who Mother mentioned ~ who he was or why he called so loudly, disturbing Mother's sleep. It was quite obvious from their faces that they were very curious to hear about it. Balu, who was sitting near Mother, solved the puzzle.

Balu: It is true that Mother couldn't sleep last night. She was so restless and all of a sudden she said in a loud voice, "Son, don't do it, Mother is here for you." It was not until five in the morning that she slept peacefully but only for an hour. We were a bit worried about Mother's mood. It remained a mystery to us as well (pointing to a young man who sat in the back of the hut shedding copious tears) until he came here today at seven in the morning. I told you that

Mother slept for an hour. All of a sudden, she got up at six, came out of her hut at six-thirty and sat outside in the sand as if waiting for someone to come. When it was five minutes to seven this young man hastily arrived at the Ashram. It was obvious that he had neither slept nor changed his clothes. Seeing Mother sitting in front of the hut, he went running to her and fell at her feet bursting into tears. The Holy Mother, with overflowing motherly affection, held him and slowly lifted him up. She wiped his tears with her own cloth and lovingly said: "Son, Mother knew that you were coming. I was waiting for you. Mother came to you last night." Hearing this, the young man again burst into tears. The Mother consoled him and talked to him for an hour and returned to her hut.

Even though the Holy Mother got up and went away, all the devotees were very curious to know about the rest of the happenings, and so to satisfy them the young man, Babu, said,

Babu: I was working as an engineer and had visited Mother a few times. I had strong faith in her. I received my engineering degree three months ago and fortunately got employed without much delay. I was in love with a young girl who was a medical student. Both of us promised to marry each other soon after the girl's college courses were over and after I was employed, even if our parents protested. Although my love for her was pure and sincere, the girl's attitude was not so. Two days ago she was married to someone else, and I had a nervous breakdown. For the last two days I have been wandering here and there as one gone mad. Last night I cried and cried, calling out to the Mother from behind the closed doors of my room. Finally I decided to commit suicide. I took the thirty sleeping pills, which I purchased the previous day and was about to swallow them. Then all of a sudden I saw the Holy Mother entering the room with outstretched arms. The door was remained closed, and so I was amazed to see the Mother entering the room in flesh and blood. As she came in, the Mother called lovingly, "My son, don't do it! Mother is here for you." She approached me and took the pills from my hand, opened the window and threw them outside. Then she said, "Don't act like a fool. You are Mother's son. Come to Vallickavu." After saying this, she disappeared. I couldn't even utter a word. I stood tongue-tied. Was it a dream or reality? I looked at the open window. It had been closed before. Still not convinced, I went out and searched for the pills outside the window and was struck with wonder to find them lying there scattered around. I had no more doubt. This happened at four-thirty in the morning. Immediately I started for Vallickavu.

Babu paused for awhile and looked at the devotees. All of them were sitting motionless like wooden statues. With a joyful smile on his face, Babu said, "Now, I hope that whole matter is clear."

It was *Bhava Darshan* day. At four-thirty in the afternoon the devotional singing started. The divine mood began at seven. Hundreds of people were present and *darshan* went on until four in the morning. The Holy Mother finally went to her hut at five o'clock after all the devotees had left.

24 October 1983

The Mother was sitting under a tree in the coconut grove which situated in the front yard of the *Ashram*. It was

about ten-thirty in the morning. Though the sun's rays were
becoming more and more intense, the shade of the trees was
there to give protection from the heat, just as the loving
guidance and help of a *Satguru* is a devotee's protection from
the scorching heat of worldliness.

Three youths who were interested in spiritual and religious matters came to see the Holy Mother. They were
sitting in front of her. On the southern side of the Ashram,
across the backwaters the people who were beating coconut
husks were quarreling with each other. It created a lot of
noise in the Ashram premises. Slowly it died down. Then
only the sound of the beating of the husks remained.

THE HINDU FAITH AND
'I', THE SUPREME PRINCIPLE

A young man: Mother, why is Hinduism so liberal and
lacking in organization?
Mother: Son, the preceptors of old presented the *Sanatana
Dharma* (eternal religion, another nane for Hinduism) not as
a narrow religion constrained to a particular caste, creed or
sect, but rather as open to anyone and everyone. All are welcome on this path. It is everyone's. Just like a compassionate
and loving mother, the *Sanatana Dharma* discards none.
This faith declares that anyone, whatever be his or her mental constitution or path, can attain God through constant
practice.

Religion should be able to satisfy everyone equally without any distinction. Take, for example, a mother who has
ten children with ten different characters. One may be a
high-thinking spiritual person, another one a scientist.
There might be an artist among them, while another will be

doing cultivation and physical labour. There can also be a rogue or a robber among the ten children. But the mother will consider all equally. While serving food she won't serve more to the spiritualist or scientist and less to the artist or the rogue. She will be able to satisfy everyone equally while serving, talking and showing love to them. Sometimes it might even seem that she loves the rogue more and gives him little concessions. Children, True religion is like this. Whatever may be the mental constitution or level of thinking of a person, true religion must be able to satisfy him fully. This is what Hinduism does. It provides a means for all. There is the path of *bhakti* (devotion) for the emotional person, and the path of *jñana* (knowledge) for the intellectual. If someone is hard-working and is interested in doing physical labour, the path of action (*karma*) is there for him. But there are some people who think that their religion alone is the best and proclaim that Liberation is possible only through their way.

Young man: Is that correct, Mother?

Mother: No, it is not. Kollam and Quilon are one and the same, are they not? The ultimate goal of all religions is one, God. He is known by different names, that is all. Is it correct if somebody says that you can go to Delhi only via one particular road? There are many roads which will lead us to Delhi. We must be ready to accept this fact instead of fighting like dogs in the name of religion.

Young man: What if a person claims that only their path is the direct way to God and all the others are indirect?

Mother: Nobody has the right to claim so. It is utter foolishness and ignorance if somebody says that. Mother would say that such people are totally ignorant about the purpose of religion. Such statements show the inability of the so-called followers to understand the teachings and life of their masters.

We (the exponents of *Sanatana Dharma*) have not declared that one path alone is suitable to attain the goal. All will reach the same place whether sitting on a bicycle or in a boat or on an autorickshaw. Whatever vehicle we use in traveling, the destination is Quilon..

Children, no great soul will say "Only through me will you be saved." Has Sri Ramakrishna said, "Follow me alone; otherwise, there is no hope?" Has Ramana Maharshi said this? Did any of the great saints and sages of the past declare this? No. A real knower of the Self will not say this. What they teach is to move forward according to your chosen path, having firm faith in it. That is what is said by the founders of all the religions.

But after a religious leader dies, the followers interpret his teachings in a different way. Doctrines like "Have faith only in our religion" or "Only through our path" are spread by the followers who have no *visalata* (broad-mindedness). Do you know what a *Mahatma* means when he says, "Believe in me?" The "I" they talk about is not the small "I" which concerns the individual. It is that "I" which is the Supreme Principle. As far as a great soul is concerned, "In me" means "In God." Taking this and interpreting it as caste or religion, the followers think in a narrow minded way. Sri Krishna told Arjuna, "Have faith in Me," that "I" which is the Supreme Principle. But now, some Hindus say that you will get Liberation only if you believe in Krishna; some others say that Shiva alone is the Liberator. This is not correct. What we (the followers of *Sanatana Dharma*) say is, whether it is Krishna or Christ or Nabi, they all help us to attain the Supreme. Whether you come through the southern side or

northern side or from the east, you can reach the *Ashram*.
Those who say, "Only our religion is true," are mistaken.
Real *Mahatmas* will never be bound by an institution. They
will go forward keeping the Supreme Truth alone as the
ideal. Therefore, the great masters of Hinduism, who were
all Realized Souls, have not insisted on any narrow rules.
They have not formed an organization. That is why, even after many aeons, the Hindu faith still exists, its roots deeply
entrenched. It is unshakable. No force can destroy it. The
infinite power of Hinduism is derived from the *sankalpa
sakti* (strong resolve) of the great saints and seers. Children,
there is no harm in having many religions and faiths but it
is harmful to think that they are different and that one faith
is higher and another lower. Do not see the differences; see
the unity in them and the great ideals which they teach.
What all religions show is how to develop compassion, love,
faith, forbearance, endurance and renunciation. That is what
is important. Religion means expansiveness, the ability to ac-
commodate anything and everything. Religion is the merging
of mind where all differences disappear.

The second youth: It is said that *Sanatana Dharma* is the
source of all other religions and that other religions sprung
from it. Is this true, Mother?

Mother: Yes, it is true. In the beginning there was only one
religion. It was from that religion that all other religions
sprang up according to the need of the different eras. In reality, there are no differences between the religions. There is
only unity. Previously, in India there was only one political
party, the Indian National Congress. It is only recently that
the other parties came into existence. At one time there was
only the *Sanatana Dharma*.

A youth: The temple authorities in our place play movie
songs instead of devotional songs through the loud speakers.

Mother: Children, you should ask the members of the temple committee, "What is this temple for, what is the purpose of it?"

Young man: Mother, if we do so, we will be left with no one to support us.

Mother: Son, don't think like that. You should tell them without getting angry, "Dear elders, you are our fathers. We are young. We would like to ask, so we can understand certain things from you. Is it right to do this in a temple? Is this place and its atmosphere meant to develop devotion and love in the hearts of people or is it meant to increase the worldly tendencies in them? As administrators of the temple, are you not responsible for keeping the temple atmosphere pure and holy? If such music is played, what then is the difference between a movie theatre and a temple?" Tell them to play devotional songs. If you say it lovingly they will come to the right path. What a pity! Worldly songs are heard from temples. They won't even play "*Harinama kirtana*" (devotional songs) early in the morning.

Young man: If these elders go to see a vulgar film, out of pride they will say, "I am going to see such and such a film." But if it is to an Ashram or other holy place that they are going, they will simply say, "I am only going somewhere." They are ashamed to say that this is where they are going.

Mother: (Laughingly) They will go secretly. Otherwise, others will tease them. Even if you have to hear their scoldings, tell them frankly that you are going to the *Ashram*. Let them scold. Our sin will be reduced. We are taking on sin when it is told in secret. We must have the courage to tell the truth. Good character is the most important thing in life. That is the foundation on which you have to build your life. Character building is what we get from *Ashrams* and *gurukulas.* Ashamed to visit such places, we consider cheap, worldly things as something great and valuable although, in truth, they utterly spoil our lives and take away our peace of mind, leaving us in the midst of darkness. Worldly things will only increase our negativity. On the other hand, *Ashrams* and spiritual people will lead you to light and bestow peace and bring tranquillity into your life. If asked, you should frankly say, "I am going to the temple or *Ashram*. We have no peace of mind. We are going to the place from where we can get it. You cannot give us mental peace. We know that you yourself don't have peace. Then what does it matter if you tease?"

THE SOCIETY WHICH DESTROYS ITSELF

Young man: Mother, they would say that they see movies to get peace of mind.
Mother: After seeing such movies, the next step is imitating what they have seen. Many people learn to steal from watching movies. Nowadays what fist-fighting the children are doing. They are practicing after returning from the movie theatre.

A few days ago a boy, having fought with another boy, fell down unconscious over there (pointing to the next house). When asked, they said that they were trying the karate which they had seen in one movie. (All laugh)

Another thing is reading cheap novels. After reading such novels, people perform bad actions in an amateur attempt to imitate what they have read, and many evil and malicious thoughts pass through their minds which later end in harmful behaviour. Because of this, even the atmosphere becomes polluted.

In olden days there were fewer people. Therefore, the atmosphere was purer. In those days if there was one house here, the next house would be far away. In an area where previously there was only one house, now there are a thousand houses. Not only that, in the olden days there were plenty of medicinal trees everywhere. No diseases would be contracted if one breathed the air which had blown over those trees and leaves. The trees grown in those days were the *peepal* tree (banyan), the country fig and the *neem* or margosa tree. They were all *ayurvedic* herbal trees. Now, all of them have been cut down and removed. Using artificial means and fertilizers which will do harm to the body, people have started growing fruit-bearing trees, plants and vegetables which are good for eating . Using these artificial and so-called modern means, they multiply the size and yield of the roots, vegetables and other plants by two or three times of what they would normally be. This is what the people are eating. It will definitely be harmful both physically and mentally. The children born to them will also be affected. Nothing is natural nowadays for human beings are after unnatural things. They cannot act or speak naturally. Everything is unnatural. Therefore, they have lost their splendour and glory. The atmosphere has become completely impure. The population and houses have increased, the air has become polluted due to the poisonous gas produced from the factories and industries, and the health of human beings is quickly deteriorating. The only way to regain the lost natural state of both Nature and human beings is through spirituality.

SATYA NASTI PARO DHARMA
There is no dharma superior to truth

Mother: In the olden days there was only truth. All families lived a truthful lives. People of those days lived truthfully even if their lives were in danger. Even if one were a servant, he would not give up truth if somebody offered millions to him. If you catch hold of truth, everything else will come back to you. Without truth, *Lakshmi* (the Goddess of prosperity), *Bhairavi* (an aspect of Mother Durga), and even *jñana* (knowledge) cannot exist. Truth is everything. Truth is God.

In olden days everyone practiced truthfulness. The wife lived for the husband and the husband for the wife. They reaped the fruits of truthfulness and self-sacrifice. They had an all-surrendering attitude, courage, love, righteousness and justice. Without truth, there is nothing, no *dharma* or *Lakshmi*.. Even if a person's life were in danger he would tell only the truth. (Laughingly) Nowadays what lies people tell even in court, while taking an oath on the *Ramayana*, *Srimad Bhagavad Gita* or *Bhagavata*! In the past there was *bhaya bhakti* (devotion endowed with reverence and fear) to *Ramayana* and other holy texts. But now, after taking an oath on the *Ramayana* saying, "This is true, what I am going to say is the truth," the first words they utter will be a lie! (All laugh) Today the *Ramayana* is only a stack of papers.

The youths and the devotees present greatly enjoyed the Holy Mother's talk. It was quite clear that they were really amazed to hear these highly enlightening words from a seemingly simple village girl who did not even have any formal education.

Young man: I have told some of my friends about Mother. But they were not interested.

Mother: Son, when it is time, a fruit will ripen. Don't squeeze it and make it ripen too early. There are people of different natures. You shouldn't try to argue with your friends. Each one's own experience is their *pramana* (valid means of knowledge). We also might not believe it if somebody tells us their experience. When we tell our experience to others, let them accept it or not. Don't insist. Don't waste time on all this, children. If someone criticizes you for coming here, tell them, "On the basis of my faith I go there. You have nothing to do with this matter. Would it be for nothing that people go to the *Ashram,* spending money from their houses? Try to consider that there may be something valuable there. I am going to the place where I will get mental peace. What about you? You give the money that you have at hand to liquor shops and tea shops. That is your habit. You don't have time and money for beneficial things. Because of that, you suffer."

Young man: Do you send the resident *brahmacharins* to give speeches?

Mother: It is no big deal to give a speech after studying books. You should speak only after having gained experience. That which comes through experience is valid. Sometimes Mother will send one or two to give a speech. Mother did send one son to study the scriptures. But the others had not studied the scriptures at that time. Still, they have conducted speeches in many places. They have shown others that one can give good speeches even without learning the scriptures. It is possible as the result of their *sadhana* and experience.

Young man: We don't have irrevocable bonds of relations like the people of other religions, do we?

Mother: They have many problems and entanglements concerning their existence as a religion. Therefore they are forced to stand together. The *rishis* (the seers) thought not to bind the Hindu religion. Where is the end to catch hold of and tie? Who do you think can seize hold of the vast sky and tie it? Therefore, they could not bind it. It lies open. Still, the fact remains that there is no unity. Because there are no bonds it still exists without decaying. Organized religion also has its drawbacks. Look at the decline of the Buddhist faith.

Look at the people of some sects of Hinduism. They say that Liberation is possible only through their God. That is an extremely narrow attitude. They are giving speeches standing in market places and street corners as if God is for sale. They will beat you if you say that there is another God other than theirs. This is an uncivilized nature. But real Hindus will accept everything. What is there to reject? Everything is God: "I am Gayatri among mantras, Himalaya among mountains, peepul tree among trees."

Two elderly people arrived, and after prostrating to the Holy Mother, they sat among the group of devotees.

Mother: Children, where do you come from?
First man: From Trivandrum (capital city of Kerala).
Mother: Children, have you eaten anything?
First man: Yes, we have eaten earlier.
Mother: Here the lunch is at twelve thirty. All children can take food from the *Ashram*. Will you be going soon?
Second Man: We came to see and speak with Mother.
Mother: Yes, it should be for *satsang* that we go to spiritual people and spiritual centres. It is good to spend some time there. *Satsang* is the best thing for spiritual advancement.

The newcomers were spiritually inclined. It seemed that they were sadhaks. The Mother also felt some kind of closeness with them. When they were about to ask something, the Mother said, "Children, have your lunch and come. Mother will talk to you later." The Holy Mother went to her hut after taking them to the dining hall.

In the afternoon the Mother called the newcomers to her hut. Getting up from the cot, the Mother sat on the floor on a mat along with them.

First man: Mother, are all *satsangs* equally good?

Mother: Son, whichever kind it is, all *satsangs* will have at least a little benefit. The gathering together of people who think of God is good, is it not? All will be thinking of the same thing. The homogeneous nature of their thoughts will lessen unnecessary thoughts and peace will be enjoyed. But the meeting should not be for arguing and disputing, as this will only increase arrogance and ego. *Satsang* should be for meditation, singing devotional songs, contemplating and discussing scriptural ideas. It is most beneficial if you get the chance to see *Jivanmuktas* (Liberated Souls) or *Avatars* (Incarnations of God). Their presence itself will benefit us.

NIRVIKALPA SAMADHI AND AN AVATAR

Second Man: Can one come back after experiencing *Nirvikalpa Samadhi* (absorption into the Absolute)?

Mother: Children, if they are people who have descended from above, they will return after experiencing *Nirvikalpa Samadhi,* but if they are people who ascended through *sadhana.* they will not return. The latter will just go (leave their body). Having thought about a particular thing, before entering into *samadhi*, one can return to the same thought which he had before entering into that state. This is possible, but only if one does it intentionally. Only those who know how can do it. Otherwise it will just be like a kite going up in the air with a broken thread. Incarnations can come back. In fact, an Incarnation doesn't have different states like *Nirvikalpa Samadhi*, the state above and below, etc. They are always That, *Purnam* (whole). The only limitations they have are the ones which they themselves have accepted for the *avatara karma*.[63]

Both the newcomers were very happy. The one who seemed to be the oldest said, "Mother, we are very blessed to be in your presence. We are ignorant children who are still very much involved in worldly affairs. Mother, please bless us to come to you every now and then so that we can unload our burdens and regain our peace and tranquillity." The Holy Mother smilingly replied,

Mother: We ourselves have taken the burden and now we ourselves have to give it back. Mother doesn't want anything from her children except the burden of their sorrows and sufferings.

The elderly people saluted the Holy Mother and took leave of her. It was fifteen minutes past six o'clock in the evening and soon the *bhajans* began.

28 October 1983

The day passed. The sun slowly moved to the western horizon ready to dive deep into the Arabian Sea. It was five

---

[63]The activities that should be launched during that particular Incarnation.

in the evening. Some *brahmacharins* were meditating in the meditation hall and others under the trees. A few went to the seashore. The *Ashram* atmosphere was calm and quiet. All of a sudden the Holy Mother, who was usually very cheerful, was afflicted with asthma. No particular symptoms were seen before this started. This created a great amount of confusion in the *Ashram*. As each moment passed the ill-ness became worse. All were very much distressed seeing the Holy Mother struggling to breathe properly. The *brahmacha-rins* ran here and there in the hope of getting some medi-cine. Although they tried different cures, no improvement was seen. Some among the householder devotees and *brah-macharins* shed tears as they watched the Mother. Some be-gan chanting Divine Names and *mantras* for healing her sickness. As if in great pain, the Holy Mother rolled on the ground. Several hours went by like this. At ten o'clock at night the Mother drifted into a seemingly sleepy mood.

29 October 1983

This sudden attack of asthma remained a mystery until the next morning. It was only seven o'clock when a lady came to the *Ashram* from Quilon, urgently stating she wanted to see Mother. She sat outside Mother's hut waiting for her to come out. That day Mother came out before the usual time. All the residents were anxious to see whether the asthma attack of the previous night was over. The Mother was very enthusiastic and cheerful as usual, so it was quite apparent that the illness had gone. Not only that, there was no trace of the attack either on her face or in her move-ments. Everyone was very happy and amazed at the same time.

The woman devotee suddenly came forward and having saluted the Mother, stood with joined palms in front of her.

Mother: Why so early daughter? Is your sickness cured?

Hearing these words, the woman stared at the Mother's face in wonderment and as if in a dream she uttered, "Mother, you saved me yesterday. So, it was true. Now it is clear. The whole day I suffered a terrible attack of asthma. In the afternoon it became worse. Unable to bear the pain and difficulty it created in my respiratory system I cried out loud calling, "Mother!" In a few minutes the illness passed. The asthmatic trouble completely disappeared. Everyone was struck with wonder. The children in the house said that it was Vallickavu Amma who removed the illness. Then they started singing the Divine Name with great devotion. I also thought, 'Who else could remove this horrible disease except Mother.' Now I have heard it from your own mouth. I came running to see you and to offer my salutations. O Mother, I have nothing else to offer."

The woman burst into tears. The Holy Mother lovingly patted her on the back and comforted her.

Later the Mother related, "Mother could not help taking her disease when she heard that daughter's heartbreaking cry."

YOGASCHITTA VRITTI NIRODAH
Yoga is control of the modifications of the mind

The *Ashram* clock rang ten. The *brahmacharins* came out of the meditation hall after their morning meditation. One young *brahmacharin*, who had joined the *Ashram* a week ear-

lier, approached the Holy Mother who was sitting under a
coconut tree, lost in meditation. The *brahmacharin* stood a
short distance away from Mother looking at her. A few minutes passed when the Mother opened her eyes, uttering,
"Shiva, Shiva." She smiled at the boy who then came closer
to the Mother and saluted her.

Before meeting the Mother, this *brahmacharin* had been
a *nirgunopasaka* (worshipper of the Formless) even though
he had worked as a priest in a temple of the Divine Mother
Kali. He started meditating on the formless Self as instructed
to him by a scholar. Before switching his meditation to the
formless Self, he had meditated upon the fierce aspect of the
Divine Mother Kali. For a long time he had chosen that
form of Mother Kali as his Beloved Deity, but never used
that form of meditation after he started the new technique.
On his first visit to the *Ashram*, he had an informal talk
with the Mother, expressing to her his decision to join the
Ashram. Before he could mention anything about his practices, the Mother took a small picture of Mother Kali from
the coconut leaf wall and, handing it to him said, "You are
not mature enough to meditate upon the Formless. Therefore, meditate on this form of the Mother. Without love,
nothing can be gained. Your mind has become very hard.
Sprinkle the water of love and make it soft." The astounded
boy was tongue tied. He looked alternately at the small picture given by the Mother and at the Holy Mother's face. It
was the very same image of Mother Kali on which he used
to meditate. Even the size of the photograph was the same.
Still unable to control his wonder, the boy said, "Mother, I
used to..." The Holy Mother interrupted him and said,
"Yes, son, Mother knows it; you used to meditate on this
form of the Divine Mother and that is why Mother gave it to

you. Attain the *Nirguna* (attributeless) through *Saguna* (God with attributes)."

Now the boy sat near Mother and said, "Mother, I would like to know something about yoga."

Mother: Son, yoga is not something that should be told. It is some thing to be experienced. It is the yoking of *jivatma* (the individual self) and *Paramatma* (the Supreme Self). Just as you cannot explain the sweetness of honey, the bliss of that unity is inexpressible. Many talk about it but have not experienced it.

Though there are many paths, there are four main ones : *bhakti yoga, karma yoga, jnana yoga and raja yoga.* The pur-pose of all *yogas* is control of the mind, which means control of thoughts. Whatever the path, attainment of the goal is possible only if the *vasanas* are attenuated.

Do you know what these different yogas are for? Differ-ent paths are needed by different people, according to each one's nature. The doctor treats the patient according to the patient's bodily constitution. Some people are allergic to in-jections; liquid medicine will be given to them. There are some others who would vomit if liquid medicine is taken; they will be given pills. But there are some for whom even allopathic treatment is not suitable. They will be told to take *ayurvedic* medicines. The aim is to cure the patient of the disease, but the treatment can be done only according to the stamina and other conditions of the body. When the dis-ciple comes to the Guru, like a good doctor the Guru knows which path is suitable for him. For some it will be *raja yoga.,* for others it is *bhakti yoga.* Each person will be given the ap-propriate teaching according to his mental state. He will be guided on that path which suits him. For an emotionally predominant person, the Guru might advise *bhakti yoga*, instructing him to direct all his thoughts towards God. For an intellectual person the Guru may suggest the path of knowledge and ask the disciple to discriminate in order to understand the ephemeral nature of the world. The path of *raja yoga* will be given to someone who is interested in observing and analyzing the functioning of the mind. He will be asked to closely observe the mind and its tricky ways, to trace where from the thoughts originate and how to control them. A dynamic person who is hard-working in nature will be asked to follow the path of *karma* yoga, dedicating all his work at the feet of the Supreme Lord, renouncing the fruit of all actions. Thus, the path of yoga differs according to the nature and taste of the disciple. But there is one more thing: It cannot be said which path is better than another because each one is unique and great in its own way. Some people may be weak by nature, others might be hard hearted. The Guru knows how to guide all these people.

Each one has qualities inherited from the past birth. Suitable treatment is needed. If we think it over carefully, *bhakti*, *raja* and *jnana yogas* , each of which says, "I am neither the mind nor the intellect," are all types of *bhakti*.. *Bhakti* comes even when you say "I am *Brahman*." It is not possible to perform *sadhana* without devotion unto the eternal and pure *Brahman* saying "I am That." *Karma marga* (path of action) is also good. What is needed is to act, seeing everything as God and renouncing the fruit. Selflessness is the goal of spirituality. All *sadhanas* are only for achieving that. No matter how much *sadhana* you do and no matter which path, no spiritual progress will be gained if there is selfishness in the mind. It cannot be said that one path is better than the other. The path will be prescribed according to *adhikari bheda* (the qualification of the student). Different paths are suitable for different people. There is no one path which is suitable for all. In fact, the apparent differences in each of the paths do not really exist. Each path merges with the other.

The path expounded by Patanjali Maharshi is known as *raja yoga*. There is importance given to *pranayama* in this path. *Kundalini yoga* also comes under this. The vital force which sleeps in the *muladhara* (bottom of the spine) is awakened through *pranayama*. The principle of both *raja yoga* and *kundalini yoga* is subjugation of the mind. The purpose of all spiritual practices is nothing but that.

SAMATVAM YOGA UCHYATE
Yoga is Equanimity

The Mother stopped talking and started singing,

> Come, O Mother,
> Who art the Enchantress of the mind.
> Give me, O Ambika, Thy Vision.
> Let Thy Form shine.
>
> When will dawn that blessed day
> When my heart will become full of
> Devotion to Thee?
> Satiated with the repetition of Thy Name
> When will blissful tears flow
> From my eyes?

The Holy Mother went into *samadhi*. She shed tears of bliss. Regaining her external awareness, the Mother said,

Mother: Son, the taste of devotion is something unique. The purpose of *bhakti yoga* which declares, "I am nothing, everything is You," is meant for mental purification. The path of *jnana yoga* which states, "I am the Self, everything is I," is also intended to attain purity of mind. The aim of *karma yoga* in which one does selfless action seeing God in everything is also for mental purity. Through the attainment of concentration of mind, *raja yoga* also aims at this. All *yogas* aim at *samatva bhava* (attitude of equality). What is known as *yoga* is *samatva*. There is no God beyond that, whatever may be the path. That state should be attained.

(To one householder devotee) The different paths are for people endowed with different natures. Look at this son. He used to do meditation on *suddha bodha* (Pure Awareness). But understanding his nature and mental constitution, Mother asked him to meditate upon the form of Kali. This will soften his mind which has become very hard due to lack of love and devotion.

One who knows how to make paper flowers beholds flowers whenever he sees a sheet of paper. That memory comes because he has learned how to make flowers. How could this vision spring forth in a person who has not learned that art? Therefore, we should first learn. That means mental purity should be gained. For obtaining that, it is said that *bhakti* is necessary. Only those who have attained mental purity can say, "*suddha bodha.*"

However, we are not mature enough for that. The ego has not been removed. Such being our condition, there is no use in walking around speaking about *suddha bodha.* In the beginning, there must be *bhakti*. Otherwise our egos will only be inflated.

Turning again to the *brahmacharin*, the Holy Mother said, "*Bhakti* alone will help to eliminate the ego. At present that is what is needed. Nothing else is needed now. Try to call God shedding tears. Don't run after different *yogas*."

The Mother sang:

> Except through devotion,
> There is no way to get
> The Lord's Vision and to know Him..

Mother: Werner says that he likes *atma dhyana* (self-inquiry). He does *sadhana* on that. Therefore, Mother tells Werner "*Atma dhyana* is the best." He is able to do it. Mother asked him to sit and meditate and he is doing accordingly.

It is good to do *sadhana* but self-observation should also be done to see whether you have attained concentration and the strength to love everyone equally, to act selflessly and to manifest other spiritual qualities.

THE EXPANSIVE "I"

Mother: Even here there are so many distinctive natures. For each one Mother shows a different path. Mother loves all ~ those who follow any path. But Mother especially likes the path of devotion and gives the most importance to that. That is how Mother grew up. There is the expansive "I" and the narrow "I". Expansive "I" is the Pure Principle (*suddha tattvam*). It doesn't have any connection with *Maya* (illusion or Nature). The narrow "I" is the mind or *jiva* (individual soul). The mind and Creation are the result of desire. It is not correct to say all that is seen is that narrow "I". In the expansive meaning, Mother is in everything that is seen. There is no Mother who is different from this Universe.

We were talking about *yoga*. All that is explained by Mother can be known through experience if one moves forward firmly holding to any one of these paths. Nothing will happen by simply hearing about it.

One Devotee: Mother, what should be done to melt the heart with God's love?

Mother: You should call God in solitude and pray, shedding tears. The mind of one who has a wound on his body will be always on that. He will always be thinking of ways to cure it. We are afflicted with the disease of *samsara* (transmigration). We should have the desire to treat and cure it. Then the prayers will become sincere and love will fill the heart.

It was on o'clock. Having told everyone to go and have their lunch, the Holy Mother entered the temple.

31 October 1983

The Mother did not sleep or rest properly after the previous night's *Bhava Darshan*. Some of the devotees were still waiting to see the Mother and to offer their salutations before leaving. Perhaps because of their intense desire the Mother came out of her hut at eight in the morning. When they left, the Mother sat in the corner of the temple verandah, keeping her feet on the footstep. The voices of those chanting of the *Lalitasahasranama* emerged from the temple. All the brahmacharins were in meditation.

A group of people from the extreme north of Kerala arrived to see the Holy Mother. There were some scholars in the group. The Holy Mother happily said, "Come children, come and sit here."

They all stepped onto the verandah and sat there, having prostrated to the Mother and offered the fruits which they brought. The Holy Mother distributed oranges to everyone as *prasad*. After some time one of the *pandits*, who looked and acted a bit egocentric, started asking certain questions to the Mother.

Scholar: What is *moksha* (Liberation)? Is it attenuation of *vasanas* or elimination of mind?
Mother: Son, attenuation of *vasanas* and *mano nasa* (elimination of mind) are one and the same. That itself is *moksha*.
Scholar: What is the way to it?
Mother: Different people have different paths. For you it is enough if you get *bhakti*. If a balloon is inflated too much it will burst. Beauty is in humility, not in being egoistic and thinking that one knows everything. This can be attained only by sowing the seeds of *bhakti*. *Bhakti*, when fully ripened and developed, becomes the huge shady tree of *jnana*. All are waiting to get that *bhakti*. We will have succeeded if *bhakti* is attained. Hollow utterances of being a *jnani* or scholar are of no use. The picture of a cow drawn on a sheet of paper won't eat grass. Those who have experience won't say that *bhakti* and *jnana* are two. When love for God comes, that is *jnana*.

There was a sudden change in the scholar. He was genuinely humbled. He clearly understood that the Mother's words were aimed at him. His next question was full of humility and reverance.

Scholar: Mother, what is needed to get love?
Mother: Faith should come. *Vairagya* (detachment) also is needed.

Scholar: Mother, is it possible to attain *bhakti* through faith?

Mother: Yes, definitely it is. Faith and love are not two. They are interdependent. Without faith we cannot love someone and vice versa. If we have complete faith and love for someone, the mere thought of that person will give us a special joy. Do we get any joy if we have no faith in him and consider him a thief? The lover opens his heart to his beloved because he has faith in her. That faith is the foundation of love. Love springs from faith.

One devotee: Mother, does love arise through *japa*?

Mother: Through *japa*, mental purity is gained. While chanting, we are replacing other thoughts with that particular *mantra*. Just as saline water loses it's salty taste by constantly adding fresh water to it, through constant repetition of a *mantra*, the number of thoughts can be reduced. In due course, all the thoughts can be eliminated except one, and that is God. Love will spring through *japa* if one has complete faith and strong intent to reach the goal.

Devotee: What change will chanting of the Divine Name bring in us?

Mother: Son, when Divine Names are chanted sincerely and with devotion, peace of mind and tranquillity will be gained. As Mother said before, it will lessen the number of thoughts. When the thoughts are fewer, you will get more peace of mind. Tension and mental agitation are caused by the numerous thought waves which, in turn, bring forth all other kinds of negative tendencies like lust, anger, jealousy and greed. Divine Names, when chanted with one-pointedness, will enable us to accept both good and bad experiences of life as God's Will and blessing. This is not possible if your prayers are only to fulfill desires. That will only help to increase your sorrows and disappointments in life. Peace of mind is the most important thing. Without it one cannot enjoy even worldly comforts. Son, when we have the desire to be healed of a disease, we will move carefully. If medicines are taken, there occurs a change in our state of health, doesn't there? So, when we chant with concentration, thinking, "I want to be healthy and wish to be healed," there occurs a change in our character. In the same manner, all our ways will change when the mind is on God. If you read the biographies of devotees and *Mahatmas* you will understand the difference between them and other people. Look at the lives of Chaitanya Mahaprabhu and Sri Ramakrishna. You will understand what change "*Nama*" (chanting the Divine Name) can bring in us.

Scholar: Mother, while taking the medicine of *Nama* to remove the disease caused by worldly existence, is it necessary to adhere to the Guru's prescription regarding diet and other personal habits?

Mother: It is absolutely necessary. In the beginning, this is indispensable, though it is not so much needed after gaining concentration of mind. One's mode of life is very important. The character of a deer which eats grass and that of a tiger which eats meat are different, aren't they? Those who do meditation should not talk about worldly things during the period of *sadhana*. In the beginning, complete silence is needed. Silence, *sattvic* food, abstinence from worldly talk, *satsang*, regularity and discipline in doing *sadhana*, all these will come under the rules and regulations which a serious *sadhak* should observe.

You should become introspective. Speak only when it is necessary. Only an introspective person can look within. Endurance will arise when the desire to cure the illness is there. In the hospital at Vallickavu, Mother has seen people going and lining up in a queue. No matter how much time they will have to wait, they will wait. It is because of the desire to get rid of their illnesses that, having walked in the hot sun all the way from their houses, undergoing many difficulties, they come and stand there for long hours. What patience they have! Their only thought is to see the doctor and get the proper medicine. Would you go see the doctor if you think that you do not have a disease? Would you stand waiting? One who thinks that he has no disease will not have the necessary patience and will not wait for such a long time. When we have patience, we will also have the attitude of sacrifice. Mere chanting of *Nama* is not enough. It should be done with concentration. Otherwise, it is like pouring water on the surface of a rock. *Japa* is beneficial only if there is concentration. To sit for ten hours with eyes closed and to chant the Divine Name with concentration for one hour are both equal. Among fireworks there is a kind of rocket which goes upward with great speed and a hissing noise and then bursts when it reaches a certain height. *Bhakti* is like that. Liberation can be attained in a moment. That call, that one loving call which causes one to forget one's mind, intellect and body ~ that will take one to the goal.

At that moment a devotee from Mavelikara[64] having walked all the way from their house in the sun and undergone many difficultiescame and prostrated to the Holy Mother. Having conversed with him for some time, the Mother sat with eyes closed for a few minutes. Everyone waited gazing at the Holy Mother's form until she came down from the ecstatic mood. Some more moments passed,

[64]A town about 25 kms. north of Mother's Ashram.

and with a smile on her countenance, the Mother opened her eyes. After a few moments of silence, one devotee asked, "Mother, what is real devotion?"

Mother: The devotion of Hanuman[65] is an example. *Bhakti* is surrendering or sacrificing oneself to Divine Love.

Devotee: What about the devotion of the Gopis?

Mother: Son, the devotion of the Gopis is also superior. But in the beginning, it was a little bit mixed with *vasanas* . Because knowledge had not yet arisen, the Gopis got angry when Akrura[66] came. They still had the attitude of duality. Why did Sri Krishna's depart from Ampadi (His birth place)? Because the Gopis had not attained complete mental purity. Mother is talking about the beginning. Later they attained a state where they could see Krishna inside, outside and everywhere. The seed has to be sown in the shade first. It can be transplanted when it has grown to a certain height, but until then, shade is necessary. Likewise, the seeds of the Gopis' love were sown and grew to a certain level under the shade of the huge tree called Krishna. Then, all of a sudden, He left them in order to teach them to see Him within and to become more expansive. It was in order to teach them self-dependence that He left. Yet in the beginning, the selfishness which the Gopis had in their love towards Krishna helped them a lot to increase their devotion.

A young man who worked as a leader in the social and spiritual field was present among the devotees. He was keenly listening to the Mother's words.

---

[65]The great monkey devotee of Sri Rama. He is revered as an Incarnation of Lord Siva who wanted to enjoy the bliss of service to Sri Rama and therefor took the humble form of a monkey.

[66]A devotee of Sri Krishna who came to give a message to the Gopis from the Lord telling them to see Him within and as identical with their Real Self.

Young leader: Mother, it is seen that many are approaching spiritual subjects with a negative attitude. Why is this so?

Mother: Son, such things will happen if spirituality is served to anyone and everyone. What Mother says is that *"Hari Sri"* (the first letters of the Malayalam alphabet) should be taught only to one who has a surrendering attitude. Only when the child approaches the teacher stretching out his fingers saying, "I don't know anything, please teach me," will the teacher make the child write the letters in the sand while holding his fingers. How could a teacher teach a child who doesn't stretch out his fingers? If you approach those who don't have humility, trying to make them understand spirituality, they will refuse to listen. Anyhow, you are doing good work in propagating *dharma*. It is God alone who entrusted this work to you. The only thing you must remember is that you have to do it selflessly.

Young leader: But Mother, there is a problem when we talk about selflessness. Suppose some aggressors forcefully pluck coconuts from the coconut trees of the Ashram and take them away. Now, what would Mother do? Would you simply allow them to take the coconuts or would you call the police? It is selfishness if you call the police, is it not?

Mother: We must keep in mind one thing: that everything is one Self. Still, a dog should be seen as a dog and treated accordingly. Holding a stick against it in order to protect oneself doesn't fall under the category of selfishness. There is no fault in driving away an ignorant dog when it comes to harm us. Mother does not say that this is selfish. And there is nothing selfish in obstructing a person who does things out of ignorance. Actually, if he is not prevented, he will become a public nuisance and will create many problems in society. What is important is that when you punish him, it should be done with a pure intention ~ that is, to correct him for his future good. It should not be done out of dislike or revenge. One shouldn't act desiring selfish ends. It is beneficial for the world if you help to punish an aggressor who forcefully climbs on somebody's coconut tree. This the is not selfishness, but *Dharma*.

A *Mahatma*, if he really wishes, can create another world. But he won't do anything against the pre-established laws of Nature. It was they (*Mahatmas*) who formulated the rules and regulations of life and if they wish they can break them. But they will not do so. Just as the supreme authority of a nation would not do anything which is against the constitution, in a like manner, great souls do everything only according to the rules and regulations set by the ancients.

Above all, as far as great souls are concerned, they look upon everyone and everything equally. They will not waste their power to achieve trivial worldly things. For them, nothing is insignificant; each and every thing has its own place. They know that even a needle has its own use.

TO THE SADHAKS

When she finished speaking, the Holy Mother noticed two *sadhaks* sitting on the bare ground.

Mother: In the beginning *sadhaks* should be careful about many things. They should use sandals while walking. The earth has gravitational power. Try sleeping on the black sand on the seashore. You will become so fatigued that you can't even get up. The gravitational power of the earth is capable of absorbing our energy. Now we are enslaved by that attractive power. We are trying to overcome this. Therefore, wherever the *sadhak* sits, he should spread something on the ground. In the initial stages a serious *sadhak* should wear clothes that cover his whole body. Do not give negative vibrations any chance to affect your body. It is said that a *sadhak* should cover his body so that if others happen to look at him, they will not see his full form. All these are nec- essary during the period of *sadhana*.. Besides that, a *sadhak* also should not gaze at anyone. Don't speak too much. A lot of vital energy will be lost through speech. In this way, only if there is much external alertness can the *sadhak* who is in the beginning stagesof his *sadhana* withstand and overcome obstacles. To a non-dualist all these observances may seem to be a kind of weakness, but such people can only speak about non-duality. Those who have reached the goal are people who have observed the disciplines in this manner.

There are also people who have attained the goal with- out all these disciplines, but they had a tremendous spiritual disposition inherited from their past birth. We who long to go from the level of the *jivatma* (individual self) to the state of *Paramatma* (Supreme Self) need all the discipline. It doesn't matter for a *Jivanmukta* (a Liberated Soul) if he lies in the sand or water. But one can do all those things only af- ter attaining a particular stage. After one attains the state of *Jivanmukti*, the power will not go out without his will be- cause his mind is fully under his control. Even if he may look at a person or an object with his eyes, he won't fix his mind there. Only if the mind is fixed will the power flow out. It is beneficial for us if he looks at us with that resolve. Until that state is attained, a *sadhak* should move very care- fully.

Young Man: Mother, then are not the charges lodged

against Sankaracharya correct, saying that he has *tindal* and *todil?*[67]

Mother: It will definitely harm to the *sadhak* if he mingles with those who do not have spiritual culture. If we live with a leper, doesn't that disease affect us also? In the beginning stages it is very advisable for the *sadhak* not to associate with others. Even if it is said that all are human beings, are all human beings the same? Some are thieves, some are innocent, and others are embodiments of compassion. There are some who have leprosy or tuberculosis, while others are perfectly healthy. It is harmful if all mingle together without any restrictions or control. Therefore, Mother cannot find any fault if Sankaracharya doesn't touch anyone. Maybe it is to set an example for *sadhaks*. All those rules are necessary for a *sadhak* before the attainment of *Jivanmukti*. In a *math* (monastery) discipline and a regular routine are indispensable. A path is needed for human beings. The birds don't need one; an *Avatar* or a *Jivanmukta* doesn't need a path; but we can proceed only with the help of *yama* and *niyama* (observance of rules and regulations prescribed by the scriptures and the great masters).

BEYOND DISCIPLINE

Mother: Some people would say that a hand fan is not necessary if there is an electric fan. A fan is not needed on the seashore. If there is *satsang*, rules and regulations of worship are not necessary. But it should be real *satsang*. Who does real *satsang?* Real *satsang* is the combining of *jivatma* and

---

[67]The Sankaracharya, the ecclesiastic head of a large section of Hindu society, observes an old custom of India existing among the higher castes forbidding the people who belong to the lower castes to touch or come close to them for fear of pollution by touch and nearness.

Paramatma; there should be a sincere and dedicated effort to attain that unity. If that kind of effort is there, then nothing else is needed. We are all seeds from fruits which have been caused to ripen unnaturally. Such seeds are a bit difficult to sprout; whereas seeds that fall from the beaks of birds onto rocks and they will germinate lying even there. The saliva which comes out from the bird's mouth is their fertilizer. They need neither sand nor water nor a protective fence to grow. Nor do they need someone to look after them. They will grow lying there, having come already enriched with fertilizers necessary for their growth. Such people are *Jivanmuktas*. They will be able to lead a life without attachment to anything. They are people who have come with fully developed spiritual qualities inherited from the previous birth (*purva samskara*). They will not become weak-minded under any circumstance. They will act only through their understanding of the subtlety of things. They will not act in accordance with external appearances. They do not need to do *sadhana*, while ordinary people do. For ordinary people it is not possible to attain the goal without *sadhana*.

As she was talking, the Mother entered into *bhava samadhi* (ecstatic trance). After some time, chanting "Shiva...Shiva...Shiva," she became her normal self. The Mother continued,

Mother: Wherever *Jivanmuktas* go, people will run after them. They do not have to search for disciples. People will go on following them. People will be attracted to them even without knowing it, just like rubbish caught in a whirlwind. That is the power of a person who does *sadhana*. Just their breath or the wind that blows over their body is enough to benefit the world.

Ordinary people must gain concentration through spiritual practices, observing the prescribed rules and regulations. Otherwise, they will collapse. Whether it is a stone or paper, the artist beholds in the object that which he can make from it. A Self-Realized soul beholds the Essence of all objects. He neither sees the differences that we see nor does he think that anything is without significance. Others may see a stone or a paper only as a useless thing. They will not see, as an artist will, the object which can be made . Therefore, move forward in this way, observing things subtly.

Young Man: Certain spiritual persons are being abused by some people for wearing silk clothes. Is there any significance of things such as silk clothes?

Mother: Son, there are good effects which come from wearing silk clothes as well as from wearing certain animal skins. They will protect us from several evil external powers. *Rudraksha,* also, has medicinal power. It is good to wear it on the body. Especially beneficial is wearing it on the neck, with the seeds touching the cavity of the throat. Applying ash from a burnt corpse is also good. It has the power to prevent germs. Ash from the burial ground (*chutala bhasmam*) will also prevent polluted air from entering the body. Different things will be needed during each stage of spiritual practice.

The Holy Mother got up and went to the hut. The Mother having gone inside, some devotees left. Others came to stay overnight in the Ashram. The western horizon slowly became pink in colour. The sun dove deep into the ocean, as if to have its evening bath. Dusk had fallen. The Ashram atmosphere was saturated with peace and tranquillity. The

brahmacharins began singing *bhajans.* The Holy Mother also
came and sat for the *bhajan.* There was no light except the
light from the oil lamps kept inside the temple. The Mother
sang in an intoxicated mood,

> O Goddess, Great Goddess, bless me.
> O Leader of all, my salutation to Thee.
>
> For how many days have we been crying
> Like this, O Treasure of Compassion,
> O Embodiment of Truth.
> Please shower Thy Grace on us, O Krishna,
> Lover of Thy devotees.
>
> For what reason have we been pushed into
> This hell and are being tortured, O Krishna,
> Who nourished the Pandavas, O Holy One?

The Mother sang like an innocent child, calling out,
"Amma...Amma!" now and then. The *bhajan* lasted for two
hours. After the *arathi* (vespers) the Holy Mother sat in the
sand by the side of the temple. Everyone offered their prostrations to her. Some went to meditate and others remained
near her.

NITYANITYAM
The Eternal and non-eternal

An Aspirant: Mother, what is meant by "*nityanitya vastu
vivekam*" (discrimination between the eternal and the non-
eternal)?
Mother: Shiva...Shiva...what do we know? Your Mother is
crazy. She is uttering something or other. Accept what you
feel is right.

If a traveller happens to stand in a bus stop, a person may look and smile at him. He will talk to him. At that time another person will come near. Thus, some people will gather together. Quickly all of them will become friends. As they are talking the bus comes. Everyone gets into it. Having travelled for sometime, when the first traveller turns around and looks, none of the friends who had gotten into the bus at the bus stop with him are there in the seats. "Alas, are they all gone? I thought that all of them would be with me until the end." The poor fellow thinks that all those people who travelled with him would be his friends forever. He is disappointed when each one of them alights and goes his own way when the bus reaches his destination. He would not have been dejected if he had understood this earlier. Whether it is your father or mother or wife, like the man's friends, they will leave you when it is their time. Disappointment will result if you live fixing your mind on ephemeral objects.

Therefore, children, don't be deluded by these external dreams. All things and people will have to go when the time comes. If you are attached, then what remains is only sorrow, is it not? Despair will not arise if you live with this understanding, and without getting tempted by external affairs. Instead of attachment, remember God with an attitude of surrender. God alone is the Eternal Truth. It should be understood that the world is not eternal. This is discrimination between the eternal and the non-eternal.

Everything will be alright if you move along this path. Suppose a person has a job in a bank. Many people will come to see him there. They will speak sweetly to him. A clever person will understand that those people are coming not because of their love towards him, but to take care of

business, to fulfill their desires. Understanding this, he will
do his duty properly without being deluded by their sweet
words and manners. He won't waste time talking. He will
even be ready to lodge a case against them if they don't repay the amount that they have taken as a loan. Many people
will come to see you when you have a position of power.
But what will happen when the position is gone? Then ad-
mirers will not be there. One should take refuge in the
eternal God after thinking about all this with discrimination.

A person may handle millions of rupees in the office or
in the bank, but he knows that it is not his wealth. He has
no attachment to it nor does he desire it. The headache is
over if we understand that none of the things in this world
are our own. One will not have any more problems if the
awareness that the wife and children are not one's own
dawns in us. What we have as our own is God alone. Perform your actions in the world thinking, "This is my duty."
Don't sit idle. You should work. In the beginning stages of
sadhana, a regular routine is needed. If you take tea today,
tomorrow a headache will come if you don't drink it. That is
because of the habit. Therefore, good habits should be developed through a regular routine.

In the beginning external rules and external attentiveness are necessary. One must move with discrimination.
That only is beneficial. Otherwise, you might simply sit and
say, "I am Brahman" (the Absolute). You can see Brahman
jumping up and down with pain if a thorn happens to
pierce your foot. (All laugh) There is no use in babbling
without attaining that state of experience.

All these years we have worked thinking that the world
was eternal. Now, having understood the truth, we should
set aside some time for the Self. Out of twenty-four hours,

we should try for at least one hour to know the Self. Spiritual practices should be performed regularly. Time lost cannot be regained. If millions of dollars are lost we can make it up by doing more business, but if even a second is lost it can never be regained. You should live understanding this.

Sadhak: Mother, you have said that we are in the *vyavahara* (empirical plane) and that we should move with subtlety. What does this mean?

Mother: The empirical plane means the level of meaningless things and actions. *Mithya* does not mean perishing but rather, everchanging. The world is transforming from one state to another. Each and every object is changing. Look at lentils: first there are whole lentils, then the broken ones, and finally we get *parippu vada*.[68] But the basic thing is not being destroyed. It is only transformed into something else.

When we say *Brahman*, everything is included. But discrimination is needed because we are rooted in *vyavahara*. In the beginning, only if we think, "This is day, this is night, this is good, that is bad, etc.," can we progress.

All that is related to *Maya* will exist in *vyavahara*. That which is *mithya*, that which is not the Truth, is changing. Proceed with subtlety.

Sadhak: Mother, is it very necessary that one should do *mantra japa* using a rosary?

Mother: Children, kids learn to count using pearl beads. Using this method they can learn quickly. In the beginning a *japa mala* (rosary) is good to fix the mind firmly on one point. Later, you can continue even without a rosary. It will become a habit. The japa will go on automatically even without our knowledge. One person used to write dipping the

---

[68] A kind of fried food made from ground grams or pulses with spices, roasted in oil.

pen in the ink bottle. For ten days the ink bottle was kept on the right side. On the eleventh day he shifted it to the left side. Even if he knows that the ink bottle is on the left side his hand will automatically move to the right side. Therefore, first *japa* should become a habit. Then it will go on while walking, sitting or sleeping. *Japa*, prayer and meditation are all good for concentration. Once compound letters are learned then there is no need to practice the letters by writing them down. But in the beginning tools and methods are indispensible. Otherwise, it is not possible to learn, my child.

Upon first showing the picture of an elephant or a horse to a child, his father or mother will explain, "This is an elephant, this is a horse." The child will think that the elephant and horse are in the picture. Only later will he understand that the elephant or the horse are not the picture itself, but something entirely different. When his father showed him the pictur e and told him, "This is an elephant" or "this is a horse," the child did not have even one iota of doubt in his words. He might even have been frightened if he was told, "Look, the elephant is going to pierce you with his tusk." Just like the child, you must have innocent and blind faith in the Guru's words. That faith will serve as a vehicle in which you can easily travel towards the goal.

Son, whatever the Guru does is only for the spiritual progress of the disciple. It is absolutely impossible for him to act otherwise. Mother is referring to a *Satguru*, not just anyone who declares himself to be a Guru. A true spiritual master may sometimes behave strangely. He may get angry at the disciple for no particular reason, blaming him for errors which he hasn't committed. But that seemingly strange behavior is not because the Guru is really angry with the student. It is the Guru's way of teaching self-surrender, patience and acceptance. For example, sometimes the Guru might ask the disciple to make a beautiful image of Krishna or Devi. The disciple, forsaking food and sleep and applying all his artistic talents, will make one in twenty days or a month. Eventually, he will bring it to the Guru. The Guru may not even look at it, or he may smash it into pieces after snatching it from the disciple. On such occasions a perfect student will remain totally calm, accepting everything as the Guru's will and realizing that it is for his spiritual good. Thus he will not respond negatively at all. Each reaction which arises from us causes a delay in attaining the goal; whereas, acceptance will cause the Grace to flow without cease. Son, the real Guru has no selfish interests at all. He or she lives in *tyaga* (renunciation); his or her whole being is *tyaga*. For the upliftment of the disciples and the good of the world, the Guru burns his or her own body (which has been taken by self will), in the flame of *tyaga* . From that blazing flame of *tyaga* each one of us can kindle a wick so that we too can become street lights on the dark path along which the entire human race walks.

Sadhak: (Bowing down to the Mother) Mother, this has cleared many of my questions.

He sat for awhile in front of the Mother with joined palms and his head bowed and then asked, "Mother, Ramana Maharshi propagated the path of *Jnana*, didn't he?"

Mother: He has said everything. When instructing foreigners, who are predominantly intellectual, according to their nature, he instructed them to enquire, "Who am I and

where did I come from." But he also said that one should attain concentration, performing proper *sadhana* to attain this
goal. First, the Guru might act according to the what the
sadhak likes. Then gradually rules and regulations concerning *sadhana* and regularity in spiritual practice will be
insisted upon. *Sadhana* is necessary if one wants to reach
the goal. Ramana Maharshi said that one needs devotion
also. Imagining each stone of Arunachala Hill as Shiva, he
criedout, "My Father, My Father!" Ramana Maharshi perceived Arunachala as Lord Shiva Himself.

He himself had done *sadhana* sitting in the Patalalinga
Cave. He also practiced silence. There is a picture of Ramana Maharshi cutting vegetables. In one or two books he
talks about worldly affairs as well, but nobody will notice all
these things. The followers always want to limit the unlimited Guru. This is a pity. *Satgurus* are expansive; but the
followers, wearing the spectacles of narrowness, try to im-
pose their own limited point of view on them. This is like
trying to put the vast ocean in a small bottle. Think sincerely
for a while. Are we trying to accept the teachings of the
Great Masters, or do we want to bring them into our little
worlds of chaos and confusion which will make others also
confused? It is not enough to pay attention to only one part
of the sayings of great souls. We must heed all that they say
and do.

Without some resolve (*sankalpa*), how is it possible to
concentrate on the Self? For that, Ramana Maharshi has in-
troduced the method of going around the hill chanting the
Divine Name. A raft is needed to cross the river. It is not
necessary after crossing the river. *Sagunaradhana* (worship of
an image of a God or Goddess) is there at Ramana's
Ashram. But some are doing nothing, saying, "I am *Brah-*

man." Having drawn the picture of a house, they want to live in it. Simply keeping Ramana's picture they do nothing, no meditation or other spiritual practices. Instead of this, why don't they chant the Divine Name so that they can become a true follower of Ramana Maharshi or any other *Mahatma?* How much he meditated! The *Mahatmas* will still retain *bhakti* even after attaining the state of *Jivanmukti.* Do you know why? To stay in this world. They will not give up *bhakti.* They accept it of their own will. The greatness of *bhakti* is something unique. They enjoy *bhakti,* having created it by self-will. You may ask, what is there for them to enjoy; is there "I," "you," etc.? But, they will retain *bhakti* to stay in the world.

One devotee: Mother, what is needed to attain concentration?

Mother: Son, there are no short cuts. Constant practice is needed. It is difficult to get one-pointedness. In the beginning, it is a great thing if by chance we get even one or two minutes of concentration when we do *sadhana* for one hour. *Sadhana* should be done continuously and sincerely without stopping until one-pointedness is gained. Once the seeds are sown, you should water them every day until the seedlings grow and reach a certain level. If you stop watering before this, they will wither away, especially if the land is dry. Through daily watering, one day they will become strong enough to withstand the heat. Then you can stop watering. We have sown the seeds of spirituality in ourselves, but due to the scorching heat of worldliness, we are very dry inside. Therefore it might take some time for the sprouts of spirituality to come out. Sprinkle them with the waters of *sadhana* regularly, without fail; and wait patiently. If you stop the *sadhana* owing to lack of concentration and patience, then no result will be gained. *Japa* is necessary.

One young man: What benefit does the world get if one sits and meditates with eyes closed?

Mother: Nature is benefited by the concentration of a *sadhak*.

Young man: How?

Mother: Son, such concentration will purify the atmosphere. At some time in the future, modern material science will discover it. We should not forget the services done by the *Mahatmas* who were *dhyanis* (meditators). They derived power from meditation, and used this power to benefit the world.

Son, in order to magnetize an iron rod, a powerful magnet needs to be rubbed on it in one direction alone. When it is rubbed for some time the iron will become a magnet too. The molecules in the iron rod, which were previously lying in disorder, are systematized by the rubbing process. But it needs another powerful magnet to do this. Mother thinks that this is what happens in meditation also. By fixing the mind firmly on one thought, such as a selected *mantra*, Divine Name or Form, the thoughts are rearranged and directed towards that one object. Thus, power is generated when thoughts constantly flow in one direction towards God.

This power is always radiating from a *Mahatma* which certainly creates spiritual energy in us when we sit in his presence. He can transmit that power to us through a mere touch, look or thought. But like the iron rod, we must allow ourselves to be magnetized, without raising any objection or words of protest.

Children, look at a river which flows into many branches. The force of the current will be very little. But if a dam is constructed closing all the small channels, the water current will increase tremendously and we can generate electricity from it. If the mind, which is flowing outwards in the form of thoughts and desires is directed to one point, infinite energy can be created. This will definitely radiate from all around you, revitalizing anything and everything. But the quantity of energy will differ depending upon each one's subtlety of mind.

Son, television stations always broadcast programs, but if you want to see them you must turn on the television and tune it in. In the same way, tuning your mind to the *Mahatma's* is necessary. If that is done, then you can experience the flow of spiritual energy from them to you ~ spiritual energy which was, in fact, always there. For this, spiritual practice is a must.

The Mother paused for a while and then distributed as *prasad* the sugar candy which had been brought by a devotee. A few grains fell and scattered on the floor. One by one the ants came and gathered there. Pointing to the ants, the Mother said,

Mother: Children, look here. First there was only one ant on the sugar candy, then many. One is enough for others to follow. If even one *vasana* remains, other *vasanas* will follow. All *vasanas* must be destroyed without leaving even one.

The Mother noticed one *brahmacharin* passing by at a distance. She called, "Come here, son." The perplexed *brahmacharin* came near her.

Mother: Son, tomorrow you should go and have your hair cut.

The *brahmacharin* nodded his head in approval and left the place silently.

A householder along with his family came in the evening. They had been devotees of the Holy Mother for quite a long time. They had a lot of problems: The wife had no obedience to her husband, and their family life was not very peaceful.

Mother: This daughter has devotion to Mother but (smilingly) what kind of *bhakti* is it? What *bhakti*, what *japa* and what kind of *dhyana* is it that has filled your husband with sorrow? Who needs the devotion of a wife who gives trouble to her husband? That is why the people of old gave more importance to mental unity than to physical beauty when considering marriage. If the wife is a pious woman endowed with patience, forbearance, devotion and endurance, she can transform the character of the husband, even if he is a rogue.

Just then a father arrived with his little daughter. The Holy Mother called the little girl and made her sit near her. The father of the girl said, "Mother, please advise her not to cry when she returns home, or insist that she wants to see Mother after having returned home from the Ashram."

Hearing this, the Holy Mother hugged the little girl and laughed with great happiness.

One devotee: How fortunate it is to cry for God. That is how all of us have understood it.

All laugh happily.

One young man: Does Mother ever recommend *prana-yama?*

Mother: During the present age *pranayama* is very difficult to practice. *Kumbhakam* (retention of the breath) will arise on its own when there is love for God. What is *pranayama* for then? With *hatha yoga* and *pranayama* insanity will result if a Perfected Master is not there to guide the aspirant.

14 November 1983

It was about nine-thirty in the morning. The Holy Mother was sitting on the cot in her small hut, facing towards the north. Four young men came to the Ashram to see the Mother. Learning from a resident that the Mother was sitting in her room, the young men peeped in from outside. The Mother saw them and said, "Come in, children."

All four of them entered the hut and sat on the carpet that was spread on the floor. The Mother got up from the cot and sat down. The young men, one by one, looked at her quite surprised. They were all educated and had read a few spiritual books which had kindled an interest in them to learn more about spirituality. Recently they had heard about the Mother and were curious to see her in person and possibly to ask certain questions. It was quite clear that the Mother's simplicity, humility and her loving call had influenced them to some extent.

Mother: (Smilingly) Children, from where do you come?

One among them: We are from Paravoor. It is near Quilon. (Pointing to one young man sitting near him) This is my friend and the other two are his acquaintances. Together we came to see Mother.

Mother: (Laughingly) Shiva, Shiva, Shiva, to see Mother? Mother is crazy. Because the children call her "Mother" she acts in some way or other, doing some crazy things. Children, have you eaten anything?

Young man: Yes.

Another young man: We came having heard about you. We have visited many Ashrams.

Mother: How far have you studied?

Young man: I have passed B.Sc. and he has a B.A.

By this time the Mother entered into a trance. A few moments went by in silence. The roaring Arabian Sea could be seen from the Mother's hut. The beating of the coconut husks by the fisherwomen could also be heard from across the backwaters. The Mother slowly opened her eyes chanting "Shiva, Shiva, Shiva," whirling her uplifted hand which formed a *mudra*.

One young man: We would like to know certain spiritual things.

Mother: (Laughingly) Shiva, Shiva, Shiva! What do we know about spirituality! He (God) knows everything. Children, you may ask. Mother may blurt out some crazy things. Accept it if you feel that it is correct. Mother would tell her children, "There is a crazy Kali here. You will know her nature only when you get closer." Shiva, Shiva! (Mother laughs)

The young men were very surprised. After a pause, the young man continued, "It is rich people more than the poor who are visiting the Ashrams, isn't it?"

Mother: Is there a rule saying that only the poor should go to visit *Bhagavan* and the rich shouldn't? The rich have their own problems, don't they? Children, more wealth means more problems. In spirituality there are no distinctions like small and big, rich and poor. For God, all are His children; none will be discarded. The rich who come into contact with Ashrams and spiritual people will do a lot of good. Doesn't it take money to do charitable things? Can the poor give it? No, they have no capacity to do so. Ashrams and spiritual people inspire the rich people do *sat karmas* (virtuous actions). It is the poor who are getting the benefit of that, aren't they? This is not so bad.

Spirituality is the right of both the poor and the rich. When remembrance of God is done with concentration, when you make one step towards God, God will make a hundred steps towards you. Are you ready for that? Son, are we getting concentration even for a minute? Without striving for that, we simply find fault with others. First try to correct our own drawbacks. You know, son, if one rich man becomes interested in spirituality, many poor people will be saved. Because of the *dharma buddhi* (charitable mind) of the spiritual person or Ashram, the poor man will also be inspired.

Young man: What must be done in order to gain concentration?

Mother: Son, to gain concentration we must be intent on reaching the goal. Suppose one person is learning to ride a bicycle. Even if he falls down several times he will again climb onto it. Why? Because he has the intent to learn. While learning, falling down or getting injured is not a problem. Concentration will arise if intent to reach the goal is there. It is not possible unless you strive hard. Your efforts will bear fruit only through concentration.

WORLDLY LOVE

At this time, a couple of householder devotees entered the hut and sat down after prostrating to the Mother.

Mother: Take the case of worldly love. Does anybody love selflessly? Is it either for the woman or for the children that one gets married? Is it not for one's own pleasure only? Is it not to satisfy his own desire that a man loves his wife and that a father loves his children? Now, let us take the case with the child. We love the child because he or she was born from our ovum and semen. But do we love him or her selflessly? If so, why do we not love the children of other people? Really we love our child only because the child was conceived by us. Even then, we are loving ourselves only. Let that be for the present. Suppose that the house catches fire. The child is inside the house and you are outside. We would only cry, calling out, "Please, somebody save my child!" We won't save the child by jumping into the fire because we know that death is certain if we jump in. So, then whom are we loving and who loves us? We love ourselves only. This is the nature of worldly love. Is this not so? Allured by this love, we wander away from God, thinking, "He loves me; she loves me." We become friendly with others only for our own pleasure. Selflessness won't arise as long as the awareness "This body is I" exists.

So, this is what people are doing. They become enticed, thinking the people whom they had seen in the bus stop were relatives. The so-called relatives will go to their own places. That Supreme Self, the Eternal Principle, that alone is the real friend. Understanding this truth, we must always contemplate it, whatever path we walk on while doing our work.

DON'T GIVE UP THE INTENT TO REACH THE GOAL

Mother: Many obstacles will arise. No matter many kicks we get, we won't get angry while waiting in the queue to buy tickets for the cinema. Why? Because our aim is to see the movie? When we are really desirous of seeing the movie, these kicks and sufferings are not a sacrifice. Suppose we are getting in a bus. There are many people trying to get in. They are pushing and pulling. Someone hits us and we hit him back. It is not out of anger. Like us, he or she just wants to get into the bus, in time to reach the office or home. That is the reason. If it was another occasion we would have quarreled and might have even lodged a case against him. But when one is intent on the goal, all differences are forgotten. While traveling, two strangers or even enemies might sit on the same seat.

In the same manner, we will sit patiently waiting until evening in the court verandah. Why? Just to win the case. That is it. No matter how rich one may be, he will sit waiting in the front yard of the court. He is not hesitant to endure any amount of suffering. Don't we understand that nothing is difficult if there is *lakshya bodha* (intent to reach one's goal)? He does not complain that the wife is sick, that the medicine has not yet been purchased or that the food is not cooked. He doesn't feel that it is a sacrifice when he lies down in the courtyard from morning until evening because he wants to win the case. That is the goal.

Those inconveniences are not considered sufferings. But when you come to the spiritual field, even a little suffering will be felt as being big. The reason is the lack of *lakshya bodha*. So when we suffer for spirituality's sake, we should think over all this. We undergo sufferings for silly things. Not only that, don't we proceed, enduring all the obstacles that arise during our effort to fulfill our desires? Impediments will arise in the spiritual path as well. We should move forward enduring everything.

Having lived so many years thinking that we are the body, we will not get concentration simply by saying that we are the Self. We are lucky if we can get even one minute of one-pointedness. Son, in the beginning you will feel it to be a bit difficult. Even the ocean can be emptied, but the mind cannot be brought under control. It is very difficult. One can move forward overcoming everything if one has *lakshya bodha*. No obstacle will be a problem if we remember the beatific vision that awaits us. Nothing is a problem when we think of that. We should try to control the mind through *tyaga* (renunciation).

Another thing is that we must have faith. Faith is what is important. But Mother doesn't say that you must believe in God. It is enough to believe in one's own Self. Our Real Nature should be known. *Atman* is eternal. The world is not eternal. You should become convinced about this. One should move forward believing in one's own Self.

MANIFESTATION OF SIDDHIS

Young man: What is Mother's opinion about the display of *siddhis* (psychic powers)?

Mother: What the *rishis* (sages) have written is that it is not correct if *sadhaks* display *siddhis*. But in today's world *siddhis* might become necessary. In the olden days, the type of education which existed was *gurukula vidyabhyasa*.[69] Even at a

---

[69]Staying in the Guru's residence, serving the Guru and spending one's time in studies and contemplation for a number of years until all the scriptures were learnt.

young age obedience to the parents and the Guru was taught. After that, the purpose of life and the reason one took birth will be understood. In the olden days it was not taught to get married and give birth to five or ten children. One virtuous child was enough. A couple produced a child having done tapas for a long time. They conceived with the semen of their *tapas shakti* (power of *tapas*). Their child would be a brilliant and intelligent one. The parents would go to the *vanaprastha*[69] after having raised him and make him fit by giving him a proper education. That was the system in the olden times. Whether one was a king or a servant, *sannyasa* (total renunciation) was the goal of life. But what about today? "I want to become a minister in the government. I want to become a doctor. I want to grab all the wealth! And then I want a scooter, a car, a house, etc." This is today's way of thinking. Trapping the mind in this restlessness and tension, we attempt to kill and rob everyone. We are ready to grab our share of wealth even by killing our own parents. Today we don't give any value to our parents. We live in the midst of such desires with a false sense of values.

In those days each step was made keeping spirituality as the goal. Today, we do not do that. Even children studying in nursery school are shouting political slogans. During *Bhava Darshan,* many children come to Mother and say, "Mother, I want to kill a person, Mother should help me." This is what tiny little children say! There is enmity in the name of political parties. The children of today think that their party should thrive even by murder. In the olden days this was not so. The attitude was "Love your neighbor as

---

[70]The third stage of life, renouncing the hearth and home and going to the forest for doing penance.

yourself," as Jesus said. Today it is just the opposite. Display of *siddhis* should be evaluated keeping this in mind.

As the young men keenly listened, the Holy Mother continued,

Mother: *Siddhis* might not have been necessary in the old days when the people had spiritual culture. Then there was selflessness and *tyaga*. Today, all is selfishness only. People are desirous of seeing *siddhis*. If they don't, they won't believe in God.

Son, in this age people will go only after desires. If the desires are fulfilled, they will believe. Thus, slowly they can be brought to the path of devotion. Nowadays, nobody would go anywhere if it were not to fulfill their desires. If there is sickness they will go to see a doctor, otherwise not. However, some who do not have any disease will also go to see doctors. Do you know what for? To get advice as to how to prevent disease. They see the doctor to learn where and when to do purification, how to live, and what food stuffs are good. They are people who have good insight into things. Now, there are people who would approach great souls with the thought, "I must know what spiritual life is." Still, they may have desires to fulfill but they will consider those as secondary. But such people can be counted only on one hand. The majority crave fulfillment of their desires. Manifestation of *siddhis* is necessary to lead them to goodness.

In the world of today, all are afflicted with the disease of worldliness. They go after desires only. They fear that the wife will err, or that the husband or the children will err. They worry about whether they will be wealthy or whether they will become grandparents, etc. They do not want spirituality other than for providing the solutions to such ordinary problems. Mostly people are of this kind. Certain things will be needed to attract such people. This is like a *katha prasangam*.[71] The story will actually be only half an hour long but it will take hours to tell it. This is because in order to attract the audience it should be embellished with humorous and appealing touches. Only then will the people be attracted. No one will listen if the story is narrated too briefly. According to the desire of the devotees or people who visit them, Some *Mahatmas* will manifest *siddhis*. Their intention is to attract people towards God. They will be attracted to God and the Divine Power when they see the display of *siddhis*.

One young householder devotee: Mother, this conversation about *siddhis* reminds me of one incident which occured in my life only two weeks ago.

With a child's curiosity the Mother asked, "What is that, son?"

Devotee: Mother, like an innocent child you pretend as if you do not know anything, though this son is fully convinced that without your knowledge nothing would happen.

Mother: Mother knows only one thing, that she doesn't know anything.

Devotee: Mother, I know you are trying to fool me. Anyhow, I like to be fooled by you.

Another devotee: We are anxiously waiting to hear the incident which you were about to tell.

Devotee: Two weeks ago my wife had a dream in which the

---

[71]A public narration of a story with accompanying music.

Mother appeared in front of her and said in a very clear voice, "Watch Resmi." That is the name of our only girl child. She is just two years old. My wife immediately got up but the child was comfortably sleeping near us. She woke me up and told me about the dream. I said, "Go back to sleep; it was probably just a dream, don't worry." Neither of us gave much importance to it. But my wife Sarada had the same dream the following two nights. Mother appeared before her, loudly repeating the same sentence: "Watch Resmi," but more loudly. On the third night, as my wife got up she screamed. The sound woke me up. When I turned on the light I saw my wife sitting on the bed, trembling and sweating. Resmi also woke up and started crying. My wife took her and held her tightly to her bosom. Like one gone mad, she went on saying, "Mother, what is going to happen to my child Resmi; what is going to happen to my Resmi? Protect her." Although the dream had seemed insignificant to me on the other two nights, I couldn't remain at peace when the same dream was repeated on the third night, especially when my wife narrated the way it happened. I myself was very confused but even then I tried to console my wife saying, "Don't worry, Mother is there to protect us." We could not sleep that night.

The next morning, Sarada and I went with Resmi to the family shrine room and offered our morning prayers to the Mother seeking her protection especially for the two year old child. Since I had no more days off, and owing to the heavy work load at the office because of the closing of the yearly accounts, I could neither come to the Mother nor could I take leave for a day. Therefore, dedicating everything at the Mother's feet and instructing Sarada to keep a careful eye on Resmi, I went to the office with a totally upset mind.

When I returned from the office that evening, I was shocked and at the same time struck with wonder upon hearing Sarada's narration of the unbelievable incident that happened that day.

At a quarter past ten my wife went to the kitchen to cook lunch. Resmi was fast asleep. Afraid of the dream's warning, Sarada didn't lay Resmi on the cot in order to avoid the possible danger of her falling down from it. Instead, she lay her down on a mattress spread on the floor. It was eleven-thirty. Sarada was immersed in cooking and other household chores. All of a sudden, as she was about to chop the vegetables, somebody pushed her strongly from behind and simultaneously she heard the Mother's voice as if scolding her, "I warned you to watch your child. Go, hurry up to the pond." Sarada rushed to the pond which was situated on the southern side of the house, only a few yards away from the room where Resmi was sleeping. Sarada screamed out loud, perceiving the horrifying sight that she saw there. Resmi was about to step into the waters of the deep pond. Sarada, like one gone mad, cried loudly and rushing towards the child, grabbed her post-haste. Hearing her loud cry, all the neighbors came running to the house. All felt relieved seeing that the child had been saved from the threat of danger.

It was only then that Sarada thought about how Resmi had happened to get there. Noticing Resmi's plastic playball floating on the surface of the water, the whole incident flashed through her mind. Before falling asleep, Resmi was playing with the ball. Upon waking, she might have again played with the ball which probably rolled out of the room to the yard through the open door. Thus each time the ball slipped away and rolled, the child followed it and eventually reached the pond.

The devotee stopped. He was silently shedding tears. After a few seconds he asked, "Mother, what you said is true. Who can help themselves from feeling attracted to you, my God, when they directly come into contact with such experiences?"

Half of the time, while the story was being narrated, the Mother was deeply immersed in *samadhi*. The Mother smilingly replied, "Son, this happened only because of your innocent devotion and faith, not because of this crazy Kali."

The Mother continued talking about *siddhis*. She said,

Mother: A *sadhak* must not show *siddhis*. If he gets deluded by *siddhis* they will cause a downfall for him. But as far as an *Avatar* is concerned, displaying *siddhis* is not a problem. The wonderful power which we call *siddhi* is God's innate nature. Power will not be wasted if a Godly person shows *siddhis*. Did not Rama and Krishna manifest *siddhis*? God is not affected by the rule that a *sadhak* shouldn't manifest *siddhis*. People may come looking for a spectacle; but nobody is really searching for that. Therefore, after having first shown *siddhis*, an *Avatar* can then teach people the essential principles.

Young man: Sri Ramakrishna didn't encourage *siddhis* at all, did he?

Mother: Children, don't compare one *Mahatma* with another. Don't ask, "If he has done like that why this one is not doing likewise?" There are no two people alike. Is Sri Rama like Sri Krishna? No. Parasurama is not like Sri Rama[72] and Hanuman is not like Parasurama. Sri Ramakrishna is not like Hanuman. The incarnation of Narasimha

---

[72]Parasurama and Sri Rama were both Avatars of Lord Vishnu and both lived at the same time.

is not like Vamana.[73] There are no real differences between Incarnations; the goal of all the Incarnations is one. Even so, the way in which they act is different. Don't compare one with another. Is it possible to tell one person's features looking at another's?

Sri Ramakrishna did say that *siddhis* should not be shown. There are two reasons for this. Firstof all, it was to *sadhaks* that he was speaking. He told them not to get deluded by *siddhis* , as they would cause one to fall spiritually. This is true. Secondly, he was setting an example to show how a true *bhakta* (devotee) should live. In order to set an ideal example of a true devotee, he did not show any miracles.

Usually *Mahatmas* won't show any *siddhis*. If ever they show them it will be a spontaneous manifestation in a befitting circumstance. They manifest *siddhis* not for the sake of spectators but naturally, according to circumstance.

Children, don't go after *siddhis*. They will turn black in a moment. The Incarnations come in order to destroy desires, not to create them. Therefore, it is good if nobody shows or gets deluded by *siddhis*. Otherwise, one may fall. Often spiritual people will desire *siddhis*., and because of that, they will be ruined. Those who approach these people also will be ruined without gaining any spiritual upliftment. When a person displays *siddhis* before us, we will also develop a desire to learn how to display them ourselves. Having learned *siddhis*, we pave the way for our own destruction. Children, calling to God, try to shed just two drops of tears . Ah, *Bhakti*! It's taste is something unique.

---

[73]Narasimha and Vamana were also both living at the same time and were both Vishnu's Avatars.

AVATAR (INCARNATION)

Another young man: Mother, is an *Avatar* a person whose mind has become perfectly good?

Mother: Son, it is not that one is an *Avatar* because his mind has become good. *Avatars* will have full awareness of God from birth itself. Others will not have it. Because the *Avatars* are in total identity with Nature, their mind is not what we usually call a mind. All minds are theirs. In other words, an *Avatar* is Himself the Universal Mind. *Avatars* will be far beyond all kinds of *dvandas* (pairs of opposites) including purity and impurity. Therefore, an *Avatar* cannot be called, "One whose mind has become good." When God descends in a human form, He or She is an *Avatar*. Therefore we cannot limit Incarnations saying, "*Avatars* will appear in such and such a period of time at such and such a place." If God is omniscient, omnipotent and all-pervading, He can easily assume any form at any time, at any place irrespective of caste, creed and sect. It depends on the urgency or need of the era.

Young man: Mother, will the infinite God come in a human form?

Mother: All forms have a limit. God, the Supreme Principle, is beyond that limit. An Incarnation (the infinite God in a limited form) existing in *Brahman* (the Infinite Reality) is like an iceberg in the ocean. All the water in the reservoir will come through the tap, but the tap itself is not the reservoir. There are limitations for whatever has a name or form. But, through this small body, God can act as He likes. That is the greatness of the form of an Incarnation. This is the reason that it is said that God and an Incarnation are one.

There is no need to assume a body and descend in order for God to act. But still, *Avatars* are beneficial for human beings for they help to bring them closer to God.

Young man: Is there any meaning in calling a person who is alive as "*Bhagavan*"?

Mother: Child, that depends on our faith. Is not a father dear and great as far as his son is concerned?

The young man's friend: Does it mean that we don't have to believe if there is no faith?

Mother: Not so, son. A mosquito will get only blood from an udder while someone else squeezes milk out of it. Faith alone is important. Two different things can come from the same udder. The thief, when he sees a post in the night, will think that it is a policeman; the girl will think that it is her beloved; one who is fearful in the night will think that it is a ghost. Is there any change in the post? The post is the post only. Yet it appears differently according to each one's nature. In which way did the Gopis see Krishna? In which way did Kamsa (an enemy of Sri Krishna) see Him? What was Arjuna's attitude?

We can see that our faith determines what we perceive. The principle is that if we believe that God is in a blade of grass, we will get power even from that. Didn't God appear from a pillar as the Man-Lion (Narasimha)? If so, can't God's Power manifest in human beings too?

INCARNATION AND AN ORDINARY SOUL

The following is an extract from a conversation which occurred on 27th December, 1981.

Devotee: Mother, what is the difference between an ordinary *jiva* (individual soul) and an Incarnation?

Mother: There are differences. A date palm that gives sweet fruit to everyone can be compared to an Incarnation. It can satisfy those who come to it hungry. People can pluck it's fruits and eat. An Incarnation is able to give peace, tranquillity and spiritual power to both those who take refuge in Him and to others as well. It makes no sense if the seed of the date palm says, "Listen, I am the date tree." The seed has to be grown with attention and care, being given water and manure properly. If properly grown, a date tree will spring forth from the seed. It makes no sense if, when it ripens, the fruit says, "I came from this date palm; therefore, I am the tree." There is a difference between the two until the fruit becomes a palm tree. It can become a date palm. As said before, it would need to be given proper care, a fence to protect it from stray animals, and water and manure. Even then, it might wither away due to the heat of the sun, or it might be eaten by some cows or other animals. This is like the difference between a *jiva* and an Incarnation. There are five hundred watt bulbs, one hundred watt bulbs and night lights. Even though all shine with the same electricity which comes from the same power station, their light will be different. We are all just sparks, not even night lights. We have not become perfect. An *Avatar* is perfect.

MOTHER'S TALKS TO WESTERN DEVOTEES

15 December 1988

Mother: Children, you have come to the Ashram because you have a pure resolve to fulfill certain desires. Mother is not trying to put forth rules and regulations or to impede your freedom, but there are some things that she must tell you so that your stay here will be fruitful.

In every corner of India you can see people in colleges. Those students who failed their examinations while studying in colleges will next go to tutorial colleges. Most of these tutorials do not give proper discipline or coaching to the students. But there are some tutorial colleges where students will get good training, and the students who go there will come out successful. Because those tutorial colleges have trained their students properly, the students are well-disciplined. So, in the beginning stages, discipline is very important. Without it we cannot attain the goal. When the goal is attained, you can surrender this discipline at the Feet of the Lord. But for now, discipline is a must.

Some of you might feel that having to follow the rules and regulations here in the Ashram is like being in a prison, but this is not true. Mother does not want to restrict your freedom. But if a child is given too much freedom, it may jump into water or fire due to lack of proper discrimination. If too much freedom is given now, one may end up in jail tomorrow. If rules and regulations are followed now, then you can be fully free tomorrow. It is for tomorrow's freedom that Mother is giving these rules and regulations today.

First of all, you must have love and respect for your *mantra*, the *mantra* that was given to you by your Master. Always repeat this *mantra* wherever you are, whatever work you are doing, irrespective of time and place. Without talking unnecessarily, chant your *mantra*, have love for your *mantra*. Your *mantra* will help you to purify your mind; it is a vehicle to take you to the Supreme. If you can repeat it silently, that is best. If you are unable to do that, then you can just repeat it softly, moving your lips.

Some may feel that even though one is repeating a *mantra*, the thoughts that continue to rise from within will dissipate one's energy. This is not true. For example, take the water in a dam. When the wind blows, there will be ripples on the surface but even then, water will not be lost. So even if there are thought waves within, the energy will not get dissipated if a *mantra* is repeated mentally. It is talking about worldly things and indulging in worldly activities that dissipates our energy.

If you simply do your spiritual practices once a day, such as after your bath or after your breakfast or lunch, it will not help you reach the goal. Constant practice is needed. No matter how much we do, it will not help us to reach the goal without constant practice. Even if you take hundreds of births and do a lot of penance, this kind of intermittent spiritual practice will not help you reach the goal. Whatever work you do, irrespective of place and time, you should be able to chant the *mantra* or reflect on the Vedic dictums or on the spiritual things that you have learned. Only then will you be able to attain the goal.

Children, do not think that all these prayers and the chanting of a *mantra* and other external practices are only for weak minds. The more you chant and the more you pray, the more the mind will become clear and pure. For example, take a washing machine. When we put dirty clothes in, the more they get rinsed, the more they will become clean. The more you chant your *mantra*, the more the mind will become clear and pure. Mother is just reminding you about certain things. You have your own freedom and you can choose to do whatever you like.

It is easy to realize God if you see God in each and every action you perform. Take the Gopis of Brindavan for example. Their business was selling milk, ghee and butter. On each and every bottle and container they would write the different names of Krishna. On the bottles of spices they would write "Madhava," and on some other bottle they would put "Keshava." When they went out selling, instead of calling out, "Butter! Ghee! Milk!" they used to call out, "Krishna! Hari! Mukunda! Madhava!" They could easily see unity in diversity. It is easy to attain God if you see God in each and every action you perform.

It does not matter which path you follow. It may be the path of *jnana*, *karma* or *bhakti* yoga. It does not matter if you are one who meditates on the formless Self or one who meditates on God with form. What is needed is to cleanse the mind. Without that, no matter how much practice you do, it will not enable you to attain Perfection. Before we sow seeds, the weeds must be removed. Only then will we get a good harvest. Negative tendencies, likes and dislikes must first be uprooted. Prayer and chanting of the Divine Name will enable us to attain that goal easily. Whether it is worshipping the Formless, or God with form, what we need is a pure resolve; then we can worship God. Even to worship the formless God we need a pure resolve.

The Realization of God is not possible in a moment. It will not simply arrive one fine morning. It requires lifelong practice. In the *Srimad Bhagavatam* there is a story about a character named Ajamila. He did all kinds of evil deeds while he was alive. Eventually, when he was breathing his last breath, he wanted to see his youngest son named Narayana. He called out "Narayana!" but instead of his young son, the messengers of Lord Narayana (Vishnu) Himself appeared before him and forbade the messengers of the Lord of Death from taking him. After reading this story, a businessman thought that it must be easy to attain God. You simply call God's Name at the end of your life and God will appear and take you to heaven. With this in mind, he named his three sons Krishna, Rama and Govinda. During his life he did all kinds of evil acts. He had a shop and committed many atrocities like cheating and lying. Finally, when he was bedridden and was breathing his last breath, he called his three sons, Krishna, Rama and Govinda. When all his sons came near him, the thought that came to his mind was, "Didn't you open the shop today? Isn't there anyone in the shop?" This was the thought that sprang up in his mind because all his life he was thinking about the shop and how to make a profit. So, the thought that you follow all of your life is the one that will spring up at the end of your life. Definitely that will be the thought that comes to you first. So do not think that God-Realization is possible in a day or two. It requires lifelong practice.

Why should Mother say all these crazy things to you? All of you have read a lot and heard a lot. Mother is telling you in order to remind you of these things, that is all. What you want is experience and Mother is asking you to do whatever is necessary to gain that experience. If we simply read and learn things, then there is no difference between us and a tape recorder. Whatever is recorded will be repeated. What we want is to apply all these scriptural statements to our lives and live them.

At the bus stop, you can see a board giving the timetable of the buses going to different destinations. If you simply stand there reading all the details, you will not catch the bus and reach your destination. If you want to reach your destination, you must find the bus and get inside. Suppose there is a billboard saying that there is a jewelry shop in the next town. If you simply read the billboard, you will not get the jewelry. You must go to that shop and purchase it.

Mother knows that you know all these things. Now what is needed is practice. The ego should be uprooted. The practice is for eliminating the ego. We always think that we are greater or better than other people. This feeling follows us wherever we go. Even if we apologize to someone, later we may think, "Oh, I shouldn't have said that. I am greater than he, so why should I apologize?" These egoistic thoughts will always pull us down. Only in the presence of a Perfect Master can we remove these egoistic thoughts and actions. This is why we go to ashrams and live in the presence of great Masters. Only they can remove the ego in us. There is a huge tree dormant in the seed, but only if the seed is buried in the ground will the tree sprout. If the seed egoistically thinks, "Why should I bow down to this dirty earth?" then its real nature cannot manifest. Only if we cultivate and develop humility is it possible to realize the Supreme Truth, our real nature.

In the beginning stages of *sadhana*, a Perfect Master is a must. Otherwise, it is impossible to remove the subtle tendencies *(vasanas)* of the mind. For example, a child is more inclined to play than to study. If he does study, it will be out of fear of his parents or teachers. But after his high school studies, he will have the desire to become an engineer or a doctor. Then he will concentrate on his studies and abandon all other play because now the awareness of a goal has arisen in him. He will automatically concentrate on his studies. Once discrimination arises, the Guru within you will be invoked. Then you do not have to depend entirely on an external Guru because you will get instructions from within. But until then, a Perfect Master is needed to guide you.

A parrot raised in a church or temple will have one type of character. It will always be chanting God's Name. But a parrot raised in the liquor shop will always use vulgar words. When you go to an ashram or when you are in the presence of a Great Soul, there will be radiant spiritual power in the atmosphere around you. We will be able to become one with that if our mind is properly tuned. Being in the world in the midst of material pleasures is like sitting at the seashore. Due to the salty breeze, our body will become coated with salt. But being in the presence of a Perfect Mater is like going to an incense factory. After leaving there, your body will smell of that fragrance. Similarly, slowly and gradually our mind will become purified due to the presence of a Great Soul.

When you are in the Ashram atmosphere, it is good if you move with utmost alertness. Selfless service and repeating your *mantra* is enough for attaining the goal. If these are lacking, no matter how much penance you do, you will not be able to attain the goal. If you do spiritual practices without performing selfless actions, it will be like building a house without any windows or doors. Be courageous. Do not be idle.

Now we do not have the requisite mental harmony. Because of that, Nature's harmony also is lost. Even now one can clearly see the after effects of this disharmony. Either there is not enough rain or there is too much. If we become harmonious within, then Nature also will be benefited and there will be harmony without.

Children, Mother is not saying that you should give up your present way of life or pleasures. But in whichever way you choose to live, you should discriminate between that which is eternal and that which will pass away. Slowly and steadily cultivate and develop detachment. If you do that, then you can enjoy peace of mind and spiritual bliss wherever you may be and whatever you may do.

GLOSSARY

ACHARA: Traditional customs and observances.

ADHARA: Substratum.

ADVAITA VEDANTA: Philosophy of Non-duality.

AGNANA: Ignorance.

AKARAM: Form.

ANANDAM: Bliss.

ANTARIKA PRAKRITI: Inner nature, as opposed to external Nature.

ANACHARAS: Contrary to custom.

ARATI: Waving burning camphor before the Deity as the conclusion of worship.

ARCHANA: Worship through repetition of Names of God.

ASANA: A seat; a posture in Hatha Yoga.

ASANA SIDDHI: Perfection in sitting unmoving in one posture for more than 3 hours.

ASURA: A demon.

ASURA SVABHAVA: Demonic nature.

ASURIC: Demonic.

ATMA BHAVA: The spiritual attitude; to be established in the Self.

ATMA DHYANA: Meditation on the Self.

ATMA GNANA: Self-knowledge.

ATMA VICHARA: Self-enquiry.

ATMACHAITANYA: Spiritual power; the illuminating soul.

ATMAN: The Self.

ATMAVIN DUKHAM: Sorrow of the soul.

AVADHUTA: A Realised Soul who has transcended all the rules and regulations of the Scriptures, tradition and society.

AVATAR: Incarnation of God.

BALA BHAVA: Attitude of a child.

BHAGAVATI: The Divine Mother.

BHAGAVAN: The Lord.

BHAJAN: Devotional singing.

BHAKTI: Devotion.

BHAKTI MARGA: The path of devotion.

BHARAT: India.

BHAYA BHAKTI: Devotion with fear and reverence.

BHEDA BUDDHI: Differentiating intellect.

BHOGA: Enjoyment.

BHUKTI-MUKTI-PRADAYINI: Giver of worldly enjoyment and Liberation.

BHAGAVATAM: Scripture about the life and deeds of Lord Vishnu's Incarnations.

BHAVA DARSHAN: The Holy Mother giving an audience in the mood of the Divine Mother or Krishna.

BHAVAS: Moods, feelings or attitudes.

BIJAKSHARAS: Seed letters preceding mantras.

BRAHMA PADA: The Absolute State; the highest position.

BRAHMACHARIN: A celibate student studying the scriptures and undergoing spiritual guidance and discipline under a Guru.

BRAHMAGNANA: Knowledge of the Absolute.

BRAHMAN: The Absolute.

BRAHMANUBHUTI: Experience of the Absolute.

BRAHMANANDA: Bliss of the Absolute.

BRAHMACHARYA: Celibacy and sense control.

CHITTA: Intellect; mind.

DAKSHINA: Reverential offering in cash or kind.

DARSHAN: Audience or vision of the Deity or holy person.

DASA BHAVANA: Attitude of being a servant.

DASATVAM: Servitude.

DASOHAM: "I am a servant."

DEHA BHAVA: The feeling that oneself is a body.

DEVATA: A god or deity.

DEVI BHAVA: Divine mood as Devi, the Goddess.

DHARMA: Righteousness.

DHYANA: Meditation.

DHYANA RUPAM: Form on which one is meditating.

DOSHA: Evil or defect.

DVARAKA: City where Sri Krishna lived.

EKAGRATA: One-pointedness.

GAURANGA: Sri Krishna Chaitanya, considered as an Incarnation of Sri Radha-Krishna, who lived in Bengal about 400 years ago.

GNANA: Spiritual wisdom or knowledge.

GNANA MARGA: The path of knowledge.

GNANI: A Knower of Truth.

GNANAGNI: The Fire of Knowledge.

GOPAS: Cowherds of Brindavan.

GOPIS: Wives of the cowherds of Brindavan; divine lovers of Sri Krishna.

GRAHASTA: One living in a house, i.e., a married person.

GRAHASTASHRAMI: A spiritual-minded grahasta.

GUDAKESA: A synonym for Arjuna; one who has conquered sleep.

GURU: Spiritual master.

GURU BHAVA: Attitude of a Guru.

GURU MAHIMA: Greatness of the Guru.

GURUKULA: Residential school of a Guru.

HRIM: A seed letter associated with the Goddess.

ISWARA AMSA: A partial manifestation of God.

ISWARA BHAVANA: The attitude that oneself is identical with the Lord.

JAGAT: The world.

JAPA: Repetition of a mantra.

JIVA: The individual soul; life force.

JIVANMUKTA: One who has achieved Liberation even while tenanting the body.

JIVATMA: Individual soul.

KALIYUGA: The present Dark Age of materialism.

KARMA: Action.

KARMA PHALA: The fruit of action.

KAURAVAS: The enemies of the Pandavas during the Mahabharata War, representing unrighteousness.

KIRTANA: Devotional singing.

KOLADI: A country folk dance.

KRISHNA BHAVA: The divine mood as Krishna.

KRÔDHA: Anger.

KUMBHAKA: Retention of breath during pranayama.

KUNDALINI DHYANA: Meditation on the kundalini.

KURUKSHETRA: The battlefield on which the Mahabharata War was fought.

KAMA VIKARA: Lustful feelings.

KAMA: Lust or desire.

LAKSHANA: Symptoms or signs.

LAKSHARCHANA: Worship by repeating the Divine Names 100,000 times.

LAKSHYA: Aim or goal.

LAKSHYA BÔDHA: A mind intent on reaching the goal.

LALITASAHASRANAMA: The 1000 Names of the Goddess Sri Lalita.

LAYA: Merger or absorption.

LEELA: Play.

MAHAMANTRA: Great mantra.

MANONASA: Destruction of the mind; permanent subsidence of the mind.

MITHYA: Unreal.

MOKSHA: Release from the cycle of rebirth.

NAVARATRI: Festival of Nine Nights dedicated to the worship of the Divine Mother.

NIRGUNA: Without qualities.

NIRGUNOPASAKA: One who meditates on the qualityless Absolute.

NIRVANA SHATKAM: A composition of Sri Sankara consisting of six stanzas on Nirvana or Final Emancipation.

NISHKRIYA: Actionless.

NISHTA: Established; regularity in practice.

NITYA: Eternal.

NITYANITYA VASTU VIVEKAM: Discrimination between the eternal and the transitory.

NAMA: The Divine Name.

OMKARA: The divine sound OM.

PADMASANA: Lotus posture.

PARAMAHAMSA: A God-realised Soul.

PARA BHAKTI: Supreme devotion.

PEETHAM: Seat or throne.

PRAMANA: Knowledge; means of knowledge; proof.

PRASAD: Consecrated offering to God or a saint.

PREMA BHAKTI: Loving devotion.

PREMA SWARUPA: Of the nature of love.

PRANA: Life force.

PUJA: Ritualistic worship.

PURANA: Ancient scriptures written by Vedavyasa.

PURNAGNANI: Fully realised soul.

PURNAKUMBHA: Lit., full pot; a pot of consecrated water offered to a holy person on their arrival at a temple, house, etc.

PURVA SAMSKARA: Previously acquired tendencies.

PURNAM: Full or perfect.

RAJAS: The principle of activity; one of the three gunas or qualities of Nature.

RASA: Taste; juice; elixir.

RADHA BHAVA: Attitude of being Sri Radha, Beloved of Sri Krishna; supreme devotion.

RAJA YOGA: The Royal yoga; the eight-fold yoga of Liberation.

SAGUNA: With attributes.

SAGUNARADHANA: Worship of God as having attributes.

SAHAJA SAMADHI: The Natural State of being established in the Supreme Reality.

SAHASRADALA PADMA: The thousand-petalled lotus chakra on the top of the head wherein resides the Supreme Lord, the Goal of all Yogas.

SAHODHARA BUDDHI: Treating all as one's brothers and sisters.

SAMA CHITTATA: Equipoised mind.

SAMATVA BHAVANA: Attitude of equality.

SAMATVA BUDDHI: Mind endowed with the equal vision of beholding all as One.

SAMATVAM YOGA UCHYATE: "Equipoise is yoga."

SAMADHI: The equipoised state of Oneness with God.

SANKALPA SAKTI: Power of resolve or creative imagination.

SANATANA DHARMA: The Eternal Religion of the Vedas.

SARVATRA SAMADA: Equal vision everywhere.

SASTRA: Scripture; science.

SAT KARMA: Good or virtuous action.

SATTVA: Principle of clarity; one of the three qualities of Nature.

SATYA NASTI PARO DHARMA: "Truth is the supreme righteousness.

SEVA: Service.

SHANTI: Peace.

SHIVOHAM: "I am Shiva."

SIDDHI: Psychic power; perfection.

SISHYA: Disciple.

SUDDHA BODHA: Pure awareness.

SUDDHA SATTVA: Pure sattva (see "Sattva" above).

SUDDHA TATTVAM: The pure Principle.

SUPRABHATAM: Good morning; verses requesting the Deity to wake up in the early morning hours.

SVADHARMA: One's own duty.

SVAYAMBHU LINGA: A self-manifest linga or symbol of Lord Shiva.

TAMAS: The principle of inertia; one of the three qualities of Nature.

TAMASIC: Pertaining to tamas (see above).

TAPAS SAKTI: The power generated by austerities.

TINDAL AND TODIL: An old custom of avoiding impure substances and people for fear of pollution.

TIRUVATIRA KALI: A village dance.

TRIGUNAS: The three gunas or qualities of Nature, sattva (tranquil), rajas (active), and tamas (inert).

TRIKARTIKA: A star or constellation.

TURIYA: The fourth state of Bliss beyond the waking, dream and deep sleep states.

VAIRAGYA: Detachment.

VANAPRASTHA: The third stage of life in which one leaves all worldly activity and devotes oneself to austerities.

VEDAS: The revealed scriptures of Hinduism.

VETTUCHEMBU: A kind of tuber root.

VIDYA DEVI: The Goddess of Knowledge.

VISALA BUDDHI: Broadmindedness.

VISALATA: Expansiveness.

VIVEKA: Discrimination.

VYAVAHARA: Empirical.

YAMA AND NIYAMA: The do's and don't of the path of Raja Yoga.

YOGASCHITTA VRITTI NIRODAH: "Yoga is the control of mental modifictions."

INDEX

A

achara (customary observances and code of conduct) 56, 59, 253-254
adhara 108
Ajamila 72, 361-362
ajnana 7, 34
alertness (see sraddha)
anachara 60
anger (see krodha)
Angiras 268-271
antarika prakriti (internal nature) 169
asana 167, 206, 246
astrology 247
atma vichara (self-inquiry) 119
Avatars 21, 161-162, 356-358

B

Balarama 21
bhakti 91, 170-171, 244-245, 301, 325, 339, 355
   bhakti marga 164
   bhaya bhakti 144, 179, 258
   parabhakti 46, 170-171
   prema bhakti 194
bhakti yoga 301, 315-316, 318-319
Bharata 72
bhava
   atma bhava 32
   bala bhava 50
   deha bhava 32
bhavana
   dasa bhavana 4
   iswara bhavana 22-23
   prapancha bhavana 36
bheda buddhi (differentiating mind) 29
bijaksharas 16
Brahma 239
Brahman 32-33
Buddha 148-258

C

celibacy 180, 261
Chottanikara Temple 12
concentration (see also sadhana) 95-96, 183-184, 256, 338-339, 345

D

dakshina 279-280
Dakshineswara 68
dasatvam (humility) 165
death 77-78, 89-90
   ceremonies after death 247-248
   life after death 203-204, 274
desire (see also sorrow) 6-7, 23, 120-121, 138-139, 350
Devi 77, 171, 179, 256, 257
devotion (see bhakti)
dharma 252-253, 261-262, 326
   for women 78-79
   Sanatana Dharma (eternal religion) 300-303
dhyana 256
   atma dhyana 119, 319
   kundalini dhyana 94
   rupa dhyana 40, 119, 169, 178

diksha 55-56
discipline (see also tapas) 252
Divine Play (see leela)

E

ego 142, 263, 363
ekagrata (one-pointedness)
    183-184

F

faith (see also sraddha) 189,
    195, 321-322, 357
fate (see also vasanas) 43-44,
    47
fear of death 27
food 56, 166-167, 186, 197,
    209

G

Gauranga 170
Gayatri 154-155, 185, 198-199
Gita 54
God
    as different from gods 11
    as servant 6-7, 156-157
    belief in 348
    God's vision 90, 142
    is compassionate only 5-6
    is of the nature of Love 242-243
    is the doer 19-21
    proof of existence 1-4, 272
    separation from God 171
    with form or formless 8-9, 73-
        74, 97-98, 176-177, 361
grace 56, 132, 246
grahasta (householder) 40-41,
    66-67, 97, 106-108,
    267, 291-296
grahastashrami 97, 111-113,
    229-230
guru (see also satguru) 27, 104,
    126, 148, 164-165,
227, 251-252, 280-
    281, 338
Guruvayur (Guruvayoor
Temple) 12, 53

H

Hanuman 354
Harischandra 182
Hinduism 300-305, 309
Hiranyakasipu 84
horoscope (see astrology)
householder (see grahasta)
humility (see dasatvam and dasa
    bhavana)

I

idols (see temple worship)
ignorance (see ajnana)
initiation (see diksha)
injustice 96
instructions for living 149-150,
    282-283
    brahmacharins and sadhaks
        129-130, 173-175, 230-233,
        240-242, 323-324, 327-329
    dietary restrictions 166-167
    do not laugh while eating 70
    do not waste time 162
    good effects of wearing certain
        things 331
    grahasta - for a householder's life
        106-108
    how to develop devotion 90-91
    in an ashram 209-210, 231
    practices for Western devotees
        358-364
    remembrance of God 80
    what to do at dusk 191
intrinsic nature (see
    swadharma)
iswara bhavana 22-23

J

japa (see mantra)
Jesus 92, 148
jivanmukti 329-331
jivatma 33-34, 329-330
jnana (knowledge) 34, 70-71,
          301
jnana yoga 301, 316, 318
jnani 35, 36, 39-40, 148

K

Kali Yuga 17, 112-113, 164-
          165, 232, 256
kama (lust) 98, 130, 180, 186,
          216, 259-260
Kamsa 84
karma 22, 143
   avatara karma 311
   karma phala 162, 247
   pitrukarma 17
   prarabdha karma 39
   sanchita karma 26
karma yoga 301, 316, 318
kirtana 32, 164, 197, 257
knowledge (see also jnana) 25,
          117-119
Krishna 10, 21, 148, 170, 179,
          181-184, 273-274,
          325, 354
krodha 98, 116, 182-183, 192
Kundalini yoga 317
Kurukshetra 273

L

Laksharchana 102
lakshya bodha (mind intent on
          reaching the goal) 5,
          183, 347-348
Lalitasahasranama 103, 171,
          257, 322-323
latent tendencies (see vasanas)
laya (dissolution of the mind)
          178

leela (Divine Play) 30, 58
liberation
   attaining liberation is not one's
          aim 224
   attainment through temple
          worship 15
   freedom from worldly existence
          50
   path to 19, 60-61, 72, 321
   what is liberation? 321
   when will it be attained? 25-26,
          41, 48, 56, 68, 132-133, 223
love
   love for Mother 173-174
   love for God 122, 138
   Mother's love 51, 86
   prema swarupa (nature of love)
          242-243
   worldly love 260, 346
lust (see kama)

M

Mahabali 224
Mahatma Ghandi 274
Mahatmas 4, 12, 22-23, 141,
          327, 354-355
manasa puja 25
mantra 15-17, 154-155, 271,
          322-324, 335-336,
          359-361
mantra diksha 56
meditation
   at night 105
   at dusk 190-191
   by the sea 58
   for jnanis 229
   headaches in 31-32
   incense during 138
   instructions 80-81, 271
   length of time to meditate 144,
          167
   on form or formless 314-315

rupa dhyana (meditation on a
form of God) 40, 119, 169,
178
satsang and meditation 145
sitting quietly after245
sleep during 228
when to meditate 149
mind
bhedi buddhi (differentiating
mind) 29
definition of 149
elimination of 21-22
mental purity 38, 50-51, 81, 95-
96, 273
peace of mind 21-22, 108-109,
253, 258
samatva buddhi (equal-mindedness) 169
mithya (an illusion) 214, 273,
335
Mother and animals
calf 98-99
goat 130
Mother and children 65-66, 158
Mother - in her own words
as Truth/God 155, 177, 237,
319
crying for God 60
divine moods 44, 57, 212
expressing desires 172
flow of love 51, 92
her will and Divine Will 105
her body 136
her displays of worry, sadness,
sorrow 193
her eating habits 78
her responsibility to look after
her children 57
how she will serve a sadhak 140
Krishna and Devi Bhava 57-58,
179, 239-240, 289-290
Mother as different from one's
birth mother 152-153

Mother's Guru 242-243, 280
Mother's purpose in life 52-53,
163, 185-186, 233
perfection 141
reading 53-54
taking diseases, pain and
suffering 77, 131-138
what she knows 50, 51
what she prayed for the Divine
Mother to bring her 68, 73

N
Narada 101, 170, 182
Narasimha 354
Navaratri 195, 243
Nealu 103
Nirvana Shatkam 113
Nisargadatta Maharaj 178, 219
nitya siddha 98
niyama 294

O
Oachira Temple 63
olden days vs. modern times
12-13, 81, 84-85, 111-
113, 115, 230, 256-
257, 259-260, 300,
306, 307, 342, 348-
350

P
Pai 109-110
pain (see sorrow)
paramatma 21, 33-34, 329-330
Parasurama 21, 354
Parvati 8
patience 148
pooja (see puja)
Prabhakara Siddha Yogi 75-77
pranava 58
pranayama 47-48, 267, 317,
343

prarabdha 39
prasad 58-59
puja 10-14, 219-220
punya and papa (merit and
	demerit) 39
Puranas 182
pushpaka vimana (airplane made
	of flowers) 18

R
Radha 170
raja yoga 316-317, 318
rajas 96, 160
Rama 21, 79, 354
Ramakrishna Paramahamsa 68,
	148, 161, 170, 208,
	302, 323, 354-355
Ramana Maharshi 174-175,
	244-245, 302, 338
Ramayana 18, 79
Ravana 84
renunciation (see also sannyasa
	and tyaga) 29-30, 132
resolve (see sankalpa)
rituals 17
Rukmini 21

S
sacrifice 147-148
sadhana 32, 33, 41, 42, 90, 97,
	133, 144-145, 148,
	155-156, 167, 181,
	198, 338
stages in 37
sahasrara 93-95, 108
samadhi 182
	nirvikalpa samadhi 310-311
	sahaja nirvikalpa samadhi 98
	sahaja samadhi xv, 103, 170
	savikalpa samadhi 98
samsara 40, 48, 320
samskara 48, 330

Sanatana Dharma 300-303
Sandeepaka 268-271
sankalpa (resolve) 17, 21, 157,
	214-215, 338
Sankaracharya (Sri Sankara)
	46, 113, 206, 244, 258
sannyasa 30
Saraswathi 239
satchidananda 15
satguru (see also guru) 41, 93-
	94, 96, 145, 336-337
satsang 25, 42, 143, 145, 150,
	310, 329-330
sattva 160, 209
Satyavati 78
Savitri 78
selfishness 81
semen 166, 180, 186, 261, 349
service 364
shakti
	kundalini 92-95
	prana 12
	sankalpa shakti 303
	tapas 349
Shiva 8, 239
siddhi 207, 348-355
sin 13, 208
Sita 21, 78-79
sorrow (see also desire)
	cause of 6, 120-121, 194-195,
		249-250, 322-323
	getting rid of 82-83, 272
	longing for God 142
	sharing of 8-9
sraddha 61, 149, 169, 171,
	192, 226-228, 248-
	251, 290
Sreekumar 85-88
Srimad Bhagavatam 17, 100,
	177-178, 242, 361-362
stories
	Ajamila and Narayana and the
		businessman 361-362

Bhagavan coming when called 72, 78-79

boy learning to climb coconut trees183-184

Brahmin who ate fish to save his life 13

Brahmin teacher who ignored the king 15-17

fisherman who built a dam and one who went fishing 250-251

Lord Krishna and Sage Narada 102

man who became a scholar due to association with scholars71

sage caught and sold by fisherman100

Shiva and the sorrows of His devotees 8

subtle beings 125-126, 207

Sugunanandan 44, 137, 211-212

suicide 23-24, 297-299

surrender 6-7, 194

sushumna 93

swadharma (intrinsic nature) 112

T

tamas 160, 197

tapas 148, 223-224, 349

temple worship 10-15, 46, 107-109, 253, 259

tendencies (see vasanas)

Thiruonam (Onam Festival) 86-88

Thousand Names (see Lalitasahasranama)

time

lack of time for spiritual practices 4-5, 31, 264

wasting/losing time 162, 171, 192-193, 334-335

Tirupathi Temple 12

Trikartika 201

tyaga 40, 132, 241, 337

U

Uriyadi 181

V

Vamana224, 355

vasanas (see also fate) 8, 22, 38, 42-43, 65, 70, 141-143, 214, 227, 341

Vedanta45

Venu 113-115, 138-139, 173-175, 178, 206-207

vijnana 70-71

Vishnu 224, 239, 361

Vishwamitra 182

Vivekananda 45, 161, 258

Vyasa 18

vyavahara 33-34, 335

W

wealth 42, 61-62, 84

Werner 139-140

women

dharma 78-79

yama 294

yoga 315-319